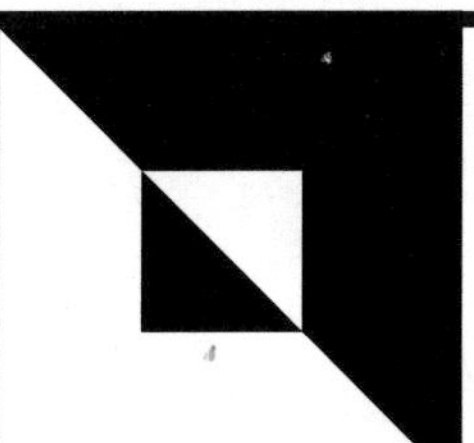

Dedication:

To My Beloved Parents

Author:

Shawn Shahfar PE , LEED AP , MBA , PMP , CEM , GBE , CSDP

Mr. Shahfar is a Principal Project Engineer and Developer for a major theme park and entertainment corporation. He has over 25 years of experience in the field of Building Design and Construction. He is also a candidate for a PhD degree in the field of Design Engineering Management and holds Master of Science degree in Business Administration (MBA), Construction Engineering Management and Mechanical Engineering. He is a Professional Mechanical Engineer (PE) in the states of California and Florida. Mr. Shahfar is also a LEED Accredited Professional (LEED AP), Project Management Professional (PMP), Certified Energy Manager (CEM), Certified Green Building Engineer (GBE), and Certified Sustainable Development Professional (CSDP). Mr. Shahfar is a Licensed General Building Contractor, Real Estate Broker, Building Appraiser and Building Inspector in California. He holds executive certification in the field of Construction Engineering Management, Project Engineering Management, and Building System Engineering. Mr. Shahfar is an active professional as well as educator in the field of Sustainable Energy Engineering and Green Design Building for domestic and international projects.

Pars Tec Company

5334 Lindley Ave. Suite #328, Encino, Ca, 91316

(818) 378-1446

www.leedpasstec.com

Disclaimer:

ISBN 978-1-60402-004-5

ISSN 1937-1268

LEEDPASS

Table of Content

LEEDPASS

(Chapter 1)

INTRODUCTION

LEEDPASS

- The goal of sustainable building is to achieve livable communities through comprehensive approaches that coordinate economic, physical, and building development.
- The Green Building is a more holistic design approach and designing an efficient system requires thinking about how all of its components interact with the world around it.
- The intent of the LEEDPASS book is to provide information that will increase the effectiveness and efficiency of your preparation to pass the LEED exam. The LEEDPASS book covers all the related topics that you will need to pass the LEED exam. The main goal is to provide a cohesive, concise, yet comprehensive study guide.
- The formatted sample questions present a practical simulation of the actual exam and would greatly assist you to test your knowledge, prior of taking the actual LEED exam.
- Based on reviews received from members of USGBC chapters, and Green Building Consultants , the LEEDPASS book is one of the most invaluable and comprehensive study material for LEED New Construction exam.
- I also recommend to purchase and read the latest version of USGBC Reference Guide while studying for the exam.
- The USGBC which is a trademark of the U.S. Green Building Council is not affiliated with publication or development of the LEEDPASS book.

- My best wishes for you to pass the exam.

Shawn Shahfar

(2008)

LEEDPASS

(Chapter 2)

ADMINSTRATIVE GENERAL NOTES

USGBC stands for (U. S Green Building Council)

LEED stands for (Leadership in Energy and Environmental Design)

SUSTAINABLE CATEGORIES:

1. Sustainable Sites.
2. Water Efficiency.
3. Energy and Atmosphere.
4. Material and Resources.
5. Indoor Environmental Quality.

ELIGIBILITY:

Commercial buildings are eligible for certification under following categories:

- NC (New Construction)
- CS (Core and Shell)
- CI (Commercial Interior)
- EB (Existing Building)

LEEDPASS
(LEED NC 2.2)

COMMERCIAL BUILDINGS:

1. Offices
2. Retail
3. Service Establishment
4. Institutional (library, school, laboratory, museum, and church)
5. Hotels
6. Residential (more than 4 stories)

LEED CERTIFICATION PROCESS:

1. The first step is to REGISTER with USGBC.
2. The LEED version 2.2 must be registered through the USGBC web site since January 2006. All communication shall be performed by emails.
3. Appoint the Project Team Administrator.
4. Select certification path for design phase and construction phase.
5. Collect technical documentation.
6. Provide technical support to the team.
7. Apply for certification.
8. Wait for USGBC review.
9. Earn the certification.

<u>CREDIT INTERPRETATION REQUEST:</u>

1. If the USGBC reference guide does <u>NOT</u> cover or explain your needs, then the CIR may be used to communicate with the USGBC.
2. If there is any CONFLICT and you need further assistance, use the CIR form to communicate with USGBC.
3. The registration fee used to cover the submission fee for two (2) CIR forms, but as of 11/15/2005, this service is <u>NOT FREE</u>.
4. The cost for each CIR form is $ 220.
5. The Project Administrator can include pictures, LEED references and technical analysis with CIR.
6. CIR can be submitted ON-LINE.
7. CIR can be reviewed by USGBC members.

<u>1. BEFORE SUBMITTING A CIR (CREDIT INTERPRETATION REQUEST):</u>

1. <u>Review and check</u> that your project complies with the intent of the credit or prerequisite.
2. Check the LEED 2.2 reference guide that has been provided by the USGBC.
3. Search the USGBC site for a similar CIR forms which could apply to your project.

4. If a similar CIR is not found, then you can submit new CIR for your project.
5. The submitted form shall include a brief interpretation request based on information in the latest reference guide.
6. Emphasize the intent of your request and offer suggestions.
7. The CIR is an online database of queries to the USGBC about issues not covered in their reference guide and elsewhere.

2. DURING CIR SUBMITTAL PROCESS:

1. Use online forms and services.
2. Do NOT mention the name of credit.
3. Do NOT state the contact information.
4. Do NOT include CONFIDENTIAL details.
5. Do NOT format it as a letter.
   (submit only required and essential background)
6. Request guidance for only ONE credit or prerequisite item.
7. Provide background and details of your project.
8. Do NOT include a lengthy project narrative. Limit your project narrative to 600 words. (4000 characters including typing spaces)
9. Do NOT include any attachments.

3. AFTER SUBMITTING CIR:

1. Credit will NOT be awarded through the CIR process.
2. The CIR process provides FEEDBACK ONLY.
3. The CIR process DOES NOT GUARANTEE any credit.
4. Do not change the language of the statement through the CIR process.

INNOVATION AND DESIGN CATEGORY:

1. EXCEPTIONAL performance by the project.
2. INNOVATIVE performance by the project.
3. It is normally awarded by increasing the original requirements to the NEXT LEVEL or DOUBLES it to a higher level.
4. The credit on one project DOES NOT MEAN it is good for other projects.

INNOVATION AND DESIGN PROCESS:

1. Identify the intent for the proposed innovation.
2. Propose all requirements for compliance.
3. Propose the submittal summary for all of the design approaches.

CERTIFICATION AWARD:

1. Receive an award letter.
2. Receive a plaque.
3. Receive a certificate.

PAYMENTS STEPS:

1. At registration and certification phases.

ADDITIONAL FEE:

1. Required for EACH appeal.
2. Required for EACH CIR.
3. Required for the LEED plaque.

THE REGITERATION FEE:

1. Impacted by construction type.
2. Impacted by building area.
3. Impacted by project type.
4. Impacted by USGBC membership.

LEEDPASS
(LEED NC 2.2)

LEED ON-LINE:

1. All work must be submitted ON-LINE.
2. The first step is project REGISTRATION.
3. The second step is REVIEW process:
    a. Option #1:
    - The second step is to submit part of documents at the DESIGN phase.

      (At this stage NO credit is awarded)
    - The third step is to submit final part of documents at the CONSTRUCTION phase.

    b. Option #2:
    - In this option, you can submit all documents at the end of CONSTRUCTION phase.
4. The Third step is the project AWARD certification.
5. The registration fee will be DIFFERENT for members and non-members.
6. The total fee for the LEED certification process will DEPEND ON the area of the building.
7. The fee shall be paid within design and construction phases.
8. The USBC will award (Credit Achievement Anticipated) or deny (Credit Denied) your request at the end of CONSTRUCTION phase.

9. The applicant can verify the status of each credit on-line.
10. Any changes to the original submittal must be resubmitted to the USGBC for further review and approval.
11. The registration fee must be <u>PAID</u> on-line.
12. After the receipt of preliminary review, the team has 25 days to submit correction or supporting documents to USGBC.

LEED CATEGORIES:

1. New Construction (NC)
2. Existing Building (EB)
3. Commercial Interior (CI)
4. Core and Shell (CS)
5. LEED for Home
6. LEED for Neighborhood Development

NEW CONSTRUCTION PROJECTS:

1. LEED for Multiple Buildings
2. LEED for Campus
3. LEED for School
4. LEED for Healthcare
5. LEED for Retail
6. LEED for Labs
7. LEED for Commercial Interior

REVIEW POLICY:

1. The request form shall be completed and submitted ON-LINE.
2. The review process will be initiated by the USGBC within 10 working days.

APPEAL PROCESS:

1. The applicant will have 25 DAYS to appeal.
2. Each appeal will cost $500.
3. Appeal can be submitted at DESIGN phase or CONSTRUCTION phase.

PROJECT REGISTRATION:

1. It is the FIRST step for the certification.
2. Once registered, the PROJECT ADMINISTRATOR will have access to the LEED online as well as to the CIR data base.
3. The project administrator will have the ability to complete and update the project data base and files ON-LINE.
4. It notifies the USGBC that the project is pursuing the LEED certification.
5. The registration fee is FIXED regardless of the building size.
6. The cost of registration is $450 for members and $600 for non-members.

LEEDPASS
(LEED NC 2.2)

REGISTRATION FORM INCLUDES:

1. Account and login Information.
2. Project Type :
   - Select Rating System
   - (LEED –NC, LEED EB and etc.)
3. Primary Contact Information
4. General Project Information:
   - Project Title
   - Project Address
   - Project Confidentiality Notes
5. Project Owner Information:
   - Project Details
   - Owner Type
   - Project Scope
   - Site Condition
   - Occupant Type
   - Gross Square Footage (excluding parking & outdoor facilities)
   - Project Budget (soft and hard cost excluding site work, furniture and equipment)
   - Current Project Phase
   - Project Type (Commercial , Laboratory, Campus)

LEED FOR CORE AND SHELL BUILDINGS:

1. The pre-certification will be given to the owner to advertise his/her project.
2. The USGBC has created the pre-certification program to promote the owner.
3. The pre-certification is granted once the early design review has been completed by the USGBC.

CERTIFICATION REVIEW PROCESS:

1. Design Phase.
2. Construction Phase.

DESIGN PHASE REVIEW:

1. The credit will NOT be awarded at design phase, but USGBC will inform the project administrator if the proposed credit is ANTICIPATED or DENIED.
2. The USGBC will offer ONE review at the end of design phase.
3. Submit all required information, before beginning of the construction phase.

<u>CONSTRUCTION PHASE REVIEW:</u>

1. This occurs after the construction phase has been completed.
2. Provide verification that all design concepts have been executed during the construction phase.
3. Any changes during the design phase must be RESUBMITTED to the USGBC for the final review and approval.

<u>RATING:</u>

- Certified 26-32
- Silver 33-38
- Gold 39-51
- Platinum 52-69

<u>MEMBERSHIP:</u>

The following groups can be a member of USGBC:

1. Government agencies
2. Educational Facilities
3. Professional Societies
4. Professional companies and building consultants.

THE POTENTIAL POINTS FOR NEW CONSTRUCTION, VERSION 2.2:

1. Sustainable Sites = 14 points
2. Water Efficiency = 5 points
3. Energy & Atmosphere = 17 points
4. Materials & Resources = 13 points
5. Indoor Environmental Quality = 15 points
6. Innovation & Design Process = 5 points

TOTAL = 69 points

THE PREREQUISITE FOR NEW CONSTRUCTION, VERSION 2.2:

1. Sustainable Sites = 1 prerequisite
2. Water Efficiency = 0 prerequisite
3. Energy & Atmosphere = 3 prerequisites
4. Materials & Resources = 1 prerequisite
5. Indoor Environmental Quality = 2 prerequisites
6. Innovation & Design Process = 0 prerequisite

TOTAL = 7 prerequisites

LEEDPASS
(LEED NC 2.2)

DOCUMENTS:

The list of items that may be required by USGBC for review process:

1. Calculation
2. Specification
3. Product Manual sheets

LEED ACTION PLAN:

1. Assign responsibility to get into construction documents.
2. The project administrator must collect information and document it (such as calculation, drawings, maps, digital photo etc.)
3. The project administrator must submit all documentation ON-LINE.

THE PROJECT ADMINSTRATOR:

1. Preferably a LEED-AP.
2. In charge of collecting, reviewing and submitting materials to USGBC.
3. Be familiar with USGBC registration, submissions and certification processes.
4. Be familiar with all references, categories, prerequisites and credits.
5. Attach team members to roles and responsibilities.

LEEDPASS
(LEED NC 2.2)

LIST OF ITEMS THAT CAN BE FOUNFD AT USGBC SITE:

1. List of registered LEED Accredited Professionals.
2. List LEED certified projects.
3. List of CIR forms.
4. Database of previous projects CIR forms.
5. Checklist templates
6. Receive a Plaque.
7. Receive a certificate.

REVIEW PROCESS:

1. Use “D” for Design phase.
2. Use “C” for Construction phase.
3. Consider 1/3 of certification fee is due at “C” phase.

<u>THE POTENTIAL EXEMPLARY POINT(S) FOR NEW CONSTRUCTION BUILDING, VERSION 2.2:</u>

1. Sustainable Sites = 6 points
2. Water Efficiency = 2 points
3. Energy & Atmosphere = 4 points
4. Materials & Resources = 6 points
5. Indoor Environmental Quality = 1 point
6. Innovation & Design Process = None

<u>THE SCORING POINTS FOR LEED EXAM VERSION 2.2:</u>

1. Lowest point = 125
2. Highest point = 200
3. Passing point = 170

GOOD LUCK

LEEDPASS

(Chapter 3)

TECHNICAL NOTES

LEEDPASS

SUSTAINABLE SITES

POINTS	REFERENCE NUMBER	INTENT OF CREDIT	STATEMENT OF CREDIT	CONCENTRATION OF CREDIT	GENERAL EXPLANATION	EXTRA CREDIT	CODE OR STANDARD	SUBMITTAL PHASE
SUSTAINABLE SITES								
0	SS P1	*To reduce pollution from construction sites by controlling the following items: 1- Soil erosion 2- Waterway sedimentation. 3- Airborne dust generation.*	*Construction Activity Pollution Prevention*	*(Mandatory)*	*1- The project shall be designed per ESC (Erosion and Sedimentation Control) standards. 2- Prevent loss of soil , pollution and sedimentation. 3- Follow EPA 2003 standards. 4-The CGP covers sites greater than 1 acre , but the LEED covers ALL sizes. Sedimentation : It can be controlled by the following methods: 1- Stabilization (seeding and mulching) 2- Structural (silt fencing, earth dikes and sediment trap)*	*n/a*	*1- EPA 2003 2- NPDES*	*Construction*

LEEDPASS
(LEED NC 2.2)

POINTS	REFERENCE NUMBER	INTENT OF CREDIT	STATEMENT OF CREDIT	CONCENTRATION OF CREDIT	GENERAL EXPLANATION	EXTRA CREDIT	CODE OR STANDARD	SUBMITTAL PHASE
1	SS 1	*1- To avoid the development of inappropriate sites. 2- To reduce environmental impact at the site.*	*Site Selection*	*Do NOT include small man-made ponds. (such as ponds for storm water retention and fire suppression) Greenfield sites : 1- It is not previously developed. 2- It is not previously graded.*	*AVOID selecting the sites : 1- Where the site elevation is lower than 5 ft above the 100 year flood level. (per FEMA) 2- Within 100 ft of the Wetland (per CFR and USAD) 3- Within 50 ft of lake, sea, river and streams. (per Clean Water Act) 4- Public parkland (unless equal or larger space is accepted by the public land owner and USAD) . The park authority projects are EXEMPT from this requirement. 5- The habitat areas for endangered and threatened species. 6- The prime farmland.*	*n/a*	*1- USAD 2- FEMA 3- CFR 4- Clean Water Act.*	*Design*

POINTS	REFERENCE NUMBER	INTENT OF CREDIT	STATEMENT OF CREDIT	CONCENTRATION OF CREDIT	GENERAL EXPLANATION	EXTRA CREDIT	CODE OR STANDARD	SUBMITTAL PHASE
1	SS 2	1- To provide channel development within the existing infrastructure. 2- To protect green fields and vegetated lands. 3- To preserve habitat and natural resources.	(Development Density & Community Connectivity) GENERAL NOTES : A) The area of a ONE story parking structure can NOT be added to the building area. B) When the parking structure is MORE than one story, then the area of only TWO story parking structures can be added to the building footprint. C) The area of both structure and stacked parking area shall be added to the building footprint. D) The boundary of project plays a major rule in this credit.	Proximity : 1- On the site map, draw 1/2 mile radius circle around the main entrance to the project. 2- Count number of building services inside the circle.	Density Development : 1- Commercial area : Minimum 60.000 sq.ft per acre on the developed site including the project site and community site. (similar to 2 story building in downtown area) 2- Residential area : 10 units per acre density within 1/2 mile. 3- Community Connectivity : 10 services within 1/2 mile, such as restaurants, churches, banks and stores. When there are two of each services inside the 1/2 mile radius, the RESTAURANT is the ONLY service that can be counted for two (2) services. The pedestrian access to the building services shall NOT be blocked by freeway, major parks OR any barriers. 4- For the calculation, do NOT include undeveloped areas such as parks, water bodies (lake) and public roads.	DOUBLE the standard OR achieve density factor of 120,000 sq.ft per acre	n/a	Design

POINTS	REFERENCE NUMBER	INTENT OF CREDIT	STATEMENT OF CREDIT	CONCENTRATION OF CREDIT	GENERAL EXPLANATION	EXTRA CREDIT	CODE OR STANDARD	SUBMITTAL PHASE
1	SS 3	1-To rehabilitate damaged sites. 2- To reduce pressure on undeveloped land.	Brownfield Redevelopment	Site Redevelopment	1- Build on contaminated sites. 2- Rebuild on the site which has been qualified as a BROWNFIELD site. 3- The SUPERFUND of CERCLA refers to the TAX BREAK. 4- Obtain contaminated risks and remedial measures for the project.	n/a	1- Local codes, 2- ASTM 1903.97 3- EPA 4- CERCLA	Design

POINTS	REFERENCE NUMBER	INTENT OF CREDIT	STATEMENT OF CREDIT	CONCENTRATION OF CREDIT	GENERAL EXPLANATION	EXTRA CREDIT	CODE OR STANDARD	SUBMITTAL PHASE
1	SS 4.1	*1- To reduce pollution generated by auto use. 2- To reduce land development required for auto use.*	*Alternative Transportation*	*Public Transportation Access*	*Case 1 : Projects which are located 1/2 mile from ONE (1) train or subway station. Case 2 : Projects which are located 1/4 mile from TWO (2) public or campus bus lines.*	*Case 1 : ONE (1) station to TWO (2) stations Case 2 : TWO (2) bus lines to FOUR (4) bus lines*	*n/a*	*Design*

POINTS	REFERENCE NUMBER	INTENT OF CREDIT	STATEMENT OF CREDIT	CONCENTRATION OF CREDIT	GENERAL EXPLANATION	EXTRA CREDIT	CODE OR STANDARD	SUBMITTAL PHASE
1	SS 4.2	1- To reduce pollution generated by auto use. 2- To reduce land development required for auto use.	Alternative Transportation	Bicycle Storage & Changing Rooms	Case 1 : 1- Provide bicycle racks within 200 yards of the building. (based on 5 % (0.05) of FTE) AND Provide changing rooms and shower rooms within 200 yards of the building. (based on 0.5 % (0.005) of FTE) Case 2 : RESIDENTIAL: Provide bicycle racks for 15 % of the tenants.	Report	n/a	Design

POINTS	REFERENCE NUMBER	INTENT OF CREDIT	STATEMENT OF CREDIT	CONCENTRATION OF CREDIT	GENERAL EXPLANATION	EXTRA CREDIT	CODE OR STANDARD	SUBMITTAL PHASE
1	SS 4.3	1- To reduce pollution generated by auto use. 2- To reduce land development required for auto use.	Alternative Transportation	Low Emitting and Fuel- Efficient Vehicles	Option 1 : 1-Provide low emission cars for the tenants. (based on 3 % of FTE) Option 2 : Provide preferred parking for low emission cars. (based on 5 % of the total parking space) Option 3 : 1- Provide charging and refuel stations. (based on 3 % of the total parking space) General notes : 1- The low emission car shall be ZEV or with energy star score of 40 . 2- Preferred parking spaces with DISCOUNTED rate. (EXCLUDE handicap parking spaces)	Report	n/a	Design

POINTS	REFERENCE NUMBER	INTENT OF CREDIT	STATEMENT OF CREDIT	CONCENTRATION OF CREDIT	GENERAL EXPLANATION	EXTRA CREDIT	CODE OR STANDARD	SUBMITTAL PHASE
1	SS 4.4	*1- To reduce pollution generated by auto use. 2- To reduce land development required for auto use.*	*Alternative Transportation*	*Parking Capacity Preferred parking spaces : 1- Handicap parking space. 2- Low-emission car parking space. 3- Parking spaces near building entrance.*	*Option 1 : (Non- Residential) 1- The number of parking spaces shall NOT exceed the local code. 2- Provide carpool parking spaces (based on 5 % of the total parking spaces) . Option 2 : (Non- Residential) 1- When preferred parking spaces are less than 5 % of FTE, then provide carpool parking space. (based on 5 % of the total parking spaces) . Option 3 : (Residential) 1- Do NOT exceed the local code standards. 2- Provide shared vehicle program. Option 4 : (Commercial & Residential) 1- NO new parking.*	*Report*	*When the local code is NOT defined: 1) Meet the Portland , Oregon Zoning Code TITLE 33 standards. 2) Obtain 25 % less than minimum requirements set by the Institute of Transportation Engineers.*	*Design*

POINTS	REFERENCE NUMBER	INTENT OF CREDIT	STATEMENT OF CREDIT	CONCENTRATION OF CREDIT	GENERAL EXPLANATION	EXTRA CREDIT	CODE OR STANDARD	SUBMITTAL PHASE
1	SS 5.1	*1- To conserve natural areas. 2- To restore damaged sites. 3- To obtain habitat spaces. 4- To promote biodiversity.*	*Site Development GENERAL NOTES : 1- The graded site should be obtained from previously developed land. 2- Exclude building footprint from developed site area. 3- This credit has high impact on ecosystem site development.*	*(Protect Habitat Spaces) GENERAL NOTES : A- This credit has the highest impact on ecosystem. B- When calculating the building area do NOT include the followings areas: 1- Parking lots area 2- Landscape area 3- Wetlands area*	*Protect the GREENFIELD sites by limiting it to: A. 40 ft beyond the building perimeter. B. 25 ft beyond the constructed areas. C. 15 ft beyond the roadway. D. 10 ft beyond the walkway. E. 10 ft from 12 inch the main utility pipe. PREVIOUSLY DEVELOPED sites : 1- Keep 50 % of the site area as a vegetated land (native) ZERO-LOT-LINE : 1-The vegetated roof can earn points in BOTH SS 5.1 and SS 2 credits. 2- The green area shall be 20 % of the site area, including the building foot print.*	*50% to 75%*	*n/a*	*Construction*

POINTS	REFERENCE NUMBER	INTENT OF CREDIT	STATEMENT OF CREDIT	CONCENTRATION OF CREDIT	GENERAL EXPLANATION	EXTRA CREDIT	CODE OR STANDARD	SUBMITTAL PHASE
1	SS 5.2	1- To create high ratio of open space compared to footprint of the building. 2- To promote biodiversity.	Site Development GENERAL NOTES : 1- It is a time consuming credit. 2- The boundary of project plays major rule in this credit. 3- The building footprint area is equal to the area of developed site minus property area.	(Maximize Open Space) Methods of calculation for the open space : 1) Use the local zoning standards 2) If NO local zoning is available, then the open space area is equal to the property area LESS than the development footprint.	Case 1 ; Where there is a local code for the open space with restriction: 1- The open space should exceed the local code requirement by 25 %. Case 2 : Where there is NO local code: (university campus and military sites) 1- The open space area should be EQUAL to the building footprint area. (for the LIFE of the building) Case 3 : Where there is a local code for open space with ZERO open space restrictions: 1- The open space area should be 20 % of the total site area. Wetland : Includes open space and pond with 1:4 slope. Urban open space : 1-Pocket parks , 2- Accessible roof decks, 3- Plazas, 4- Courtyard.	Case 1 : 25 % to 50 % Case 2 : EQUAL to DOUBLE Case 3 : 20 % to 40 %	n/a	Design

POINTS	REFERENCE NUMBER	INTENT OF CREDIT	STATEMENT OF CREDIT	CONCENTRATION OF CREDIT	GENERAL EXPLANATION	EXTRA CREDIT	CODE OR STANDARD	SUBMITTAL PHASE
1	SS 6.1	1- To limit disruption of natural hydrology. 2- To reduce impervious cover. 3- To increase on-site infiltration. 4- To manage storm water runoff. 5- To reduce and eliminate water pollution. 6- To eliminate sources of contaminants. 7- To remove pollutants from storm water runoff.	(Stormwater Design) For reduction of the impervious surface : 1- Use non-structural, <u>alternative surface</u> method: Rain garden, vegetated swales, disconnection of impervious area and pervious pavement, and rainwater recycling. 2- Use non-structural, <u>surface</u> method: Vegetated roof, pervious pavement, cisterns, manhole devices and grid pavers. <u>Minimize impervious surface by following methods</u> : 1- Retention ponds 2 -Smaller footprint ponds 3- Green roof	(Quantity Control) <u>Humid watershed</u> : 1 inch rain fall and 40 inches per year. <u>Semi-arid watershed</u> : 0.75 inch rain fall and 20 to 40 inches per year. <u>Arid watershed</u> : 0.50 inch rainfall and less than 20 inches per year.	<u>Case 1</u> : 1- The impervious surface area is <u>LESS</u> than or equal to 50 % of the total site area. 2- The pre-development discharge rate should <u>NOT</u> exceed the post-development discharge rate. (for storm water follow rate calculation, use <u>2 years</u> rainfall factor) <u>Case 2</u> : 1- The impervious surface is <u>MORE</u> than <u>50 %</u> of the total site area. 2- The post-development discharge rate shall be <u>25 % LESS</u> than pre-development discharge rate. <u>Make sure to calculate CFS and CF factors.</u>	n/a	1- BMP 2- EPA 3- TRAP 4- TSS	Design
1	SS 6.2			(Quality Control) <u>Mechanical treatment</u> : 1- Constructed wetland 2- Vegetated filtration 3- Swales <u>Structural measure methods</u> ; 1- Manhole 2- Treatment devices 3- Rainwater cisterns	1- Capture and treat 90 % of the <u>ANNUAL</u> storm water runoff. 2- Remove 80 % of TSS. 3- Use BMP to treat the storm water system per following methods: A) <u>The sustainable design</u> : 1- Implement the low impact development. 2- Promote environmental sensitive design. B) <u>The natural and mechanical treatments</u> : 1- Use constructed wetland. 2- Use vegetated filter and open channel. C) <u>The alternative surface</u> : 1- Use vegetated roofs and swales. 2- Use grid pavers.	n/a		Design

POINTS	REFERENCE NUMBER	INTENT OF CREDIT	STATEMENT OF CREDIT	CONCENTRATION OF CREDIT	GENERAL EXPLANATION	EXTRA CREDIT	CODE OR STANDARD	SUBMITTAL PHASE
1	SS 7.1	1- To reduce heat islands. 2- To minimize the impact on microclimate and wildlife habitat.	Heat Island Effect GENERAL NOTES : 1- SRI of 100 means 100 percent of solar radiation is reflected back to atmosphere. 2- The emissivity relates to the heat radiation of materials.	(Non-roof) Infrared or thermal emittance : 1- It is normally 0.90 (between 0 and 1) 2- It is a comparison factor to the black body radiation.	Option 1 : 1- Obtain full shading for 50% of the site within a period of 5 years. 2- Provide the open grid area paving for parking, roads, sidewalks and yards with SRI EQUAL to or GREATER than 29. Option 2 : 1- Design 50 % of the parking space under roof or at underground level. 2- Provide paving for the parking space with SRI equal to or greater than 29. SRI : Solar Reflectance Index is the amount of solar radiation observed or reflected by element. White (SRI =100) , Black (SRI= 0)	Option 1: 50 % up to 100 % Option 2 : 50 % up to 100%	ASTM	Construction
1	SS 7.2			(Roof) GENERAL NOTES : The heat island effect can be created by the followings: 1- Deciduous trees 2- Aledo materials 3- Evapotranspoira-tion	Option 1 : Design 75 % of the roofing material per following standards: SRI=78 (for 2/12 or less slope) SRI= 29 (for more than 2/12 slope) Option 2 : Design 50 % of the roofing with vegetation elements such as green roof. Option 3 : Combination of both options 1 & 2	Option 1: 75 % up to 100%	ASTM	Design

POINTS	REFERENCE NUMBER	INTENT OF CREDIT	STATEMENT OF CREDIT	CONCENTRATION OF CREDIT	GENERAL EXPLANATION	EXTRA CREDIT	CODE OR STANDARD	SUBMITTAL PHASE
1	SS 8	1- To minimize light trespass from building and project site. 2- To reduce sky-glow. 3- To reduce site development on nocturnal condition.	Light Pollution Reduction (this credit DOES NOT apply to the three story or less buildings, warehouses and manufactured homes) Control devices includes : 1- Occupancy sensors 2- Manual override unit 3- Sweep timers Lighting pollution factors : 1- Glare 2- Illumination level	LZ1 : 1. Dark 2. The density is less than 200 people per square mile. LZ2 : 1. Low (RESIDENTIAL) 2. The density is between 200 to 3000 people per square mile. LZ3 : 1. Medium (COMMERCIAL) 2. The density is more than 3000 people per square mile. LZ4 : 1. High (CITY) 2. The density is more than 100,000 people per square mile.	Interior lighting : 1- The interior lighting shall NOT be transferred to the outdoor area . 2- The non-emergency lights shall be turned down at non-business hours. Exterior lighting : 1- It shall ONLY be provided for the comfort and safety. 2- It shall NOT exceed over 80 % of the exterior lighting guideline published by the ASHRAE 90.1, 2004 standard. 3- It shall NOT exceed over 50 % of the landscape and the facade lighting guideline published by the ASHRAE 90.1,2004 standards. 4- It shall comply with pre-curfew guides.	n/a	1- ASHRAE/ IESNA 90.1 2004, 2- ANSI 3- California Energy Code TITLE 24 4- Curfew guidelines	Design

LEEDPASS

WATER EFFICIENCY

POINTS	REFERENCE NUMBER	INTENT OF CREDIT	STATEMENT OF CREDIT	CONCENTRATION OF CREDIT	GENERAL EXPLANATION	EXTRA CREDIT	CODE OR STANDARD	SUBMITTAL PHASE
WATER EFFICIENCY								
1	WE 1.1	*1- To limit or eliminate the use of potable water for landscape irrigation. 2- To limit or eliminate the use of natural surface or subsurface water for landscape irrigation.*	*(Water Efficient Landscaping) Gray water : 1- Shower 2- Sink 3- Bathtubs 4- Bathroom wash basin 5- Cloth washer Black water : 1- Toilet 2- Kitchen sink 3- Dishwasher. Non potable water : 1- Treated water 2- Captured rainwater 3- Recycled waste water Types of water used for load calculation in this credit : 1- Gray water 2- Strom water 3- Shower waste water Water reduction factors : 1- Species 2- Micro climate 3- Density*	*(50 % Reduction) Reduce water consumption use by followings : 1- Native plants 2- Vegetated swales 3- Adapted plants Various factors impact this credit : 1- Species factor 2- Microclimate factor 3- Density factor*	*1- Select plants with high species factor. 2- Design high efficiency micro-irrigation systems. 3- For irrigation system use the following: A) Captured rainwater. B) Recycled wastewater. C) Treated water. 4- Use non-potable treated water from the public agency. 5- Reduce the potable water consumption for the irrigation system by 50 % compare to the BASELINE standards. 6- Use month of July for evapotranspiration rate calculation. 7- For baseline calculation do NOT include building footprint, paved surface area and water bodies.*	*n/a*	*n/a*	*Design*
1	WE 1.2			*(No Potable Use OR No Irrigation) Temporary irrigation : Install it for the establishment of landscape which will be removed within ONE year.*	*Option 1: DO NOT use ANY potable water. Option 2: DO NOT use ANY irrigation system. Use following methods for the landscaping system : 1- Captured rainwater. 2- Recycled wastewater. 3- Recycled gray water. 4- Treated water. Minimize the site area covered with the turf by the following methods : 1- Composting 2- Mulching 3- Alternative mowing*	*n/a*	*n/a*	*Design*

POINTS	REFERENCE NUMBER	INTENT OF CREDIT	STATEMENT OF CREDIT	CONCENTRATION OF CREDIT	GENERAL EXPLANATION	EXTRA CREDIT	CODE OR STANDARD	SUBMITTAL PHASE
1	WE 2	*1- To reduce generation of wastewater.* *2- To reduce demand of potable water* *3- To increase recharge of local aquifer.*	*Innovative Wastewater Technologies* *GENERAL NOTES :* *1- This credit requires baseline calculation.* *2- This credit is normally applied to projects located close to urban and developed sites.*	*Treatment system :* *1- Transport* *2- Store* *3- Treat* *4- Dispose* *Calculation factors :* *1- Daily use rate* *2- Occupancy* *3- Number of workdays* *Consider following items for the load calculation :* *1- Time: 8 hr per day for FTE occupants* *2- Occupancy type:* *A) Student* *B) Retail customer* *C) Visitor* *D) FTE* *Consider the following daily use factors for MALE and FEMALE occupants :* *1- ONE to ONE ratio* *2- Male: WC=1, UR=2* *3- Female: WC= 3*	*Option 1 : Use following methods to reduce 50 % of the potable water use in the building:* *1- Select water conserving fixtures.* *2- Reuse non-potable water for flushing the plumbing fixtures.* *3- Reuse treated water.* *Option 2 : Treat and reuse 50 % of the wastewater used on the site per tertiary standards.* *Treated water must be reused & infiltrated by the following methods :* *1- Biological system.* *2- Constructed wetland.* *3- High efficiency filtration for waste water. (tertiary treatment)*	*Option 1 : More than 50 % reduction* *Option 2 : Treat 100 % instead of 50 %*	*n/a*	*Design*

POINTS	REFERENCE NUMBER	INTENT OF CREDIT	STATEMENT OF CREDIT	CONCENTRATION OF CREDIT	GENERAL EXPLANATION	EXTRA CREDIT	CODE OR STANDARD	SUBMITTAL PHASE
1	**WE 3.1**	*1- To maximize water efficiency. 2- To reduce burden on municipal water supply agency. 3- To reduce burden on wastewater system.*	*Water Use Reduction GENERAL NOTES : 1- This credit requires baseline calculation.*	*20 % Reduction*	*For the water reduction calculation : 1- DO NOT include irrigation water. 2- Include water closet, urinal, shower and kitchen sink in this calculation. 3- Use other fixtures for EXTRA credit. Method of selection : 1- Use special fixtures, flow sensors and metering control devices for plumbing system. Shower head capacity : Conventional = 2.5 GPM , Low: 1.8 GPM Lavatory capacity : Conventional = 2.5 GPM, Low: 1.8 GPM, Ultra-Low: 0.5 GPM Kitchen sink capacity : Conventional = 2.5 GPM Low-flow=1.8 GPM*	*Option 1 : 30 % up to 40% Option 2 : Reduce the use of non-regulated water to 10 % of the total regulated water.*	*Energy Policy Act 1992*	*Design*
1	**WE 3.2**			*30 % Reduction*	*Continuation of WE 3.1 notes : Water closet capacity: 1.6 GPF Urinal capacity: 1 GPF Faucets capacity: 2.5 GPM Aerator capacity: 2.5 GPM Metering faucets capacity: 0.25 Gallon per Cycle Residential : (Daily use factor per person) Flush fixture : 5 times / day Shower ; 1 time / day Kitchen sink: 4 times / day*			*Design*

LEEDPASS

ENERGY

&

ATMOSPHERE

POINTS	REFERENCE NUMBER	INTENT OF CREDIT	STATEMENT OF CREDIT	CONCENTRATION OF CREDIT	GENERAL EXPLANATION	EXTRA CREDIT	CODE OR STANDARD	SUBMITTAL PHASE
	ENERGY & ATMOSPHERE							
0	EA P1	1- To verify the design is installed, calibrated and performing according to BOD, OPR and construction documents.	Fundamental Commissioning of the Building Energy Systems	(Mandatory) The fundamental report shall include : 1- Executive summary 2- History of deficiencies 3- Evaluation 4- Submittal process 5- Operation and Maintenance 6- As-built drawings The fundamental report shall include : 1- OPR 2- BOD 3- Plan 4- Specification 5- Verification 6- Report	1- Check if the building energy system is INSTALLED, CALIBRATED, PERFORMING and OPERATING based on BOD and OPR. The minimum requirements for the designated commissioning authority : 1- Experienced for TWO (2) similar projects. 2- An independent person. 3- For LESS than 50, 000 sq.ft buildings, the commissioning process can be performed by the member of design or construction team. Provide commissioning process for the following systems : 1- HVAC systems. 2- Domestic hot water system. 3- Renewable energy (wind, solar, etc). 4- Lighting systems.	n/a	n/a	Construction

POINTS	REFERENCE NUMBER	INTENT OF CREDIT	STATEMENT OF CREDIT	CONCENTRATION OF CREDIT	GENERAL EXPLANATION	EXTRA CREDIT	CODE OR STANDARD	SUBMITTAL PHASE
0	EA P2	To establish minimum level of energy efficiency standards.	Minimum Energy Performance GENERAL NOTES : The following factors are identical for BOTH design and baseline calculations: 1- Occupancy rate 2- Number of workdays 3- Daily use rate	(Mandatory) Provide occupancy control devices for the following rooms : 1- Class rooms 2- Meeting rooms 3- Break rooms Building system includes ; 1- HVAC system 2- Lighting system 3- Building envelope	Option 1 : 1- The design of building system shall comply with ASHRAE-IESNA 90.1- 2004 standards. Option 2 : 1- The design of building system shall comply with the local codes or DOE regulations instead of ASHRAE standards. Consider the following factors for energy calculation : 1- Window area: It shall be LESS than 50 % of the total wall area. 2- Skylight area : It shall be LESS than 5 % of the total roof area.	n/a	1- ASHRAE-IESNA 90.1 2004 2- DOE	Design

POINTS	REFERENCE NUMBER	INTENT OF CREDIT	STATEMENT OF CREDIT	CONCENTRATION OF CREDIT	GENERAL EXPLANATION	EXTRA CREDIT	CODE OR STANDARD	SUBMITTAL PHASE
0	EA P3	*To reduce ozone layer issues.*	*Fundamental Refrigerant Management*	*(Mandatory)* *GENERAL NOTES :* *Do NOT include HVAC units with LESS than 0.5 lbs of refrigerant in the BASELINE building calculation.*	*1- NEW building: Implement ZERO use of CFC.* *2- EXISTING building: Replace HVAC units and fire suppression systems designed with CFC refrigerants.* *3- The production of HVAC units with CFC refrigerant was stopped in 1995 and it will be phased out by 2011.* *4- The mechanical system, which will be CONNECTED to the existing chilled water system, has to be selected with CFC - FREE refrigerants.* *The NON-FEASIBLE units : Includes mechanical units with greater than 10 years payback.* *Select refrigerants material with :* *1- Short environmental lifetime* *2- Small ODP* *3- Small GWP*	*n/a*	*EPA (Montréal Protocol 1987)*	*Design*

POINTS	REFERENCE NUMBER	INTENT OF CREDIT	STATEMENT OF CREDIT	CONCENTRATION OF CREDIT	GENERAL EXPLANATION	EXTRA CREDIT	CODE OR STANDARD	SUBMITTAL PHASE
10	EA 1	1-To increase the level of energy performance compared to the mandatory standards 2- To reduce excessive energy use.	(Optimize Energy Performance) PROJECTS REGISTERED AFTER 06/26/2007 : 1) The project shall exceed the requirements of the ASHRAE - IESNA 90.1-2004 standards. 2) The project shall achieve at least TWO (2) POINTS under this credit. GENERAL NOTES : 1- Minimum increase for new buildings is 14 % (10.5+ 3.5 = 14) and minimum increase for existing buildings is 7 % (3.5+3.5=7). 2- Option # 1 requires baseline calculation. 3- The demand-controlled ventilation system can be utilized for this credit.	Increase the energy performance by the following methods : 1- Reduce the demand load. 2- Reduce the footprint of the building. 3- Provide controlling sensor for the mechanical system. 4- Use the harvest energy. 5- Increase the efficiency of the mechanical system. 6- Recover the waste energy. 7- Use demand - controlled system.	Option 1 : (Whole Building Simulation) 1- NEW building: Start at 10.5 % increase, compared to the baseline, requiring 3.5 % increase for each additional point. (up to 42 %) 2- EXISTING building: Start at 3.5 % increase, compared to the baseline, requiring 3.5 % increase for each additional point. (up to 35 %) 3- ALL costs shall be included in the energy calculation. 4- This credit offers 1 to 10 points. 5- Everything must be compared to the baseline of the ASHRAE 90.1 standard. 6- The DEFAULT process energy is 25 % of the total energy. 7- Provide FOUR (4) orientation simulations for each baseline. Provide lighting sensor for the following: Class rooms, conference rooms and break rooms.	NEW building (45.5 %) & EXISTING building (38.5 %)	Option 1 : Simulation method : 1- It shall comply with ASHRAE-IESNA 90.1 2004, ANSI standards. 2- It does NOT cover : Buildings with 3 stories or less , warehouses and manufactured homes. 3- It covers : Building envelope, HVAC systems, service water heating systems , power systems and lighting systems.	Design

POINTS	REFERENCE NUMBER	INTENT OF CREDIT	STATEMENT OF CREDIT	CONCENTRATION OF CREDIT	GENERAL EXPLANATION	EXTRA CREDIT	CODE OR STANDARD	SUBMITTAL PHASE
10	EA 1 (cont.)		*Optimize Energy Performance (Continuation of EA 1)* *GENERAL NOTES :* *1- The life cycle analysis includes first cost, installation cost and maintenance cost.* *2- This credit requires the lengthiest technical and managerial analysis.* *3- For daylight control use photoelectric daylight sensor.* *4- The average Energy Star for building materials is normally 50 .* *5- The photoelectric daylight sensor can be utilized in this credit.* *The factors that impacts performance energy calculation :* *1- Building area* *2- Building orientation* *3- Number of floors*	*The regulated system :* *HVAC system, hot water services and interior lighting* *The non-regulated system :* *Exterior lighting, plug load, process load and garage ventilation.*	*Continuation of EA 1 :* *Option 2 : (Prescriptive Method)* *1- The design shall comply with the ASHRAE 2004 standard for SMALLER buildings.* *2- The building area shall be under 20,000 sq.ft .* *3- This method ONLY applies to office building occupancy.* *4-The building shall comply with the LOCAL climate zone standards.* *5- This option offers up to 4 points .* *6- The energy cost calculation is NOT required for this method.* *Energy Calculation Software :* *Trane, carrier, DOE* *Energy Star = EPA + DOE codes*	*n/a*	*Continuation of Option 1 :* *1- Do NOT include on-site renewable energy (solar panels, wind turbine) for the PERFORMANCE calculation.* *2- Do NOT include on-site recovered energy (chiller and waste heat recovery) for the PERFORMANCE calculation.* *3- For the PROPOSED calculation, the windows COULD be distributed equally, but in the baseline calculation, the windows SHALL be distributed equally.*	*Design*

POINTS	REFERENCE NUMBER	INTENT OF CREDIT	STATEMENT OF CREDIT	CONCENTRATION OF CREDIT	GENERAL EXPLANATION	EXTRA CREDIT	CODE OR STANDARD	SUBMITTAL PHASE
10	EA 1 (cont.)		Optimize Energy Performance (Continuation of EA 1) Alternative fuel : 1- Diesel 2- Petroleum gas 3- Natural gas Process load can be generated from following items : 1- Water pumps 2- Office equipment 3- Elevator machine 4- Washer and dryer GENERAL NOTES : 1- In this credit option # 3 requires baseline calculation. 2- In selection of HVAC units consider SHGC, SEER and COP factors. 3- Do NOT include recover waste energy sources in building performance calculation.	The harvest energy applies to : 1- Building orientation. 2- Location of windows. 3- Natural ventilation design. The recover waste energy system includes : 1- Exhaust air waste energy. 2- Water heat load factor. 3- Cogeneration system.	Option 3 : (Performance Compliance) 1- The design shall comply with Core Performance Guideline published by New Building Institute. 2- It is applicable for buildings under 100,000 sq.ft. 3- It is NOT applicable for warehouses, health care and laboratory projects. 4- It shall comply with section ONE and section TWO of Core Performance. 5- It can earn up to 5 points . (3 points for office, school and retail projects) AND (2 points for other types of projects) Option 4 : (Prescriptive method): 1- Projects registered after 07/26/07 may NOT use this option. It offers 1 point and shall comply with ASHRAE, BENCHMARK 1.1.	Option 3 : Implement THREE strategies EXCLUDING cool roofs, night venting and additional commission-ing from section THREE of the Core Performanc e guideline and earn TWO (2) additional points.	Option 3 : New Building Institute. Option 4 : ASHRAE, Benchmark 1.1 for the LARGER building.	Design

POINTS	REFERENCE NUMBER	INTENT OF CREDIT	STATEMENT OF CREDIT	CONCENTRATION OF CREDIT	GENERAL EXPLANATION	EXTRA CREDIT	CODE OR STANDARD	SUBMITTAL PHASE
1	EA 2	1- To increase on-site renewable energy. 2- To reduce impacts on fuel energy use. 3- To offset building energy cost.	On-Site Renewable Energy GENERAL NOTES : 1- Organic materials can be utilized for this credit.	Types of renewable energy : 1- Solar 2- Wind 3- Geothermal 4- Biomass 5- Bio-gas 6- Low impact hydro-photovoltaic To assign dollar value use : 1- Local utility rates 2- Virtual energy VIRTUAL ENERGY : It is equal to the annual energy COST divided by annual energy CONSUMPTION.	1- Achieve the annual energy saving of 2.5 % , 7.5 % and 12.5 % and earn ONE point for each increment. (up to 3 points) The following systems are eligible for this credit : 1- Electrical system 2- Geothermal energy system 3- Solar thermal system 4- Photovoltaic panel system 5- Wind turbine system 6- Solar panel system The following systems are NOT eligible for this credit : 1- Architectural feature (passive solar, daylight) 2- Geo-exchange	Annual saving of 17.5 %	1- ASHRAE 90.1-2004 2- DOE 3- CBECS 4- EIA 5- REC	Design

POINTS	REFERENCE NUMBER	INTENT OF CREDIT	STATEMENT OF CREDIT	CONCENTRATION OF CREDIT	GENERAL EXPLANATION	EXTRA CREDIT	CODE OR STANDARD	SUBMITTAL PHASE
1	EA 3	*1- Implement commissioning process after verification phase.*	*Enhanced Commissioning* *GENERAL NOTES :* *1- This is a time consuming credit.*	*GENERAL NOTES :* *1- It is a costly credit* *2- It is a time consuming credit .* *3- Implement BOD, OPR and environmental factors for this credit.*	*All EA-P1 requirements PLUS followings :* *1- Review submittal.* *2- Prepare project manuals.* *3- Arrange to review the building operation within 10 months of the sustainable completion.* *4- Review drawings and specification at 50 % of design phase.* *5- Provide training for the final users.* *(S for Submittal, M for Manual, A for Arrange, R for Review and T for Training)* *(SMART)* *MEMORIZE IT*	*n/a*	*n/a*	*Construction*

POINTS	REFERENCE NUMBER	INTENT OF CREDIT	STATEMENT OF CREDIT	CONCENTRATION OF CREDIT	GENERAL EXPLANATION	EXTRA CREDIT	CODE OR STANDARD	SUBMITTAL PHASE
1	EA 4	*1- To reduce ODP and GWP and comply with the Montreal Protocol*	*Enhanced Refrigerant Management*	*Refrigerant comparison :* *1- CFC (High)* *2- HCFC (Medium)* *3- HFC (Low)* *ODP : The CFC has the highest and the HFC has the lowest.* *GWP : The CFC has the highest and the HFC has the lowest.* *Efficiency :* *1- The CFC has HIGHER than the HCFC.* *2- The HCFC has HIGHER than the HFC.*	*Option 1 : Do NOT use any type of refrigerant.* *Option 2 : Minimize or eliminate emission per the following:* *1- Select HVAC system with low ODP and GWP refrigerants.* *2- Select long-life mechanical units.* *3- Do NOT install fire suppression system with CFC and HCFC refrigerants and halon products.* *4- Comply with the ASHRAE standards. (the HFC has ZERO ODP and will be phased out by 2030)*	*n/a*	*1- Clean Air Act 1990* *2- EPA*	*Design*

POINTS	REFERENCE NUMBER	INTENT OF CREDIT	STATEMENT OF CREDIT	CONCENTRATION OF CREDIT	GENERAL EXPLANATION	EXTRA CREDIT	CODE OR STANDARD	SUBMITTAL PHASE
1	EA 5	1- Develop a plan to measure and check the building energy consumption.	Measurement & Verification The following items apply to this credit : 1- Whole building computer simulation 2- Occupancy period 3- Energy conservation and measurement GENERAL NOTES : 1- This is a time consuming credit.	1- Ongoing accountability of the Building Energy Consumption. 2- Develop and implement the measurement and verification plan for mechanical, electrical and plumbing systems. 3- A suitable credit for LARGE projects. 4- The M& V process shall apply to irrigation systems, mechanical systems and lighting performance in the building.	1- The IPMP Volume III offers 4 options , but for the LEED certification process, we ONLY need to comply with TWO options. (B) & (D) Option B : Covers the energy conservation for the SMALLER projects. Option D : Covers the calibrated energy simulation for the LARGER projects. 2- Measurement and Verification : Install a metering device to measure the energy consumption rating. The result of M& V is valid for ONE year. Performance factor : The PREDICATED measurement DIVIDED by the ACTUAL measurement. Efficiency : The BASELINE measurement DIVIDED by the ACTUAL measurement.	n/a	1- IPMVP 2- EVO 3- ECM	Construction

POINTS	REFERENCE NUMBER	INTENT OF CREDIT	STATEMENT OF CREDIT	CONCENTRATION OF CREDIT	GENERAL EXPLANATION	EXTRA CREDIT	CODE OR STANDARD	SUBMITTAL PHASE
1	EA 6	1- To encourage the use of renewable energy based on NET-ZERO pollution.	Green Power GENERAL NOTES : 1- This credit requires a baseline calculation.	Types of Green Power sources : 1- Solar 2- Wind 3- Geothermal 4- Biomass 5- Bio-gas 6- Low-impact hydro 7- Photovoltaic	1- Renewable sources are defined by the CRS. 2- Determine the baseline for electricity use from EA credit 1 or DOE database. Case 1 : OPEN electrical market: 1- Obtain 35 % of the annual consumption load from green power source. The Green Pro Certificate is NOT required for the purchased power. 2- Purchase the contract for TWO years. Case 2 : CLOSED electrical market: Obtain 35 % of annual consumption load from the green power source without ANY contract. Case 3 : When the green power source is NOT available: Purchase 35 % of the annual consumption load for TWO years (which adds up to 70 % of projected energy use) .	Case 1 : 35 % up to 70 % (OR) 2 years up to 4 years	1- DOE 2- CBECS 3-CRS	Construction

LEEDPASS

MATERIAL

&

RESOURCES

POINTS	REFERENCE NUMBER	INTENT OF CREDIT	STATEMENT OF CREDIT	CONCENTRATION OF CREDIT	GENERAL EXPLANATION	EXTRA CREDIT	CODE OR STANDARD	SUBMITTAL PHASE
MATERIAL AND RESOURCES								
0	MR P.1	*1- To reduce waste generated by occupants.* *2- To reduce waste hauled to or disposed of in landfills.* *3- Provide accessible area for collection of recyclables materials at the site.*	*Storage & Collection of Recyclables*	*Mandatory*	*Methods of approach :* *1- Separation* *2- Collection* *3- Storage* *Collection sources :* *1- Cardboard baler* *2- Recycling chutes* *3- Collection bins* *4- Aluminum can crusher* *Recyclable materials :* *1- Paper* *2- Glass* *3- Metal* *4- Plastic* *5- Cardboard*	*n/a*	*CIWMB 1999*	*Design*

LEEDPASS
(LEED NC 2.2)

POINTS	REFERENCE NUMBER	INTENT OF CREDIT	STATEMENT OF CREDIT	CONCENTRATION OF CREDIT	GENERAL EXPLANATION	EXTRA CREDIT	CODE OR STANDARD	SUBMITTAL PHASE
1	MR 1.1	*1- To extend life cycle of existing buildings. 2- To reduce waste and environmental impacts on new buildings. 3- To retain cultural resources. 4- To reduce constructability issues for manufacturing processes. 5- To conserve natural resources. 6- To avoid any constraints for transporting materials to the site.*	*Building Reuse*	*Maintain 75 % of the EXISTING walls, floors and roof.*	*1- <u>REUSE</u> the existing building material. 2- <u>REMOVE</u> the elements with the contamination risk factors. 3- <u>EXCLUDE</u> windows, doors and non-structural material for this credit. 4- The calculation for this credit is based on the area or volume (square ft or cubic ft) of the reuse building material. 5- Do <u>NOT</u> include MEP (Mechanical, Electrical, Plumbing) units and elevator machines in the calculation. 6- Do <u>NOT</u> include hazardous material in the calculation. 7- This credit is <u>NOT</u> applicable if the <u>ADDITION</u> footprint area is <u>DOUBLE</u> the building footprint area. <u>The building structure includes</u> : Floor, frame, roof and exterior structure.*	*n/a*	*(code is n/a) The estimate shall be based on the following: 1- For the <u>STRUCTURAL</u> items: use (sq.ft) & 2- For the <u>SHELL</u> elements use (sq.ft)*	*Construction*
1	MR 1.2			*Maintain 95 % of the EXISTING walls, floors and roof.*				
1	MR 1.3			*Maintain 50% of the interior material with <u>NON-STRUCTURAL</u> elements.*	*1- The interior elements include: Wall, partition, doors, ceiling, floor covering and ceiling. 2- The calculation shall be based on the building footprint <u>AREA</u> (sq.ft). 3- Do <u>NOT</u> include MEP (Mechanical, Electrical, Plumbing) units and elevator machines in the calculation. 4- This credit is totally <u>INDEPENDENT</u> from MR.1.1 and MR.1.2 credits.*			

POINTS	REFERENCE NUMBER	INTENT OF CREDIT	STATEMENT OF CREDIT	CONCENTRATION OF CREDIT	GENERAL EXPLANATION	EXTRA CREDIT	CODE OR STANDARD	SUBMITTAL PHASE
1	MR 2.1	1- To divert debris from disposal in the landfill. 2- To redirect recyclable material to the manufacturer. 3- To redirect reusable material to the site.	(Construction Waste Management) For the calculation EXCLUDE the following items : 1- Soils from the site. 2- Vegetations from the site. 3- Rocks from the site. 4- Hazardous material. 5- The elevator machines. 6- Cleaning debris GENERAL NOTES : 1- In order to earn points, full or partial of wasted material can be donated to the specified agency. 2- This credit is mostly used for projects located far from developed and urban areas.	Divert 50 % Divert materials includes : 1- Reused and salvaged materials , if it is NOT included in MR credit 3.1, 3.2. Salvaged material includes : Flooring, paneling, beams, and cabinetry.	The waste management materials includes following items : 1- Salvaged materials 2- Refurbished materials 3- Recycled materials 4- Reuse materials Divert materials include following items : 1- Recycled , refurbished and salvaged items that can be delivered back to the manufacturer. 2- Recycled , refurbished and salvaged items that can be reused at the site. Include following items in the calculation : The on-site salvaged and reused materials that have NOT been utilized for MR 3.1 & MR 3.2 credits.	95%	(code is n/a) The estimate shall be based on following factors : 1- Weight (lb) or 2- Volume (Cubic ft)	Construction
1	MR 2.2			Divert 75 % Diversion process includes the followings : 1- Salvage of materials on-site. 2- Donation of materials. Divert materials do NOT include the following : 1- Rocks 2- Soil 3- Vegetation elements				

POINTS	REFERENCE NUMBER	INTENT OF CREDIT	STATEMENT OF CREDIT	CONCENTRATION OF CREDIT	GENERAL EXPLANATION	EXTRA CREDIT	CODE OR STANDARD	SUBMITTAL PHASE
1	MR 3.1	*1- To reduce waste material.* *2- To reduce the processing of the virgin materials.*	*Material Reuse* *__GENERAL NOTES__ :* *1- Salvaged materials from nearby buildings may be utilized in this credit.*	*5% of the total construction material is from reused items.*	*1- The reuse process means bring it back to its original capacity and reduce the use of the original sources.* *2- Do __NOT__ include recycled materials in the calculations.* *3- Include salvaged and refurbished materials in the calculations.* *4- Do __NOT__ include MEP (Mechanical, Electrical, Plumbing) units and elevator machines in the calculations.* *5- The comparison factor is based on the __REPLACEMENT__ cost divided by the total __CONSTRUCTION__ cost.* *6- The material cost is normally __45 %__ of the building cost.* *7- The reused material __DOES NOT__ need to be supplied from the site.* *8- Any approved __REUSE__ material can be utilized in this credit.* *9- Applies to MR 5.1 & MR 5.2 credits.*	*15%*	*1- The estimate shall be based on the cost ($)* *2- UBC* *3- LCA*	*Construction*
1	MR 3.2			*10 % of the total construction material is from reused items.*				

POINTS	REFERENCE NUMBER	INTENT OF CREDIT	STATEMENT OF CREDIT	CONCENTRATION OF CREDIT	GENERAL EXPLANATION	EXTRA CREDIT	CODE OR STANDARD	SUBMITTAL PHASE
1	MR 4.1	1- To reduce impact of extraction process. 2- To reduce processing of virgin material. 3- To increase demand for building products with recycled content. 4- To use materials with recycled content.	(Recycled Content) GENERAL NOTES : The value of recycled material shall be validated by CFR. The total cost shall include the following : 1- Collection cost 2- Reprocessing cost 3- Marketing cost Urban maintenance : 1- Leaves 2- Grass clipping 3- Tree trimming Discarded materials : 1- Interior furniture 2- Wood cabinetry 3- Roof decking The following processes shall be verified by CFC : 1- Collection 2- Reprocessing 3- Marketing	10 % of the total construction material is from recycled materials with this mixture: (post consumer + 1/2 pre-consumer)	1- Post consumer : The building materials which have already been used and will be reused for other applications, such as plastic, paper, glass and metal. 2- Pre-consumer : Material from manufacturer site which has NOT been used and will NOT be reused for any other applications, such as grain rubber, metal scrap, seed hulls, wheat straw, sawdust and fly ash, EXCLUDING the in-house industrial scrap. 3- Calculate the comparison factor by DIVIDING the total QUALIFIED material cost ($) to the total CONSTRUCTION material cost ($). 4- Do NOT include MEP (Mechanical, Electrical, Plumbing) units and elevator machines in the calculation.	30%	(ISO 14021-1999) Calculate per the followings methods : 1- The estimate for the post consumer and pre-consumer materials shall be based on the WEIGHT (Lb) 2- The estimate for the total construction material shall be based on the COST ($) 3- Include the permanent INSTALLED material in BOTH cost and weight calculations.	Construction
1	MR 4.2			20 % of the total construction material is from recycled materials with this mixture: (post consumer + 1/2 pre-consumer)				

POINTS	REFERENCE NUMBER	INTENT OF CREDIT	STATEMENT OF CREDIT	CONCENTRATION OF CREDIT	GENERAL EXPLANATION	EXTRA CREDIT	CODE OR STANDARD	SUBMITTAL PHASE
1	MR 5.1	1- To increase job demand within the region. 2- To reduce transportation issues. 3- To use indigenous resources.	Regional Materials <u>GENERAL NOTES</u> : The following materials shall be excluded from calculation of this credit: 1- Rework 2- Reuse 3- Scrap (salvaged materials from nearby buildings may be utilized in this credit)	10 % of construction material is extracted, processed and manufactured regionally.	1- Utilize the building material or products that have been extracted, harvested and manufactured within <u>500</u> mile radius. 2- Calculate the comparison factor by DIVIDING the total cost of <u>QUALIFIED</u> material cost from the total cost of material. 3- Do <u>NOT</u> include the MEP (Mechanical, Electrical, Plumbing) units and elevator machines in the calculation. 4- For the <u>PRE-CONSUMER</u> calculation <u>EXCLUDE</u> rework, reward and scrap materials. 5- If part of the product is <u>NOT</u> supplied by the sources within <u>500</u> miles radius, then use the weight percentage method. 6- Utilize the salvaged material from sources within <u>500</u> miles radius. 7- This methodology is also applicable for MR 3.1 and MR 3.2 credits.	40%	(Code is n/a) 1- The estimate shall be based on the cost ($)	Construction
1	MR 5.2			20 % of construction material is extracted, processed and manufactured regionally.				

POINTS	REFERENCE NUMBER	INTENT OF CREDIT	STATEMENT OF CREDIT	CONCENTRATION OF CREDIT	GENERAL EXPLANATION	EXTRA CREDIT	CODE OR STANDARD	SUBMITTAL PHASE
1	MR 6	*1-To reuse long cycle materials.* *2- To reduce the use of finite raw materials.*	*Rapidly Renewable Materials*		*1- Utilize rapidly renewable materials based on 2.5 % of total construction cost.* *2- Utilize rapidly renewable material with 10 years life cycle.* *The following items consider as RAPIDLY renewable materials :* *1- Bamboo flooring* *2- Wool carpeting* *3- Cork flooring* *4- Cotton batt insulation* *5- Linoleum flooring* *6- Wheat board cabinets*	*5%*	*n/a* *1- The estimate shall be based on the cost of materials*	*Construction*

POINTS	REFERENCE NUMBER	INTENT OF CREDIT	STATEMENT OF CREDIT	CONCENTRATION OF CREDIT	GENERAL EXPLANATION	EXTRA CREDIT	CODE OR STANDARD	SUBMITTAL PHASE
1	MR 7	*To encourage the forest management program.*	*Certified Wood*	*FSC responsibility :* *1- To enforce forest Management process.* *2- To protect health and safety of forest workers.* *3- To prohibit the use of pesticides.* *TYPES of certifications :* *1- The Forest Management for all trades.* *2- The Chain of Custody (COC) for the supplier.*	*1- Use 50 % of wood materials with the FSC certificate for structural items, sub-flooring materials , doors and building finishes.* *2- Calculate the comparison factor by DIVIDING the total cost of certified wood materials to the total cost of NEW wood materials.* *3- Do NOT include MEP units and elevator machines in the calculation.* *4- INCLUDE building furniture and furnish materials in the calculation.* *5- The contractor does NOT need to obtain a certification number, but the supplier needs to obtain a certification number.* *6- When part of product requires certification number, then the whole product shall obtain a certification number.*	*95%*	*FSC certification seal* *1- Estimate per cost of materials ($)*	*Construction*

LEEDPASS

INDOOR ENVIRONMENTAL QUALITY

POINTS	REFERENCE NUMBER	INTENT OF CREDIT	STATEMENT OF CREDIT	CONCENTRATION OF CREDIT	GENERAL EXPLANATION	EXTRA CREDIT	CODE OR STANDARD	SUBMITTAL PHASE
INDOOR ENVIRONMENTAL QUALITY								
0	EQ P1	1- To establish minimum requirements for indoor air quality.	Minimum IAQ Performance	(Mandatory) Three methods of ventilation system : 1- Active : Mechanical system 2- Passive : Natural ventilation 3- Mixed-Mode : Both	Design Ventilation : 1- Design the HVAC system to exceed or comply with the ASHRAE 62.1-2004 standard or the LOCAL codes. (whichever is more stringent) 2- For the mechanical system use sections 4 thru 7 of the ASHRAE 62.1, 2004 standard. 3- For the natural ventilation use section 5.1 of the ASHRAE 62.1, 2004 standard. 4- Design the HVAC system to balance the ventilation rate. 5- The opening for the naturally ventilated space shall be 4 % of the total floor area.	n/a	ASHRAE 62.1, 2004	Design

POINTS	REFERENCE NUMBER	INTENT OF CREDIT	STATEMENT OF CREDIT	CONCENTRATION OF CREDIT	GENERAL EXPLANATION	EXTRA CREDIT	CODE OR STANDARD	SUBMITTAL PHASE
0	EQ P2	1- To minimize the exposure of building occupants to tobacco smoke.	Environmental Tobacco Smoke (ETS) Control	(Mandatory) For RESIDENTIAL buildings : 1- Minimize the pathway for ETS transfer between apartments. 2- All doors shall be weather stripped. 3- Prohibit smoking in the common areas.	Option 1 : 1- Prohibit smoking in the building. 2- The designated smoking areas shall be 25 ft away from the main building entrance and exterior windows. Option 2 : 1- Prohibit smoking in the building, except at designated areas. 2- Locate the designated smoking areas 25 ft away from outside air intake for HVAC system and main building entrance. 3- Enclose the ventilated area with deck-to- deck partition. 3- Run sampling process for 15 minutes . 4- When door is closed, the exhaust system shall provide 5 Pa of negative pressure to the adjacent areas.	n/a	1-ANSI 2- ASTM 3-California Title 24, 2001	Design

POINTS	REFERENCE NUMBER	INTENT OF CREDIT	STATEMENT OF CREDIT	CONCENTRATION OF CREDIT	GENERAL EXPLANATION	EXTRA CREDIT	CODE OR STANDARD	SUBMITTAL PHASE
1	EQ 1	*1- To monitor ventilation system by CO_2 sensors.* *2- To sustain well-being and comfort zone for building occupants.*	*Outdoor Air Delivery Monitoring*	*Install permanent monitoring system for the outdoor air system.*	*Mechanical ventilated area :* *1- The system shall be monitored by a CO_2 sensor.* *2- Install the monitoring alarm system for 10 % of the occupied space.* *3- Provide CO_2 sensor with density factor of 25 persons per 1000 sq.ft .* *4- Locate the CO_2 sensor at 3 ft to 6 ft above the finish floor OR in the return air system.* *5- Provide monitoring device for the areas with less than 25 persons per 1000 sq.ft .* *6- Measure air quality based on (+/- 15 %) of the ASHRAE 62.1,2004 standard.* *Natural Ventilation :* *1- Provide the CO_2 sensor for 90 % of the occupied space.*	*n/a*	*ASHRAE 62.1, 2004*	*Design*

POINTS	REFERENCE NUMBER	INTENT OF CREDIT	STATEMENT OF CREDIT	CONCENTRATION OF CREDIT	GENERAL EXPLANATION	EXTRA CREDIT	CODE OR STANDARD	SUBMITTAL PHASE
1	EQ 2	*1- To increase the ventilation rate in the building. 2- To provide a comfort zone space for the occupants. 3- To provide additional outdoor air ventilation system.*	*Increased Ventilation*		***Mechanical ventilation*** *:* *1- Increase the ventilation rate by 30 % above ASHRAE 62.1 2004 standards.* *2- Use heat recovery method where it is appropriate to recover the wasted energy created by ventilation system.* ***Natural ventilation*** *:* ***Case 1:*** *Meet CIBSE standard.* ***Case 2*** *: Design the system for 90 % of occupied area based on ASHRAE 62.1, 2004 standard.* ***General note*** *(for both options) :* *1- Outside air : Use 0.30 cfm per sq.ft* *2- Breathing zone : Cover areas within 3 ft to 6 ft above the finish floor and 2 ft from the exterior walls.*	*n/a*	*1- ASHRAE 62.1, 2004 2- Carbon Trust Good Practice Guide 3- CIBSE 4- CDVR*	*Design*

POINTS	REFERENCE NUMBER	INTENT OF CREDIT	STATEMENT OF CREDIT	CONCENTRATION OF CREDIT	GENERAL EXPLANATION	EXTRA CREDIT	CODE OR STANDARD	SUBMITTAL PHASE
1	EQ 3.1	*1-To improve indoor air quality during construction and renovation phases. 2- To provide comfort zone space for construction team and building occupants during the construction phase. 3- To protect HVAC units during the construction phase.*	*Construction IAQ Management Plan*	*During construction*	*Develop and implement IAQ management plan by the following methods :* *1- Install MERV- 8 filter in the return duct plenum of permanent mechanical systems.* *2- Meet or exceed SMACNA requirements during the construction phase.* *3- Replace air filter prior of occupancy.* *4- Protect on-site material from moisture damages.* *5- Avoid contamination.* *6- Comply with standards of EQ 3.2 & EQ 5 credits.*	*n/a*	*1- SMACNA 2- ASHRAE 52.2,1999*	*Construction*

POINTS	REFERENCE NUMBER	INTENT OF CREDIT	STATEMENT OF CREDIT	CONCENTRATION OF CREDIT	GENERAL EXPLANATION	EXTRA CREDIT	CODE OR STANDARD	SUBMITTAL PHASE
1	EQ 3.2	1- To improve indoor air quality during construction and renovation phases. 2- To provide comfort zone for construction team and building occupants during the construction phase. 3- To protect HVAC units during the construction phase.	(Construction IAQ Management Plan) GENERAL NOTES : 1- The commissioning process may occur during the flush-out period, if NO contaminated materials have been transferred into the building during the flush-out process. 2- It is a time consuming credit.	Before occupancy : 1- The air sample testing has a minimum impact on the schedule, but it is a COSTLY procedure. 2- Use EQ 3.1 and EQ 5 credits to prepare specifications and schedules. 3- Start the flush- out process AFTER following tasks: A) Final punch-list B) Cleaning C) Final testing	Develop and implement the Indoor Air Quality Management Plan by : Option 1 : (FLUSH - OUT) 1- AFTER the construction is completed, supply 14,000 cubic ft per sq.ft of air within 60 F & 60 % RH into the building. 2- BEFORE the occupancy period, supply 3,500 cubic ft per sq.ft of air into the building. 3- DURING the occupancy period, supply 0.30 cfm per sq.ft of air for 3 hours till total of 14,000 cf per sf of flushing is accomplished inside the building. Option 2 : Air testing (EPA Method) 1- Run the HVAC system at the NORMAL operation mode and take sample for every 25,000 sq.ft. 2- Collect sample at 3 ft to 6 ft above the finish floor for minimum of 4 hours .	n/a	Option 2 : EPA	Construction

POINTS	REFERENCE NUMBER	INTENT OF CREDIT	STATEMENT OF CREDIT	CONCENTRATION OF CREDIT	GENERAL EXPLANATION	EXTRA CREDIT	CODE OR STANDARD	SUBMITTAL PHASE
1	EQ 4.1	*1-To reduce odorous and irritating contaminants in air. 2- To reduce harmful airborne containments in air. 3- To provide comfort zone for building occupants.*	*(Low- Emitting Materials) Design phase : 1- Note the VOC limit in the specification. 2- Ask for the cut-sheet, MSD and certification. Construction phase : 1- Discuss the VOC limit at the pre-bid meetings. 2- Discuss the VOC limit in the bid-award meetings. 3- Include the VOC limit in the contractual documents and purchase orders. 4- The contractor responsibility includes preparation of MSD and evidence for waste management plans.*	*Adhesives & Sealants*	*1- The VOC limit shall stay BELOW the SCAQMD rule # 1168 standards. 2- It shall comply with the Green Seal standard. (GS-36)*	*n/a*	*1-SCAQMD 2- Green seal standard*	*Construction*
1	EQ 4.2			*Paints & Coating*	*1- The VOC limit shall stay BELOW the SCAQMD rule # 1113 standards. 2- It shall comply with the Green Seal standards. (GS-11 & GC-3) 3- The primer shall meet the VOC limit for NON-FLAT paint.*	*n/a*	*1-SCAQMD 2-Green seal standard.*	*Construction*
1	EQ 4.3			*Carpet Systems*	*1- The carpet and cushion shall comply with the GREEN LABEL PLUS program which is offered by the Carpet and Rug Institute. 2- The adhesive for the carpets shall comply with the standard of EQ 4.1. credit and shall be limited to the VOC of 50 gram per liter. 3- The test result submitted for the LEED certification process shall be LESS than 2 YEARS old.*	*n/a*	*1- CRI 2- California Department of Health Services. 3- Green label program*	*Construction*

POINTS	REFERENCE NUMBER	INTENT OF CREDIT	STATEMENT OF CREDIT	CONCENTRATION OF CREDIT	GENERAL EXPLANATION	EXTRA CREDIT	CODE OR STANDARD	SUBMITTAL PHASE
1	EQ 4.4	*1-To reduce odorous and irritating containments in air. 2- To reduce the harmful airborne containments in air. 3- To provide comfort zone for building occupants.*	*Low-Emitting Materials*	*Composite Wood & Agrifiber Products*	*1- The low-emitting materials shall be furnished with NO added urea-formaldehyde resins. 2- The composite wood materials includes particle board, plywood, wheat board and strawboard panel. 3- The agrifiber board materials includes cereal straw, sugarcane, sunflower husk, walnut shell and coconut husk. 4- If the lamination process is completed at the site then the final product shall be fabricated with NO added urea-formaldehyde resin.*	*n/a*	*n/a*	*Construction*

POINTS	REFERENCE NUMBER	INTENT OF CREDIT	STATEMENT OF CREDIT	CONCENTRATION OF CREDIT	GENERAL EXPLANATION	EXTRA CREDIT	CODE OR STANDARD	SUBMITTAL PHASE
1	EQ 5	*1-To minimize the exposure of hazardous particulates and chemical pollutants.*	*Indoor Chemical & Pollutant Source Control*	*Mechanical System :* *1- It shall be provided with MERV 13 or more efficient filters.* *2- The filtration system shall comply with ASHRAE 52.2 1999 standard.*	*GENERAL :* *1- Provide 6 ft of entryway.* *2- Install grates and grilles.* *3- Provide roll-out matt if the building is maintained weekly.* *CHEMICAL GAS AREA :* *Provide the following design standards:* *1- Self locking door and hard lid ceiling.* *2- Deck to deck partition.* *3- Select the exhaust system for 0.50 CFM per sq.ft.* *4- The air circulation module shall NOT be provided for HVAC system.* *5- When doors are fully CLOSED, the exhaust system shall provide 5 Pa of NEGATIVE pressure to the adjacent area.*	*n/a*	*ASHRAE 52.2, 1999*	*Design*

POINTS	REFERENCE NUMBER	INTENT OF CREDIT	STATEMENT OF CREDIT	CONCENTRATION OF CREDIT	GENERAL EXPLANATION	EXTRA CREDIT	CODE OR STANDARD	SUBMITTAL PHASE
1	EQ 6.1	*1- Provide high level of lighting control for EACH occupant in the building.* *2- Promote productivity and comfort for the building occupants.*	*Controllability of Systems* *GENERAL NOTES :* *1- This credit is suitable for LARGE projects.* *Regularly occupied space :* *1- Offices* *2- Conference rooms* *3- Cafeterias* *Non-regularly occupied space :* *1- Restrooms* *2- Mechanical rooms* *3- Storage rooms* *Regularly occupied space for RESIDENTIAL buildings :* *1- Dimming rooms* *2- Media rooms* *3- Kitchens*	*Lighting*	*1- Ensure 90 % of the FTE occupants have the individual lighting control system.* *2- Provide a control system that can be shared in the group.* *3- The PERMANENT wiring system is NOT required for the TASK lights.* *4- The NON- REGULATED areas: Corridors, hallway, break rooms and kitchens.* *5- The SHARED areas: Conference rooms, class rooms and training rooms.* *6- The energy assumption for the lighting system shall comply with ASHRAE 90.1 standard.*	*n/a*	*ASHRAE- IESNA 90.1, 2004*	*Design*

POINTS	REFERENCE NUMBER	INTENT OF CREDIT	STATEMENT OF CREDIT	CONCENTRATION OF CREDIT	GENERAL EXPLANATION	EXTRA CREDIT	CODE OR STANDARD	SUBMITTAL PHASE
1	EQ 6.2	*1- To provide high level of thermal control for EACH occupant. 2- To promote productivity for the building occupants.*	*Controllability of Systems GENERAL NOTES : Control system for thermal comfort: 1-Tempreature sensor 2- Humidity sensor 3- Automatic sweep.*	*(Thermal Comfort)*	*1- Ensure 50 % of the FTE occupants have full thermal control by using an INDIVIDUAL thermostat, diffuser or radiant panel. 2- The range of temperature & humidity in the occupied space shall comply with the ASHRAE 55-2004 standards. 3- The operable window can be utilized instead of individual control system. Operable window : 1- The operable window shall be located within 20 ft of each space. 2- It shall be furnished with individual control system. 3- It shall comply with ASHRAE 62.1,2004 standards. 4- The area of window shall be EQUAL or MORE than 4 % of total floor area. Non-occupied area includes : 1- Janitorial and storage room. 2- Equipment room and closet.*	*n/a*	*1- ASHRAE 55-2004 2- ASHRAE 62.1,2004*	*Design*

POINTS	REFERENCE NUMBER	INTENT OF CREDIT	STATEMENT OF CREDIT	CONCENTRATION OF CREDIT	GENERAL EXPLANATION	EXTRA CREDIT	CODE OR STANDARD	SUBMITTAL PHASE
1	EQ 7.1	*1- To provide comfortable thermal environment for building occupants over period of time. 2- To promote productivity in occupied space.*	*Thermal Comfort __GENERAL NOTES__ : 1- This credit is suitable for __LARGE__ projects.*	*Design*	*1- The design shall meet the ASHRAE 55-2004 standards. 2- Use PMV (Predicted Mean Vote) Model. 3- Ensure the supply air temperature, return air temperature, zone radiant temperature, fan air speed, and relative humidity are all in compliance with the following standards: 1- EQ prerequisite 1 2- EQ.1 3- EQ.2*	*n/a*	*ASHRAE 55-2004*	*Design*
1	EQ 7.2			*Verification*	*1- The general survey should be preformed within __6 to 18__ months after occupancy period. 2- If more than __20 %__ of the occupants complain about the system, then the responsible party shall perform another verification process. 3- The verification process should comply with the ASHRAE 55-2004 standards.*	*n/a*	*ASHRAE 55-2004*	*Design*

POINTS	REFERENCE NUMBER	INTENT OF CREDIT	STATEMENT OF CREDIT	CONCENTRATION OF CREDIT	GENERAL EXPLANATION	EXTRA CREDIT	CODE OR STANDARD	SUBMITTAL PHASE
1	EQ 8.1	1- To connect indoor space and outdoor space for building occupants. 2- To introduce daylight and views into the occupied spaces.	(Daylight & Views) 1. For the measurement option consider the following factors : The size of wall opening , the size of vertical trees next to the building, the orientation and height of adjacent buildings, the location of the courtyard, the location of wall louvers, the area of adjustable blinds, the area of interior walls, the orientation of the building, the type and size of exterior glass, the type of shading devices, the layout and perimeter of the building. 2. The utility rooms, closet, storage areas and bathrooms are NOT REGULARLY occupied spaces for the RESIDENTIAL projects. 3. The boundary of site plays major rule in this credit.	(Daylight 75 % of space) For Daylight calculation consider the followings: Daylight glazing area: Includes any openings at 7'-6" above finish floor or higher. Provide daylight design for the following rooms : 1- Office spaces 2- Meeting rooms 3- Cafeterias The daylight design is NOT required for the following rooms : 1- Copy rooms 2- Storage rooms 3- Equipment rooms 4- Laundry 5- Restrooms	Provide daylight design for 75% of the occupied space: Option 1 : Calculation Consider the glazing factor of 2 % for the exterior windows. Option 2 : Simulation Demonstrate computer program for minimum of 25 FC @ 30 inches AFF. Option 3 : Measurement Provide minimum of 25 FC in 75 % of the occupied areas on 10-ft grid floor. The variables for the daylight design : 1- The building floor area. 2- The area of windows. 3- The geometry of windows. 4- The height and visible transmittance of windows. The visible transmittance equal to VISIBLE light divided by TOTAL light through a surface. Glazing factor : It is equal to space illumination factor divided by exterior illumination factor	95%	NFRC	Design

POINTS	REFERENCE NUMBER	INTENT OF CREDIT	STATEMENT OF CREDIT	CONCENTRATION OF CREDIT	GENERAL EXPLANATION	EXTRA CREDIT	CODE OR STANDARD	SUBMITTAL PHASE
1	EQ 8.2	*1- To connect indoor space and outdoor space for the building occupants. 2- To introduce daylight and views into the occupied spaces.*	*Daylight & Views GENERAL NOTES : 1- Regularly occupied space for this credit includes offices, conference rooms and cafeterias. 2- Movable partitions consider as FIXED item for this credit.*	*Views for 90 % of space Windows area : Includes any windows between 2'-6" to 7'-6" AFF. Areas that can NOT be contributed : Any opening below 2'-6" AFF*	*Provide view for 90 % of the occupied spaces : 1- Achieve sight line to outdoor via the windows located 2'-6" to 7'-6" AFF. 2- In the PLAN view, the design area shall be located within the sight lines drawn from the building perimeters. 3- In the SECTION view, the sight line shall PASS through the windows located between 2'-6" to 7'-6" AFF. 4- DO NOT include furniture and partitions in the view and daylight calculation. 5- The elevation of the seating area shall be calculated at 42 inches AFF. Private Office : 1- When 75 % of the office area has a view to the outside then include TOTAL office area in the calculation. 2- When LEES THAN 75 % of the office area has a view to the outside, then use the PERCENT method.*	Case by case	*n/a*	*Design*

LEEDPASS

INNOVATION IN DESIGN

POINTS	REFERENCE NUMBER	INTENT OF CREDIT	STATEMENT OF CREDIT	CONCENTRATION OF CREDIT	GENERAL EXPLANATION	EXTRA CREDIT	CODE OR STANDARD	SUBMITTAL PHASE
INNOVATION & DESIGN PROCESS								
1	ID 1.1	*1- To promote exceptional performance above the LEED design standards. 2- To promote innovative performance which is not addressed in the LEED design standards.*	*Innovation in Design*		*1- Points are awarded for the exceptional performance above requirements set by the LEED rating system. 2- Innovative performance in the Green Building (Environmental) categories which is NOT specifically addressed by the LEED rating system. 3- It shall be submitted in the writing. 4- It shall be applicable for other projects. The formula proposed for the innovative performance shall work for similar cases. 5- If the innovation performance is accepted for ONE project, it DOES NOT mean automatic approval for other projects. 6- Provide narrative statement and submittal for each point. 7- One of the tasks for LEED AP is to manage CIR forms and coordinate the decision making process.*	*n/a*	*n/a*	*Design & Construction*
1	ID 1.2							*Design & Construction*
1	ID 1.3							*Design & Construction*
1	ID 1.4							*Design & Construction*

LEEDPASS
(LEED NC 2.2)

POINTS	REFERENCE NUMBER	INTENT OF CREDIT	STATEMENT OF CREDIT	CONCENTRATION OF CREDIT	GENERAL EXPLANATION	EXTRA CREDIT	CODE OR STANDARD	SUBMITTAL PHASE
1	ID 2	*1- To support and encourage design integration required by USGBC and LEED design standards. 2- To streamline application and certification processes.*	*LEED Accredited Professional*		*1- At least ONE primary member of team shall be a LEED AP. 2- To educate and facilitate the team. 3- The submittal package should include the followings : A- Name of LEED AP. B- The LEED AP's company name. C- The description of LEED AP's project role. D- The copy of the LEED AP's certificate.*	*n/a*	*n/a*	*Construction*

LEEDPASS

(Chapter 4)

CODE TABLES

LEEDPASS
(LEED NC 2.2)

Reference Standard or Agency	Reference Number	Statement of Credit
Advanced Building- Bench Mark 1.1 Method	EA 1	Optimize Energy Performance
ANSI	SS 8	Light Pollution Reduction
	EQ P2	Environmental Tobacco Smoke Control
ASHRAE / IESNA 90.1, 2004 (For energy consumption)	SS 8	Light Pollution Reduction
	EA P2	Minimum Energy Performance
	EA 1	Optimize Energy Performance
	EA 2	On-Site Renewable Energy
	EQ 6.1	Controllability of System (Lighting)
ASHRAE 2004 Prescriptive Method	EA 1	Optimize Energy Performance

LEEDPASS
(LEED NC 2.2)

Reference Standard or Agency	*Reference Number*	**Statement of Credit**
ASHRAE 52.2, 1999 ***(For filter selection)***	***EQ 3.1***	**Construction IAQ Management Plan** **(During Construction, MERV 8)**
	EQ 5	**Indoor chemical & Pollutant Source Control** **(MERV 13)**
ASHRAE 55,2004 ***(For temperature and humidity control)***	***EQ 6.2***	**Controllability of Systems** **(Thermal Comfort)**
	EQ 7.1	**Thermal Comfort** **(Design)**
	EQ 7.2	**Thermal Comfort** **(Verification)**
ASHRAE 62.1, 2004 ***(For quality of air and ventilation rating)***	***EQ 1***	**Outdoor Air Delivery Monitoring**
	EQ P1	**Minimum IAQ Performance**
	EQ 2	**Increase Ventilation**
	EQ 6.2	**Controllability of Systems** **(Thermal Comfort)**

LEEDPASS
(LEED NC 2.2)

Reference Standard or Agency	*Reference Number*	**Statement of Credit**
ASTM	*SS 3*	**Brownfield Redevelopment**
	SS 7.1 & 7.2	**Heat Island Effect (Roof and no-roof)**
	EQ P2	**Environmental Tobacco Smoke Control**
BMP	*SS 6.1 & 6.2*	**Stormwater Design**
California Department of Health Services	*EQ 4.3*	**Low-Emitting Materials (Carpet Systems)**
California Energy Code Title 24, 2001	*SS 8*	**Light Pollution Reduction**
	EQ P2	**Environmental Tobacco Smoke Control**
Carpet and Rug Institute	*EQ 4.3*	**Low-Emitting Materials (Carpet Systems)**
CBECS	*EA 2*	**On-Site Renewable Energy**
	EA 6	**Green Power**
CDVR	*EQ 2*	**Increased Ventilation**

LEEDPASS
(LEED NC 2.2)

Reference Standard or Agency	*Reference Number*	Statement of Credit
CERCLA	*SS 3*	**Brownfield Redevelopment**
CFR	*SS 1*	**Site Selection (for wetland)**
CIBSE	*EQ 2*	**Increased Ventilation**
CIWMB 1999	*MR P1*	**Storage & Collection of Recyclables**
Clean Air Act 1990	*EA 4*	**Enhanced Refrigerant Management (Montreal Protocol 1987)**
Clean Water Act	*SS 1*	**Site Selection**
CRS	*EA 6*	**Green Power**
DOE	*EA P2*	**Minimum Energy Performance**
	EA 2	**On-Site Renewable Energy**
	EA 6	**Green Power**

LEEDPASS
(LEED NC 2.2)

Reference Standard or Agency	*Reference Number*	**Statement of Credit**
ECM	*EA 5*	**Measurement & Verification**
EIA	*EA 2*	**On-Site Renewable Energy**
Energy Policy Act 1992	*WE 3.1 &3.2*	**Water Use Reduction**
EPA	*SS P1*	**Construction Activity Pollution Prevention**
	SS 3	**Brownfield Redevelopment**
	EA P3	**Fundamental Refrigerant Management (EPA refers to Montreal Protocol 1987)**
	EA 4	**Enhanced Refrigerant Management**
	EQ 3.2	**Construction IAQ Management Plan (Before Occupancy)**
	SS 6.1	**Stormwater Design (Quantity Control , impervious surface) (EPA refers to BMP)**
	SS 6.2	**Stormwater Design (Quality Control , treat or capture) (EPA refers to BMP)**
EVO	*EA 5*	**Measurement & Verification**
FEMA	*SS 1*	**Site Selection (for flood)**

LEEDPASS
(LEED NC 2.2)

Reference Standard or Agency	*Reference Number*	Statement of Credit
FSC	*MR 7*	Certified Wood
Green Label	*EQ 4.3*	Low-Emitting Materials (Carpet Systems)
Green Seal	*EQ 4.1*	Low-Emitting Materials (Adhesives & Sealants)
	EQ 4.2	Low-Emitting Materials (Paints & Coatings)
IPMVP	*EA 5*	Measurement & Verification
ISO	*MR 4.1*	Recycled Content
	MR 4.2	Recycled Content
LCA	*MR 3.1 & 3.2*	Material Reuse
Montreal Protocol 1987	*EA P3*	Fundamental Refrigerant Management
New Building Institute	*EA 1*	Optimize Energy Performance

LEEDPASS
(LEED NC 2.2)

Reference Standard or Agency	Reference Number	Statement of Credit
Oregon Zoning Code	SS 4.4	Alternative Transportation (Parking Capacity)
NFRC	EQ 8.1	Daylight & Views
NPDES	SS P1	Construction Activity Pollution Prevention
REC	EA 2	On-Site Renewable Energy
SCAQMD	EQ 4.1	Low-Emitting Materials (Adhesives & Sealants)
	EQ 4.2	Low-Emitting Materials (Paints & Coatings)
SMACNA	EQ 3.1	Construction IAQ Management Plan (During Construction)
TRAP	SS 6.1, 6.2	Stormwater Design
The Institute of Transportation Engineers	SS 4.4	Alternative transportation (Parking Capacity)
TSS	SS 6.1 & 6.2	Stormwater Design
UBC	MR 3.1 & 3.2	Material Reuse
USAD	SS 1	Site Selection

LEEDPASS

(Chapter 5)

DECISION MAKER TABLES

LEEDPASS
(LEED NC 2.2)

Reference Number	Statement	Decision Makers		
SS P1	Construction Activity Pollution Prevention		Contractor	Civil Engineer
SS 1	Site Selection	Owner		Civil Engineer
SS 2	Development Density & Community Connectivity	Owner		LEED AP
SS 3	Brownfield Redevelopment	Owner		Civil Engineer
SS 4.1	Alternative Transportation	Owner		LEED AP
SS 4.2	Alternative Transportation			LEED AP & Architect

LEEDPASS
(LEED NC 2.2)

Reference Number	Statement	Decision Makers		
SS 4.3	Alternative Transportation	Owner		LEED AP & Architect & MEP Engineer
SS 4.4	Alternative Transportation	Owner		Civil Engineer
SS 5.1	Site Development	Owner	Contractor	Civil Engineer
SS 5.2	Site Development	Owner		Civil Engineer
SS 6.1	Stormwater Design			Civil Engineer
SS 6.2				Civil Engineer

LEEDPASS
(LEED NC 2.2)

Reference Number	***Statement***	***Decision Makers***		
SS 7.1	***Heat Island Effect***		***Contractor***	***LEED AP & Landscape Architect & Civil Engineer***
SS 7.2			***Contractor***	***LEED AP***
SS 8	***Light Pollution Reduction***			***LEED AP & Lighting Designer***

LEEDPASS
(LEED NC 2.2)

Reference Number	Statement	Decision Makers		
WE 1.1	Water Efficient Landscaping			Landscape Architect
WE 1.2		Owner		Landscape Architect
WE 2	Innovative Wastewater Technologies			MEP Engineer
WE 3.1	Water Use Reduction			MEP Engineer
WE 3.2				MEP Engineer

LEEDPASS
(LEED NC 2.2)

Reference Number	***Statement***	***Decision Makers***		
EA P1	***Fundamental Commissioning of the Building Energy Systems***	***Owner***	***Contractor***	***Commissioning Agent***
EA P2	***Minimum Energy Performance***			***MEP Engineer***
EA P3	***Fundamental Refrigerant Management***	***Owner***		***MEP Engineer***
EA 1	***Optimize Energy Performance***			***MEP Engineer***
EA 2	***On-site Renewable Energy***			***MEP Engineer***
EA 3	***Enhanced Commissioning***	***Owner***	***Contractor***	***Commissioning Authority***

LEEDPASS
(LEED NC 2.2)

Reference Number	Statement	Decision Makers		
EA 4	Enhanced Refrigerant Management			MEP Engineer
EA 5	Measurement & Verification			MEP Engineer & Facility Engineer & Manufacturer
EA 6	Green Power	Owner		LEED AP

LEEDPASS
(LEED NC 2.2)

Reference Number	***Statement***	***Decision Makers***		
MR P1	***Storage & Collection of Recyclables***	***Owner***		***Architect***
MR 1.1	***Building Reuse***	***Owner***	***Contractor***	***Architect***
MR 1.2		***Owner***	***Contractor***	***Architect***
MR 1.3			***Contractor***	***Architect***
MR 2.1	***Construction Waste Management***		***Contractor***	
MR 2.2			***Contractor***	

LEEDPASS
(LEED NC 2.2)

Reference Number	*Statement*	*Decision Makers*		
MR 3.1	*Material Reuse*		*Contractor*	*Architect*
MR 3.2			*Contractor*	*Architect*
MR 4.1	*Recycled Content*		*Contractor*	*Architect*
MR 4.2			*Contractor*	*Architect*
MR 5.1	*Regional Materials*		*Contractor*	*Architect*
MR 5.2			*Contractor*	*Architect*

LEEDPASS
(LEED NC 2.2)

Reference Number	***Statement***	***Decision Makers***		
MR 6	***Rapidly Renewable Materials***		***Contractor***	***Architect***
MR 7	***Certified Wood***		***Contractor***	***Architect***

LEEDPASS
(LEED NC 2.2)

Reference Number	Statement	Decision Makers		
EQ P1	Minimum IAQ Performance			MEP Engineer
EQ P2	Environmental Tobacco Smoke (ETS) Control	Owner		LEED AP
EQ 1	Outdoor Air Delivery Monitoring			MEP Engineer
EQ 2	Increased Ventilation		Contractor	MEP Engineer
EQ 3.1	Construction IAQ Management Plan		Contractor	MEP Engineer
EQ 3.2	Construction IAQ Management Plan		Contractor	MEP Engineer

LEEDPASS
(LEED NC 2.2)

Reference Number	*Statement*	*Decision Makers*		
EQ 4.1	*Low-Emitting Materials*		*Contractor*	*Architect*
EQ 4.2			*Contractor*	*Architect*
EQ 4.3			*Contractor*	*Architect*
EQ 4.4	*Low-Emitting Materials*		*Contractor*	*Architect*
EQ 5	*Indoor Chemical & Pollutant Source Control*		*Contractor*	*LEED AP & MEP Engineer*
EQ 6.1	*Controllability of Systems*			*MEP Engineer*
EQ 6.2	*Controllability of Systems*			*MEP Engineer*

LEEDPASS
(LEED NC 2.2)

Reference Number	Statement	Decision Makers		
EQ 7.1	Thermal Comfort			MEP Engineer
EQ 7.2		Owner		Building Management
EQ 8.1	Daylight & Views			LEED AP & Lighting Designer & Architect
EQ 8.2	Daylight & Views			LEED AP & Lighting Designer & Architect

LEEDPASS
(LEED NC 2.2)

Reference Number	*Statement*	*Decision Makers*		
ID 1.1	*Innovation in Design*	*Owner*	*Contractor*	*All Disciplines*
ID 1.2		*Owner*	*Contractor*	*All Disciplines*
ID 1.3		*Owner*	*Contractor*	*All Disciplines*
ID 1.4		*Owner*	*Contractor*	*All Disciplines*
ID 2	*LEED Accredited Professional*	*Owner*	*Contractor*	*LEED AP*

LEEDPASS

(Chapter 6)

EXEMPLARY
TABLES

LEEDPASS
(LEED NC 2.2)

Reference Number	*Credit Statement*	*Exemplary Performance*
EA 1	Optimize Energy Performance	42 % up to 45.5 % for the new buildings & 35 % up to 38.5 % for the existing buildings
EA 2	On-site Renewable Energy	12.5 % up to 17.5 %
EA 6	Green Power	35 % up to 70 % or 2 years up to 4 years
EQ 8.1	Daylight & Views (for daylight credit)	75 % up to 95 %
EQ 8.2	Daylight & Views (for view credit)	Case by Case
MR 2.1 & MR 2.2	Construction Waste Management - Divert	50 % , 75 % up to 95%
MR 3.1 & MR 3.2	Material Reuse	5 % ,10 % up to 15 %
MR 4.1 & MR 4.2	Recycled Content	10 % , 20 % up to 30%

LEEDPASS
(LEED NC 2.2)

Reference Number	*Credit Statement*	*Exemplary Performance*
MR 5.1 & MR 5.2	Regional Materials	10 % ,20 % up to 40%
MR 6	Rapidly Renewable Materials	2.5 %, 10 year up to 5 % , 10 year
MR 7	Certified Wood	50% up to 95 %
SS 2	Development Density & Community Connectivity	DOUBLE the average density requirements OR 60,000 sq.ft per acre up to 120,000 sq.ft per acre
SS 4.1	Alternative Transportation	ONE (1) station up to TWO (2) stations OR TWO (2) bus lines up to FOUR (4) bus lines
SS 4.2 to SS 4.4	Alternative Transportation	Provide Report
SS 5.1	Site Development - Protect of Restore Habitat	50 % up to 75 %
SS 5.2	Site Development - Maximize Open Space	25 % up to 50 % , Equal up to Double , 20 % up to 40 %

Reference Number	*Credit Statement*	*Exemplary Performance*
SS 7.1	**Heat Island effect- Non-Roof**	**50 % up to 100 %**
SS 7.2	**Heat Island effect- Roof**	**75 % up to 100 %**
WE 2	**Innovative Wastewater Technologies**	**50 % up to 100 %**
WE 3.1 & WE 3.2	**Water Use Reduction**	**20 %, 30 % up to 40 %**

LEEDPASS

(Chapter 7)

CONSTRUCTION PHASE TABLES

LEEDPASS
(LEED NC 2.2)

Reference Number	*Construction Phase Submittal*
EA 3	**Enhanced Commissioning**
EA 5	**Measurement & Verification**
EA 6	**Green Power**
EA P 1	**Fundamental Commissioning**
EQ 3.1 & EQ 3.2	**Construction IAQ Management Plan**
EQ 4.1	**Low-Emitting Materials (Adhesive-Sealants)**
EQ 4.2	**Low-Emitting Materials (Paints-Coatings)**
EQ 4.3	**Low-Emitting Materials (Carpet System)**
EQ 4.4	**Low- Emitting Materials (Composite Wood & Agrifiber Products)**
ID 1.1 to ID 1.4	**Innovation in Design**
MR 1.1 to MR 1.3	**Building Reuse**

LEEDPASS
(LEED NC 2.2)

Reference Number	*Construction Phase Submittal*
MR 2.1 to MR 2.3	**Construction Waste Management**
MR 3.1 & MR 3.2	**Material Reuse**
MR 4.1& MR 4.2	**Recycled Content**
MR 5.1& MR-5.2	**Regional Materials**
MR 6	**Rapidly Renewable Materials**
MR 7	**Certified Wood**
SS 5.1 & SS 5.2	**Site Development**
SS 7.1	**Heat Island Effect - Non Roof**
SS P 1	**Construction Activity Pollution Prevention**

LEEDPASS

(Chapter 8)

PREREQUISITE TABLES

LEEDPASS
(LEED NC 2.2)

Reference Number	*Prerequisite Statement*
EA P1	Fundamental Commissioning of the Building Energy systems
EA P2	Minimum Energy Performance
EA P3	Fundamental Refrigerant Management
EQ P1	Minimum IAQ (Indoor Air Quality) Performance
EQ P2	Environmental Tobacco Smoke (ETS) Control
MR P1	Storage & Collection of Recyclables
SS P1	Construction Activity Pollution Prevention

LEEDPASS

(Chapter 9)

PROJECT PLANNING

Reference Number	*Statement*	*Initiated at this phase of project*	*Submit to the USGBC at this phase of project*	*Project Life Cycle*		
				Tasks @ Design Phase	*Tasks @ Construction Phase*	*Tasks @ Post Construction Phase*
SUSTAINABLE SITES						
SS P1	*Construction Activity Pollution Prevention*	*Schematic Design*	*Construction*	*1- Check plan in accordance with LEED's requirements.*	*1- Monitor the performance of General Contractor. 2- Document all measurement. 3- Perform weekly site visits.*	*1- Compile all documents. 2- Ensure all LEED prerequisites has been completed by the Civil Engineer. 3- Check all drawings. 4- Confirm the compliance of the path chosen. 5- Describe all tasks implemented in the project. 6-Complete all requirements on-line.*

LEEDPASS
(LEED NC 2.2)

Reference Number	Statement	Initiated at this phase of project	Submit to the USGBC at this phase of project	Project Life Cycle		
				Tasks @ Design Phase	Tasks @ Construction Phase	Tasks @ Post Construction Phase
SS 1	Site Selection	Pre- Design	Design	1- Perform weekly site visits. 2- Determine if this credit is achievable. 3- Insure the Civil Engineer has completed all required components. 4- Verify all credit compliances. 5- Document all credit compliances. 6-Complete all requirements on-line.	NONE	NONE
SS 2	Development Density & Community Connectivity	Pre- Design	Design	1- Evaluate both options for LEED compliance. 2- Compile all required data. 3- Ensure the compliance of all required data. 4- Complete all requirements on-line.	NONE	NONE

Reference Number	Statement	Initiated at this phase of project	Submit to the USGBC at this phase of project	Project Life Cycle		
				Tasks @ Design Phase	Tasks @ Construction Phase	Tasks @ Post Construction Phase
SS 3	Brownfield Redevelopment	Pre- Design	Design	1- Verify the site is classified as a Brownfield. 2- Verify the Civil Engineer has completed all necessary components on line. 3- Complete all requirements on-line.	NONE	NONE
SS 4.1	Alternative Transportation	Pre- Design	Design	1- Create a map for the project site. 2- Locate public transportations on the map. 3- Complete the LEED components on-line.	NONE	NONE

Reference Number	Statement	Initiated at this phase of project	Submit to the USGBC at this phase of project	Project Life Cycle		
				Tasks @ Design Phase	Tasks @ Construction Phase	Tasks @ Post Construction Phase
SS 4.2	Alternative Transportation	Schematic Design	Design	1- Determine number of full -time occupants. 2- Review location of bicycle storage. 3- Review location of showers and changing rooms. 4-Complete all requirements on-line.	NONE	NONE
SS 4.3	Alternative Transportation	Schematic Design	Design	1- Review different options to comply with this credit. 2- Review design of refueling stations. 3- Document construction of refueling stations. 4- Complete the LEED components on-line.	NONE	NONE

Reference Number	Statement	Initiated at this phase of project	Submit to the USGBC at this phase of project	Project Life Cycle		
				Tasks @ Design Phase	Tasks @ Construction Phase	Tasks @ Post Construction Phase
SS 4.4	*Alternative Transportation*	*Schematic Design*	*Design*	*1-Design the LEED project per local zoning requirements. 2- Calculate the parking requirements. 3- Complete the LEED components on-line.*	*NONE*	*NONE*
SS 5.1	*Site Development*	*Schematic Design*	*Construction*	*1- Review limits of site disturbance.*	*1- Inspect site fencing. 2- Document site fencing.*	*1- Complete the LEED components on-line.*
SS 5.2	*Site Development*	*Schematic Design*	*Design*	*1- Complete the LEED components on-line.*	*NONE*	*NONE*
SS 6.1	*Storm water Design*	*Schematic Design*	*Design*	*1- Evaluate different options provided by the Civil Engineer. 2- Complete the LEED components on-line.*	*NONE*	*NONE*

LEEDPASS
(LEED NC 2.2)

Reference Number	Statement	Initiated at this phase of project	Submit to the USGBC at this phase of project	Project Life Cycle		
				Tasks @ Design Phase	Tasks @ Construction Phase	Tasks @ Post Construction Phase
SS 6.2	Storm water Design	Schematic Design	Design	1- Evaluate different options provided by the Civil Engineer. 2- Complete the LEED components on-line.	NONE	NONE
SS 7.1	Heat Island Effect (Non-Roof)	Schematic Design	Construction	1- Evaluate different options provided by the team . 2- Complete the LEED components on-line.	NONE	NONE
SS 7.2	Heat Island Effect (Roof)	Schematic Design	Design	1- Review roofing materials. 2- Review green roofing material. 3- Verify roofing material meet the SRI number. 4- Compare the SRI number with slope of roof. 5- Complete the LEED components on-line.	NONE	NONE

Reference Number	Statement	Initiated at this phase of project	Submit to the USGBC at this phase of project	Project Life Cycle		
				Tasks @ Design Phase	Tasks @ Construction Phase	Tasks @ Post Construction Phase
SS 8	Light Pollution Reduction	Schematic Design	Design	1- Complete the LEED components on-line.	NONE	NONE

Reference Number	*Statement*	*Initiated at this phase of project*	*Submit to the USGBC at this phase of project*	*Project Life Cycle*		
				Tasks @ Design Phase	*Tasks @ Construction Phase*	*Tasks @ Post Construction Phase*
WATER EFFICIENCY						
WE 1.1	*Water Efficient Landscaping*	*Schematic Design*	*Design*	*1- Review landscape design. 2- Review water consumption budget. 3- Reduce potable water consumption. 4- Complete the LEED components on-line.*	*NONE*	*NONE*
WE 1.2	*Water Efficient Landscaping*	*Schematic Design*	*Design*	*1- Review landscape design. 2- Review water consumption budget. 3- Reduce potable water consumption. 4- Complete the LEED components on-line.*	*NONE*	*NONE*

Reference Number	Statement	Initiated at this phase of project	Submit to the USGBC at this phase of project	Project Life Cycle		
				Tasks @ Design Phase	Tasks @ Construction Phase	Tasks @ Post Construction Phase
WE 2	Innovative Wastewater Technologies	Schematic Design	Design	1- Review potable water demand. 2- Determine available options. 3- Prepare cost analysis. 4- Prepare life cycle analysis. 5- Complete the LEED components on-line.	NONE	NONE
WE 3.1 WE 3.2	Water Use Reduction	Schematic Design	Design	1- Review water consumption budget. 2- Determine minimum standards by implementing the Energy Policy Baseline Budget. 3- Determine percentage reduction compared to Baseline Budget. 4- Complete the LEED components on-line.	NONE	NONE

Reference Number	Statement	Initiated at this phase of project	Submit to the USGBC at this phase of project	Project Life Cycle		
				Tasks @ Design Phase	Tasks @ Construction Phase	Tasks @ Post Construction Phase
ENERGY & ATMOSPHERE						
EA P1	Fundamental Commissioning of the Building Energy Systems	Construction Administration	Construction	1- Review commissioning plan.	1- Complete the LEED components on-line.	NONE
EA P2	Minimum Energy Performance	Design Development	Design	1- Review mechanical design. 2- Review plumbing design. 3- Review electrical design. 4- Complete the LEED components on-line.	NONE	NONE

Reference Number	***Statement***	***Initiated at this phase of project***	***Submit to the USGBC at this phase of project***	***Project Life Cycle***		
				Tasks @ Design Phase	***Tasks @ Construction Phase***	***Tasks @ Post Construction Phase***
EA P3	***Fundamental Refrigerant Management***	***Design Development***	***Design***	***1- Review mechanical design. 2- Review plumbing design. 3- Review electrical design. 4- Provide cost analysis for all HVAC units. 5- Complete the LEED components on-line.***	***NONE***	***NONE***
EA 1	***Optimize Energy Performance***	***Schematic Design***	***Design***	***1- Review the Energy Cost Budget. 2- Check if there are possibilities for the project to earn higher scores. 3- Complete the LEED components on-line.***	***NONE***	***NONE***

LEEDPASS
(LEED NC 2.2)

Reference Number	Statement	Initiated at this phase of project	Submit to the USGBC at this phase of project	Project Life Cycle		
				Tasks @ Design Phase	Tasks @ Construction Phase	Tasks @ Post Construction Phase
EA 2	On-site Renewable Energy	Schematic Design	Design	1- Review mechanical design. 2- Review plumbing design. 3- Verify prerequisite requirements. 4- Complete the LEED components on-line.	NONE	NONE
EA 3	Enhanced Commissioning	Schematic Design	Construction	1- Check that all LEED's requirements are included in the scope of work.	1- Review commissioning plan.	1- Complete the LEED components on-line.

Reference Number	Statement	Initiated at this phase of project	Submit to the USGBC at this phase of project	Project Life Cycle		
				Tasks @ Design Phase	Tasks @ Construction Phase	Tasks @ Post Construction Phase
EA 4	Enhanced Refrigerant Management	Design Development	Design	1- Review selection of HVAC units with the Mechanical Engineer. 2- Complete the LEED components on-line.	NONE	NONE
EA 5	Measurement & Verification	Design Development	Construction	1- Review measurement and verification plan.	1- Complete the LEED components on-line.	NONE

Reference Number	Statement	Initiated at this phase of project	Submit to the USGBC at this phase of project	Project Life Cycle		
				Tasks @ Design Phase	Tasks @ Construction Phase	Tasks @ Post Construction Phase
EA 6	*Green Power*	*Occupation*	*Design*	*1- Determine total annual electrical load. 2- Contact Green-e providers. 3- Provide RFP (Request For Proposal) from Green-e providers. 4- Obtain signed contract between owner and Green-e provider. 5- Complete the LEED components on-line.*	*NONE*	*NONE*

Reference Number	*Statement*	*Initiated at this phase of project*	*Submit to the USGBC at this phase of project*	*Project Life Cycle*		
				Tasks @ Design Phase	*Tasks @ Construction Phase*	*Tasks @ Post Construction Phase*
MATERIAL AND RESOURCES						
MR P1	*Storage & Collection of Recyclables*	*Schematic Design*	*Design*	*1- Review location of recycling area. 2- Review size of recycling area.*	*1- Document all tasks during the construction phase. 2-Complete the requirements on-line.*	*NONE*
MR 1.1 MR 1.2 MR 1.3	*Building Reuse*	*Pre- Design*	*Construction*	*1- Review demolition plan. 2- Determine size of reused area. 3- Verify all related credit compliances.*	*1- Document all tasks during the construction phase. 2-Complete the requirements on-line.*	*NONE*

Reference Number	Statement	Initiated at this phase of project	Submit to the USGBC at this phase of project	Project Life Cycle		
				Tasks @ Design Phase	Tasks @ Construction Phase	Tasks @ Post Construction Phase
MR 2.1 MR 2.2	*Construction Waste Management*	*Construction Documents*	*Construction*	*1- Implement waste management plan. 2- Determine waste stream. 3- Review potential local recycling centers and haulers.*	*1- Monitor waste recycling plan on a weekly basis. 2- Update construction waste management plan.*	*1- Complete the LEED components on-line.*
MR 3.1 MR 3.2	*Material Reuse*	*Construction Documents*	*Construction*	*1- Review material schedule. 2- Determine any options to use salvaged materials. 3- Determine any options to use refurbished materials. 4- Determine any options to use reuseable materials. 5- Ask bidders to include list of salvaged materials in their bids. 6- Ask bidders to include list of refurbished materials in their bids. 7- Ask bidders to include list of reuseable materials in their bids.*	*1- Document all materials that comply with requirements of this credit. 2-Complete the requirements on-line.*	*NONE*

LEEDPASS
(LEED NC 2.2)

Reference Number	Statement	Initiated at this phase of project	Submit to the USGBC at this phase of project	Project Life Cycle		
				Tasks @ Design Phase	Tasks @ Construction Phase	Tasks @ Post Construction Phase
MR 4.1 MR 4.2 MR 4.3	*Recycled Content*	*Schematic Design*	*Construction*	*1- Gather recycled content information.*	*1- Compile and verify all construction data for the building materials. 2- Determine if this credit compliance is met.*	*1- Complete the LEED components on-line.*
MR 5.1 MR 5.2	*Regional Materials*	*Schematic Design*	*Construction*	*1- Determine if the credit compliance is achieved. 2- Gather product information from all bidders.*	*1- Compile construction data for the building materials. 2- Verify construction data on the building materials.*	*1- Complete the LEED components on-line.*

LEEDPASS
(LEED NC 2.2)

Reference Number	Statement	Initiated at this phase of project	Submit to the USGBC at this phase of project	Project Life Cycle		
				Tasks @ Design Phase	Tasks @ Construction Phase	Tasks @ Post Construction Phase
MR 6	Rapidly Renewable Materials	Schematic Design	Construction	1- Determine if the credit compliance is achieved. 2- Gather product information from all bidders.	1- Compile construction data on all building materials. 2- Verify construction data on all building materials.	1- Complete the LEED components on-line.
MR 7	Certified Wood	Schematic Design	Construction	1- Calculate cost of wood materials. 2- Evaluate amount of certified wood that will be utilized in this project. 3- Calculate amount of certified wood. 4- Gather all information on wood material from the bidders.	1- Gather all construction data on wood materials from the bidders.	1- Complete the LEED components on-line

Reference Number	*Statement*	*Initiated at this phase of project*	*Submit to the USGBC at this phase of project*	*Project Life Cycle*		
				Tasks @ Design Phase	*Tasks @ Construction Phase*	*Tasks @ Post Construction Phase*
INDOOR ENVIRONMENTAL QUALITY						
EQ P1	*Minimum IAQ Performance*	*Schematic Design*	*Design*	*1- Check if the Mechanical Engineer has included all required information per basis of design. 2- Complete the LEED components on-line.*	*NONE*	*NONE*
EQ P2	*Environmental Tobacco Smoke (ETS) Control*	*Pre- Design*	*Design*	*1- Check if smoking is allowed in the building. 2- Complete the requirements on-line.*	*NONE*	*NONE*
EQ 1	*Outdoor Air Delivery Monitoring*	*Schematic Design*	*Design*	*1- Complete the LEED components on-line.*	*1- Compile all information on design. 2- Verify the type of CO2 sensors.*	*NONE*

LEEDPASS
(LEED NC 2.2)

Reference Number	Statement	Initiated at this phase of project	Submit to the USGBC at this phase of project	Project Life Cycle		
				Tasks @ Design Phase	Tasks @ Construction Phase	Tasks @ Post Construction Phase
EQ 2	Increased Ventilation	Schematic Design	Design	1- Compare the mechanical design with the content of this credit. 2- Complete the LEED components on-line.	NONE	NONE
EQ 3.1 EQ 3.2	Construction IAQ Management Plan	Construction Administration	Construction	1- Coordinate the construction IAQ management plan with all bidders.	1- Check the site weekly. 2- Ensure the construction IAQ management plan is properly implemented in the field.	1- Complete the LEED components on-line.
EQ 4.1 EQ 4.2 EQ 4.3 EQ 4.4	Low- Emitting Materials	Design Development	Construction	1- Review specification. 2- Gather material listing from all bidders.	1- Ensure specified materials were installed by the contractor. 2- Collect documentation for all specified materials on a weekly basis.	1- Complete the LEED components on-line.

LEEDPASS
(LEED NC 2.2)

Reference Number	Statement	Initiated at this phase of project	Submit to the USGBC at this phase of project	Project Life Cycle		
				Tasks @ Design Phase	Tasks @ Construction Phase	Tasks @ Post Construction Phase
EQ 5	Indoor Chemical & Pollutant Source Control	Design Development	Construction	1- Ensure the exhaust fan is installed for airborne ventilation system. 2- Ensure the MERV 13 air filters are installed for the HVAC systems.	1- Document entryway system is installed properly. 2- Document exhaust system is installed properly. 3- Document filtration system is installed properly.	1- Complete the LEED components on-line.
EQ 6.1 EQ 6.2	Controllability of Systems	Design Development	Construction	1- Review lighting controls design.	1- Verify if the lighting installation was completed per plan. 2- Complete the LEED components on-line.	1- Ensure all requirements have been met for this credit.

LEEDPASS
(LEED NC 2.2)

Reference Number	Statement	Initiated at this phase of project	Submit to the USGBC at this phase of project	Project Life Cycle		
				Tasks @ Design Phase	Tasks @ Construction Phase	Tasks @ Post Construction Phase
EQ 7.1	Thermal Comfort - Design	Design Development	Construction	1- Review thermal comfort design. 2- Ensure the HVAC design comply with standards of this credit.	1- Complete the LEED components on-line.	NONE
EQ 7.2	Thermal Comfort - Verification	Design Development	Construction	1- Review thermal comfort design. 2- Ensure HVAC design complies with ASHRAE standards.	1- Complete the LEED components on-line.	1- Conduct thermal comfort survey. 2- Perform corrective action as required by this credit.
EQ 8.1	Daylight & Views	Schematic Design	Design	1- Review lighting design. 2- Complete the LEED components on-line.	1- Verify any changes to building floor plan. 2- Study different options to increase the effectiveness of the daylight in the building.	1- Ensure all requirements have been met for this credit.

LEEDPASS
(LEED NC 2.2)

Reference Number	Statement	Initiated at this phase of project	Submit to the USGBC at this phase of project	Project Life Cycle		
				Tasks @ Design Phase	Tasks @ Construction Phase	Tasks @ Post Construction Phase
EQ 8.2	Daylight & Views	Schematic Design	Design	1- Check interior building design. 2- Check direct line of sight. 3- Complete the LEED components on-line.	1- Verify any changes to the building floor plan. 2- Study different options to increase the effectiveness of the daylight in the building.	1- Ensure all requirements have been met for this credit.

Reference Number	*Statement*	*Initiated at this phase of project*	*Submit to the USGBC at this phase of project*	*Project Life Cycle*		
				Tasks @ Design Phase	*Tasks @ Construction Phase*	*Tasks @ Post Construction Phase*
INNOVATION IN DESIGN						
ID 1.1 ID 1.2 ID 1.3 ID 1.4	*Innovation in Design*	*All phases of project*	*Design & Construction*	*1- Case by case*	*1- Case by case*	*1- Case by case*
ID 2	*LEED Accredited Professional*	*All phases of project*	*Construction*	*1- Case by case*	*1- Case by case*	*1- Case by case*

LEEDPASS

(Chapter 10)

FINAL FACT TABLES

FINAL FACTS			
Item Number	***Topic***	***Remarks***	***Page Number per USGBC Reference Guide version 2.2 (Oct 2007)***
1	***Prevent the loss of soil***	***Protect topsoil by stocking***	***23***
2	***Strategies for the sedimentation control***	***It includes TWO methods:*** ***1- Stabilization*** ***2- Structural***	***23***
3	***The stabilization processes***	***It includes THREE processes:*** ***1- Temporary*** ***2- Permanent seeding*** ***3- Mulching***	***24***
4	***The Structural Control***	***It includes FOUR methods:*** ***1- Earth dikes*** ***2- Silt fencing*** ***3- Sediment trap*** ***4- Basins***	***24***
5	***The Civil Engineer***	***Identifies:*** ***1- Erosion-prone areas*** ***2- Soil stabilization***	***24***
6	***READ THE ENTIRE SHEET***		***29***
7	***READ THE ENTIRE SHEET***		***35***

FINAL FACTS			
Item Number	***Topic***	***Remarks***	***Page Number per USGBC Reference Guide version 2.2 (Oct 2007)***
8	***To develop the density of project***	***Evaluate: 1- The project site 2- The surrounding developments***	***36***
9	***The main factors for calculating the density of project***	***1- DO NOT include undeveloped public areas such as parks and bodies of water. 2- DO NOT include public roads and right-of-way areas.***	***36***
10	***Community Connectivity- (for RESIDENTIAL projects)***	***At least 10 units per acre***	***38***
11	***Community Connectivity- (for COMMERCIAL projects)***	***At least 10 community services within 1/2 mile radius.***	***38***
12	***Pedestrian access***	***It shall NOT be blocked by walls, highways and other barriers.***	***38***
13	***Bicycle Storage- (for RESIDENTIAL projects)***	***It shall be designed for 15 % or more of FTE.***	***55***
14	***Transient occupants***	***It includes: 1- Students 2- Visitors 3- Customers***	***56***

FINAL FACTS			
Item Number	***Topic***	***Remarks***	***Page Number per USGBC Reference Guide version 2.2 (Oct 2007)***
15	***The shower facilities***	***It shall be designed for 0.5 percent (0.005) of FTE.***	***57***
16	***Full time occupant***	***Assume 8 hrs per day***	***57***
17	***Parking Capacity (for COMMERCIAL projects)***	***It should NOT exceed local zoning standards.***	***65***
18	***Parking Capacity (for COMMERCIAL projects)***	***EXCLUDE handicapped spaces.***	***66***
19	***Greenfield site***	***It is NOT previously developed or graded.***	***69***
20	***For previously developed or graded sites***	***Protect 50 % of the site. (EXCLUDING building footprint)***	***69***
21	***READ THE ENTIRE SHEET***		***73***

FINAL FACTS			
Item Number	***Topic***	***Remarks***	***Page Number per USGBC Reference Guide version 2.2 (Oct 2007)***
22	***When imperviousness area is EQUAL to or LESS than 50 %***	***The rate and quantity of Post-Development area shall be EQUAL to or LESS than Pre-Development area.***	***77***
23	***When imperviousness area is GREATER than 50 %***	***DECREASE the volume of storm water runoff by 25 percent.***	***77***
24	***Storm water***	***It is NOT required to convey and receive water from municipality's sources.***	***81***
25	***Quality Control (NON-structural measures)***	***It includes: 1- Vegetation swales 2- The disconnection of impervious areas and pervious pavement***	***86***
26	***Quality Control (Structural measures)***	***It includes: 1- Rainwater cisterns 2- Manholes 3- Treatment devices***	***86***
27	***Minimize impervious surfaces***	***It includes: 1- Smaller footprint 2- Pervious material 3- Green roofs 4- Filter strip 5- Retention ponds***	***86***
28	***READ THE ENTIRE SHEET***		***91***

FINAL FACTS			
Item Number	*Topic*	*Remarks*	*Page Number per USGBC Reference Guide version 2.2 (Oct 2007)*
29	Shade area calculation	The calculation shall be performed at 10 am, 12 noon, 3 pm. (summer solstice)	92
30	EXEMPLARY performance for Heat Island effect	Locate 100 percent of the parking space under covered area.	93
31	Solar Reflectance Index	Measures of material's ability to REJECT solar heat	95
32	Heat Island Effect- roofing material	Use material shown on page 97 for 75 percent of roofing area.	97
33	Solar Reflectance	100 percent means the entire energy is reflected back into the atmosphere.	102
34	Exterior lighting	It shall NOT exceed 80 percent of the lighting power density. (Per ASHRAE 90.1-2004 standard)	103
35	To model the lighting design for the site	Use computer model	104

FINAL FACTS			
Item Number	***Topic***	***Remarks***	***Page Number per USGBC Reference Guide version 2.2 (Oct 2007)***
36	***ASHRAE standards 90.1-2004***	***It includes: 1- Building envelope 2- HVAC system 3- Hot water heating system 4- Building lighting design***	***105***
37	***Building Control***	***It includes: 1- Automatic sweep timers 2- Occupancy sensors 3- Programmed master lighting 4- Electrical control panels***	***105***
38	***Building Control***	***It includes manual override capabilities that enable lighting system for after hours.***	***106***
39	***Water-conserving systems***	***It is mandated by Energy Policy Act of 1992.***	***115***
40	***Reduce potable water***	***Potable water shall be reduced by 50 percent with attribution of plant species factor, irrigation efficiency and use of captured rainwater or recycled wastewater.***	***117***

FINAL FACTS			
Item Number	***Topic***	***Remarks***	***Page Number per USGBC Reference Guide version 2.2 (Oct 2007)***
41	***Potential technology to reduce irrigation requirements***	***Use high-efficiency equipment.***	***117***
42	***Requirements for NO Potable Use or NO Irrigation.***	***Use only:*** ***1- Captured rainwater*** ***2- Recycled wastewater*** ***3- Recycled gray water*** ***4- Treated water***	***118***
43	***Evapotranspiration rate (ET)***	***Use ET for the month of July.***	***122***
44	***Landscape area***	***Landscape area = (total site area) - (paved surface area + building footprint area + water bodies area + patios area, etc.)***	***127***
45	***READ THE ENTIRE SHEET***		***129***
46	***Gray water system***	***1- Higher code requirement than rain water system*** ***2- More expensive than rainwater system***	***130***

FINAL FACTS			
Item Number	***Topic***	***Remarks***	***Page Number per USGBC Reference Guide version 2.2 (Oct 2007)***
47	***Design case***	***Compare proposed design condition with baseline standards.***	***132***
48	***Low-flow water closet***	***Consider <u>3 daily</u> uses for <u>EACH FEMALE</u>.***	***133***
49	***Energy calculation***	***The usage rates, occupancy and number of workdays are <u>IDENTICAL</u> for <u>BOTH</u> design and baseline cases.***	***133***
50	***Aquastic system***	***1. Ecologically designed treatment system 2. Utility adiverse community of biological organisms 3. Treat waste water to advanced levels***	***137***
51	***Gray water***	***Used water from bathtubs, shower, bathroom, clothes washer, and laundry tubs***	***138***
52	***Process water***	***Water used for industrial use such as chillers and cooling towers***	***139***

FINAL FACTS			
Item Number	***Topic***	***Remarks***	***Page Number per USGBC Reference Guide version 2.2 (Oct 2007)***
53	***Tertiary Treatment***	***Highest form of waste water***	***139***
54	***On-site wastewater treatment system***	***Uses localized treatment system to transport and dispose wasted water.***	***139***
55	***Standard fixture uses by the occupancy type***	***Table 2 (columns): Includes calculation for FTE, student, visitor, retail customer and resident. (MEMORIZE IT)***	***143***
56	***Sample design case water use calculation***	***Table 4 (columns) : Includes calculation for daily uses, flow rate, duration, occupants and water use. (MEMORIZE IT)***	***144***
57	***Metering Controls***	***Manual on/automatic off controls used to limit the flow time of water***	***148***

FINAL FACTS			
Item Number	***Topic***	***Remarks***	***Page Number per USGBC Reference Guide version 2.2 (Oct 2007)***
58	***Fundamental commissioning***	***It includes: 1- Owner Project Requirements 2- Basis Of Design 3- Commissioning specification 4- Performance verification documentation 5- Commissioning report***	***154***
59	***Successful commissioning***	***To improve energy efficiency of building by 5 % to 10 %.***	***160***
60	***Commission Process***	***Improves 5 % to 10 % efficiency***	***160***
61	***Minimum Energy Performance***	***The study shall be based on ASHRAE 90.1-2004 standards.***	***165***
62	***Methods of calculation for minimum energy standard***	***There are TWO types of calculation: 1- Performance 2- Prescriptive***	***165***

FINAL FACTS			
Item Number	***Topic***	***Remarks***	***Page Number per USGBC Reference Guide version 2.2 (Oct 2007)***
63	***ASHRAE/IESNA 90.1***	***It covers: 1- Parking garage ventilation 2- Freeze protection 3- Exhaust air recovery***	***166***
64	***ASHRAE/IESNA 90.1***	***Apply to multi-family structures of four habitable stories***	***166***
65	***Mandatory Minimum Energy Performance (table 2)***	***It includes: 1- Building envelope 2- Heating, ventilating and air conditioning system 3- Service water heating system 4- Power system 5- Lighting system***	***169***
66	***Prescriptive Requirements (table 2)***	***It is utilized for smaller building. (<u>LESS</u> than 25,000 sq. ft)***	***169***
67	***Performance Compliance Approach***	***For this approach use Performance Rating Report***	***169***
68	***Mandatory Measures of ASHRAE/IESNA, 90.1***	***It includes : 1- Building envelope 2- HVAC System 3- Lighting 4- Service water heating***	***169***

FINAL FACTS			
Item Number	***Topic***	***Remarks***	***Page Number per USGBC Reference Guide version 2.2 (Oct 2007)***
69	***Documents needed for prescriptive requirements of ASHRAE 90.1***	***1- Building envelope compliance 2- Service water heating compliance 3- HVAC compliance***	***169***
70	***HVAC compliance documentation Part 1 of ASHRAE/IESNA 90.1/ 2004***	***Refers to small building, less than 25,000 sq. ft.***	***169***
71	***Energy Star Rating***	***Issued by EPA.***	***170***
72	***Variable factors for refrigerants***	***Lifetime, ODP and GWP***	***172***
73	***READ THE ENTIRE SHEET***		***175***
74	***READ THE ENTIRE SHEET***		***176***
75	***In option 2 of EA Credit 1, Optimize Energy Performance***	***Refers to building less than 20,000 sq. ft.***	***176***

FINAL FACTS			
Item Number	***Topic***	***Remarks***	***Page Number per USGBC Reference Guide version 2.2 (Oct 2007)***
76	***READ THE ENTIRE SHEET***		***177***
77	***Performance Rating Method***	***It is determined based on: 1- Building type 2- Building area 3- Quantity of floors 4- Heating fuel sources***	***181***
78	***Performance Rating Method***	***It includes: 1- Building type 2- Building area 3- Quantity of floors 4- Heating fuel source***	***181***
79	***Which ratio does not increase the energy performance***	***Default Ratio***	***182***
80	***Advanced Building Benchmark Version 1.1***	***It refers to New Building Institute***	***184***
81	***Baseline Building Performance***	***Use AVERAGE projected annual energy cost which is calculated by FOUR baseline design simulations. (One for each orientation)***	***185***
82	***On-Site Renewable Energy and site recovered energy***	***Do NOT include COST in Building Performance.***	***188***

FINAL FACTS			
Item Number	**Topic**	**Remarks**	**Page Number per USGBC Reference Guide version 2.2 (Oct 2007)**
83	On-Site Renewable Energy	It includes: 1- Power generated by photovoltaic or wind turbines. 2- Thermal energy collected by the solar panels.	188
84	Energy rates in EA credit, Optimize Energy Performance	It applies to : 1- ASHRAE/IESNA 90.1 2- Local utility schedules 3- Department of Energy	188
85	Cost of proposed building performance method	It includes : 1- Cost of process energy 2- Cost of non-regulated energy 3- Cost of lighting system	188
86	On-site renewable energy systems	1- Thermal energy collected by solar panels 2- Power generated by photovoltaic 3- Power generated by wind towers	188
87	Site-recovered energy	1- Heat recovered with chiller heat recovery systems 2- Waste heat recovery units on distributed generation systems	188
88	Process Load	1- Interior lighting 2- Receptacle equipment 3- Refrigerator heat load	195

FINAL FACTS

Item Number	Topic	Remarks	Page Number per USGBC Reference Guide version 2.2 (Oct 2007)
89	On-Site Renewable Energy- Estimated electricity use	Use information from EA credit 1 (Optimize Energy Performance) or CBECS (the survey by DOE).	203
90	On-Site Renewable Energy - Produced at site	It is a FREE energy and shall NOT be considered as ENERGY COST.	204
91	Items that are not eligible as on-site renewable energy system	1- Daylight strategies 2- Passive solar systems 3- Architectural features	205
92	Virtual energy rate	It is equal to annual energy cost for the specified fuel DIVIDED by the annual energy consumption for the same fuel.	207
93	READ THE ENTIRE SHEET		211
94	Difference between fundamental and enhanced commissioning	It includes THREE tasks: 1- Attending design review meetings. 2- Reviewing construction submittals. 3- Reviewing project manual	212
95	The commissioning process	It is indicated in TWO sections: 1- EA Prerequisite 1 2- EA credit 3	213

FINAL FACTS

Item Number	Topic	Remarks	Page Number per USGBC Reference Guide version 2.2 (Oct 2007)
96	The commissioning process	1- It shall be performed per Owner Project Requirements (OPR) 2- It MINIMIZES the NEGATIVE environmental impacts.	213
97	The commissioning process	It reduces: 1- Construction change orders 2- Repairs cost 3- Energy cost 4- Maintenance cost 5- Operation cost	216
98	The commissioning Process	1- Reduce repairs and construction change orders 2- Reduce energy cost 3- Reduce maintenance cost	216
99	Select air conditioning equipment	With REDUCED refrigerant charge and INCREASED equipment life.	218
100	READ THE ENTIRE SHEET		233
101	Number of paths to calculate the amount of the electrical energy (Green-e certified)	TWO (2)	234
102	Required information for green power credit	1- Design energy cost 2- Default electricity consumption	235

FINAL FACTS			
Item Number	***Topic***	***Remarks***	***Page Number per USGBC Reference Guide version 2.2 (Oct 2007)***
103	***Material qualifying for MR credit 3.1 and 3.2***	***It can NOT be applied to:*** ***1- MR credit 1.1*** ***2- MR credit 1.2*** ***3- MR credit 1.3*** ***4- MR credit 2.1*** ***5- MR credit 2.2*** ***6- MR credit 4.1*** ***7- MR credit 4.2*** ***8- MR credit 6*** ***9- MR credit 7***	***240***
104	***Materials used for MR Credit 3.1, 3.2***	***Can be used for MR Credit 5***	***240***
105	***The MR credit metrics, Construction Waste Management (Table 2)***	***It is calculated based on WEIGHT or VOLUME of building materials.***	***241***
106	***Non-hazardous materials for recycling***	***1- Paper*** ***2- Metal*** ***3- Corrugated cardboard*** ***4- Glass*** ***5- Plastic***	***243***
107	***Recycling activities***	***It impacts the ENVIRONMENTAL quality.***	***244***
108	***Building Reuse - Existing building structure***	***It shall be calculated based on surface AREA .***	***247***
109	***Building Reuse***	***It shall include INVENTORY list for the existing condition.***	***250***
110	***Existing building materials that do not meet MR Credit 1 standards***	***May apply towards the achievement of MR Credit 2. (By weight)***	***250***

FINAL FACTS			
Item Number	***Topic***	***Remarks***	***Page Number per USGBC Reference Guide version 2.2 (Oct 2007)***
111	***Existing building materials that can not be contributed to MR credit 1.1 and 1.2 credits***	***1- Non-structural roofing 2- Unsound materials from a structural perspective 3- Window assemblies***	***250***
112	***MR credit 1.3***	***The achievement of MR credits 1.1, 1.2 is not required for MR credit 1.3***	***251***
113	***Construction Waste Management - Divert from disposal***	***Excavated soil and clearing debris <u>DO NOT</u> contribute to this credit.***	***255***
114	***Construction Waste Management - Divert from disposal***	***The diversion may include: 1- <u>DONATION</u> of building materials. 2- <u>SALVAGE</u> of building materials on the site.***	***255***
115	***Materials that do not contribute to MR Credit 2.1, Construction Waste Management credit***	***1- Excavated soil 2- Land cleaning debris***	***255***
116	***Materials which can contribute to MR Credit 2.1, 2.2 Construction Waste Management credits***	***Materials reused or salvages on site, if they are not included in MR 3 credit***	***257***
117	***Material Reuse (calculation)***	***<u>It DOES NOT</u> include: 1- MEP (Mechanical, Electrical, Plumbing)units 2- Elevator machines***	***263***

FINAL FACTS			
Item Number	***Topic***	***Remarks***	***Page Number per USGBC Reference Guide version 2.2 (Oct 2007)***
118	***Material Reuse (cost of material)***	***It includes :*** ***1- ACTUAL cost of building materials.*** ***2- REPLACEMENT VALUE cost of building materials.***	***263***
119	***Cost of on-site materials***	***1- Actual cost*** ***2- Replacement cost***	***265***
120	***Fixed items which can be contributed to MR credit 3.2, Material Reuse credit***	***1- Must no longer be able to serve original function.*** ***2- It has be reconditioned or installed for different locations***	***265***
121	***Material Cost***	***It is normally 45 percent of total construction cost as described by CSI master format 1995-division 2-10.***	***266***
122	***Construction cost standard***	***CSI Main format 1995, Division 2-10***	***266***
123	***Recycled Content***	***Designer may include furniture as part of recycled content materials***	***269***
124	***The comparison of Post-Consumer and Pre -Consumer material***	***It identifies by WEIGHT ratio.***	***271***
125	***Post-consumer waste***	***1- Construction debris*** ***2- Discarded products*** ***3- Urban Maintenance***	***274***

FINAL FACTS			
Item Number	***Topic***	***Remarks***	***Page Number per USGBC Reference Guide version 2.2 (Oct 2007)***
126	***Discarded products***	***It includes : 1- Furniture 2- Cabinetry 3- Decking***	***275***
127	***Urban Maintenance***	***It includes: 1- Leaves 2- Grass clipping 3- Tree trimmings***	***275***
128	***Pre-consumer content***	***1- Planter shaving 2- Biogases 3- Trimmed materials***	***275***
129	***Reused and Salvaged Material - Point of extraction***	***The point of extraction refers to area where building material was originally SALVAGED .***	***280***
130	***Reused and Salvaged Material - Point of Manufacturer***	***The point of manufacture refers to area where the VENDOR has salvaged building materials.***	***280***
131	***READ THE ENTIRE SHEET***		***287***
132	***READ THE ENTIRE SHEET***		***295***

FINAL FACTS			
Item Number	***Topic***	***Remarks***	***Page Number per USGBC Reference Guide version 2.2 (Oct 2007)***
133	***EQ, Prerequisite 1, Minimum IAQ Performance (for ventilation system)***	***1- Use the Ventilation Rate Procedure or local code, whichever is more stringent. 2- Meet minimum requirement of ASHRAE 62.1 - 2004 3- Balance the system to optimize for energy efficiency***	***295***
134	***Residential units***	***All doors leading to common hallways shall be weather stripped if common area is NOT pressurized with respect to the residential units.***	***301***
135	***READ THE ENTIRE SHEET***		***323***
136	***SMACNA Standards***	***It covers: 1- Control measures 2- Construction management 3- Communication with building's occupants***	***324***
137	***READ THE ENTIRE SHEET***		***329***
138	***Air sample testing***	***The following shall be in place before air sample testing: 1-Carpet 2- Door 3- Millwork***	***330***

FINAL FACTS			
Item Number	**Topic**	**Remarks**	**Page Number per USGBC Reference Guide version 2.2 (Oct 2007)**
139	Flush-out procedure	1- May begin after construction work is completed. 2- All cleaning shall be completed before flush-out process 3- Commissioning may occur during flush-out process	331
140	Minimum outside air requirement is selected by one of the following standards	1- ASHRAE 62.1 - 2004 2- EQ Prerequisite 1 3- Local codes	332
141	Task lighting shall be counted in these areas	1- Private office 2- Reception stations 3- Ticket booths	364
142	Consider the following items for Daylight design	1- Room darkening shades 2- Glare control 3- Lighting level controls 4- Floor area 5- Visible light transmittance 6- Area geometry and height of windows	365
143	Certified Wood- calculation	It includes NEW wood products.	387
144	Consider following items for controllability of systems	1- Operable windows 2- Mechanical systems 3- Hybrid systems	387
145	Ratio of light visible transmittance	1. Total transmitted light verses total incident light	387

FINAL FACTS			
Item Number	***Topic***	***Remarks***	***Page Number per USGBC Reference Guide version 2.2 (Oct 2007)***
146	***Required written documents for ID Credit 1.1 through 1.4***	***1- Identify the intent of your proposal 2- Proposed requirements for compliance 3- Proposed submittals to demonstrate compliance 4- Design strategies and approaches***	***387***
147	***Innovation in Design***	***It includes exceptional performance and innovative performance which are NOT specifically addressed by LEED rating system.***	***397***
148	***Innovation in Design***	***By exceeding LEED standards and demonstrating improvements for ENVIRONMENTAL benefit.***	***398***
149	***Innovation in Design***	***At least ONE principal shall be a LEED AP.***	***401***
150	***Requirements for IQ credit 2***	***1- Name of LEED AP 2- Copy of LEED AP Certificate 3- Name of company***	***402***

LEEDPASS

(Chapter 11)

PRACTICE QUESTIONS

1. Which **THREE** of the following may apply to WE Credit 1, Water Efficient Landscaping credit?

   A._____ Landscape Coefficient
   B._____ Species Factor
   C._____ Microclimate Factor
   D._____ Density Factor
   E._____ Environmental Factor

2. Which **THREE** of the following credits may require the BASELINE calculation for the building energy consumption?

   A._____ WE Credit 2, Innovative Wastewater Technologies
   B._____ SS Credit 6.1, Storm water Design
   C._____ EA Credit 1, Optimize Energy Performance
   D._____ WE Credit 3, Water Use Reduction
   E._____ SS Credit 8, Light Pollution Reduction

3. Which **TWO** of the following methods may apply to the sedimentation process?

   A._____ Stabilization
   B._____ Environmental
   C._____ Structural
   D._____ Landscape
   E._____ Irrigation Factor

4. Which **ONE** of the following may apply to the stabilization method of sedimentation process?

   A._____ Structural
   B._____ Silt fencing
   C._____ Seeding
   D._____ Earth dikes
   E._____ Mulching

5. Which **THREE** of the following may apply to the structural method of sedimentation?

   A._____ Earth dikes
   B._____ Seeding
   C._____ Silt fencing
   D._____ Sediment trap
   E._____ Mowing Factor

6. Which **THREE** of the following locations shall be AVOIDED for SS Credit 1, Site Selection credit?

   A._____ Within 200 ft of river
   B._____ Within 100 ft of wetland
   C._____ Prime farmland
   D._____ Within 50 ft of streams
   E._____ Within 100 ft of streams

7. Which **THREE** of the following standards are referenced in SS Credit1. Site Selection credit?

   A._____ FEMA
   B._____ ASHRAE
   C._____ CFR
   D._____ USAD
   E._____ EPA

8. Which **THREE** of the following choices are NOT qualified for SS Credit 2, Development Density and Community Connectivity credit?

   A._____ Site area with 65,000 sq.ft per acre density
   B._____ Undeveloped areas such as parks, water bodies
   C._____ Pedestrian access with partial blocking.
   D._____ Site area with 50,000 sq.ft per acre density
   E._____ Site area with 75,000 sq.ft per acre density

9. Which **ONE** of the following establish the 100 year flood table for SS Credit 1, Site Selection credit?

   A._____ EPA
   B._____ FEMA
   C._____ CFR
   D._____ ASHRAE
   E._____ USDA

10. Which **TWO** of the following are referenced in SS Credit 3, Brownfield Redevelopment credit?

   A._____ CFR
   B._____ EPA
   C._____ ASTM
   D._____ FEMA
   E._____ SCAQMD

11. Which **TWO** of the following are true for SS Credit 4.1, Alternative Transportation, and Public Transportation Access credit?

A._____ The site shall be located ½ mile from one train or subway station
B._____ The site shall be located 1 mile from one train or subway station
C._____ The site shall be located ¼ miles from two bus lines
D._____ The site shall be located ½ miles from two bus lines
E._____ The site shall be located ¼ miles from one subway station

12. Which **TWO** of the following are true for SS Credit 4.2 Alternative Transportation, Bicycle Storage and Changing Room credit?

A._____ The bicycle rack shall be provided within 200 yards of the building
B._____ The bicycle rack shall be provided for 0.010 of FTE
C._____ The bicycle rack shall be provided within 250 yards of the building
D._____ The bicycle rack shall be provided for 0.05 of FTE
E._____ The bicycle rack shall be provided for 0.015 of FTE

13. Which **TWO** of the following are true for parking spaces of low emission cars in SS Credit 4.3 Alternative Transportation credit, Low- Emitting and Fuel-Efficient Vehicles credit?

A._____ Provide parking spaces for low emission cars based on 0.05 of the total parking space
B._____ Provide parking spaces for low emission cars based on 0.005 of FTE
C._____ Parking spaces for low emission cars shall exclude handicap parking spaces
D._____ Provide parking spaces for low emission cars based on 0.10 of the total parking spaces
E._____ Provide parking spaces for low emission cars based on 0.005 of the total parking spaces

14. Which **TWO** of the following are true for the NON-RESIDENTIAL project in SS Credit 4.4, option # 1, Alternative Transportation, and Parking Capacity credit?

A._____ Exceed the local code requirements
B._____ Provide carpool parking spaces based on 0.01 of the total parking spaces
C._____ Do not exceed the local code requirements
D._____ Provide the carpool parking spaces based on 0.05 of the total parking space
E._____ Provide the carpool parking spaces based on 0.005 of the total parking space

15. Which **THREE** of the following are true for SS Credit 5.1, Site Development, Protect of Restore Habitat credit?

A._____ Restore 30 % of the developed site area as the vegetated land
B._____ The graded site shall be obtained from previously developed land
C._____ Exclude building footprint from developed site area
D._____ Restore 50 % of the developed site area as the vegetated land
E._____ Restore 45 % of the developed site area as the vegetated land

16. Which **TWO** of the following are true for SS Credit 5.2, Site Development, Maximize Open Space credit? (there is NO local code)

A._____ Open space shall be 50 % of the building foot print
B._____ Open space shall be 35 % of the building foot print
C._____ Open space should be the same size as the building foot print
D._____ Open space shall remain for the life of the building
E._____ Open space shall be 45 % of the building foot print

17. Which **THREE** of the following methods may reduce the IMPERVIOUS surface in SS Credit 6.1, Storm water Design, Quantity Control credit?

A._____ Green roof surface
B._____ Non-structural alternative surface
C._____ Open-grid surface
D._____ Non-structural surface
E._____ Closed-grid surface

18. Which **TWO** of the following are considered as non-structural ALTERNATIVE surface methods in SS Credit 6.2, Storm water Design, Quality Control credit?

A._____ Density factor
B._____ Vegetated swales
C._____ Rain garden
D._____ Rainwater recycling
E._____ Open-grid surface

19. Which **TWO** of the following tasks are the PRIMARY roles of the LEED AP beyond receiving one point in ID Credit 2, LEED Accredited Professional credit?

A._____ Review the cost analysis
B._____ Manage CIR documentation processes
C._____ Coordinate decision making processes
D._____ Quality control management
E._____ Manage scope verification processes

20. Which **THREE** of the following may apply to SS Credit 7.1, Heat Island Effect, Non-Roof credit?

A._____ Provide paving material (SRI less than 29) for open grid space
B._____ Provide full shading for 50 % of the site within a period of 5 years
C._____ Design 50 percent of the parking space under roof or at underground level
D._____ Provide paving material (SRI equal or greater than 29) for open grid space
E._____ Provide 5 year shade for 30 percent of site area

21. Which **ONE** of the following may apply to SS Credit 7.2, Heat Island Effect, Roof credit?

A._____ Design 35 percent of roof with vegetation elements
B._____ Design 55 percent of roof with vegetation elements
C._____ Design 50 percent of roof with vegetation elements
D._____ Design 45 percent of roof with vegetation elements
E._____ Design 60 percent of roof with vegetation elements

22. Which **THREE** of the following are considered as NON-POTABLE water for WE Credit 1.1, Water Efficient Landscaping credit?

A._____ Drinking water
B._____ Treated water
C._____ Captured rainwater
D._____ Recycled waste water
E._____ Condenser water

23. Which **THREE** of the following may apply to WE Credit 1.1, Water Efficient landscaping credit?

A._____ Treated water
B._____ Recycled wastewater
C._____ Hydraulic system
D._____ Captured rainwater
E._____ Cooling tower system

24. Which **THREE** of the following may apply to WE Credit 1.2, Water Efficient Landscaping, No Potable Use or No Irrigation credit?

A._____ Gray water
B._____ Black water
C._____ Treated water
D._____ Waste water
E._____ Condensate water from HVAC units

25. Which **THREE** of the following may apply to WE Credit 1.2, Water Efficient landscaping, No Potable Use or No Irrigation credit?

A._____ Alternative mowing
B._____ Swales
C._____ Composting
D._____ Mulching
E._____ Seeding

26. Which **THREE** of the following could be included in the waste load calculation of WE Credit 2, Innovative Wastewater Technologies credit?

A._____ Student
B._____ Contractor
C._____ Retail customer, visitor
D._____ FTE and part timers
E._____ Building inspector

27. Which **THREE** of the following percentages may apply to WE Credit 3.1, Water Use Reduction credit? (Including Exemplary Performance - Extra credit)

A._____ 40 percent
B._____ 20 percent
C._____ 30 percent
D._____ 25 percent
E._____ 35 percent

28. Which **ONE** of the following may apply to WE Credit 3.1 and WE Credit 3.2, Water Use Reduction credits?

A._____ FEMA
B._____ CFR
C._____ Energy Policy Act 1992
D._____ ASTM
E._____ None of above

29. Which **TWO** of the following may apply to the commissioning authority in EA P1, Fundamental Commissioning of The Building Energy Systems?

A._____ Licensed contractor
B._____ Professional Engineer
C._____ Experienced person for 2 similar projects
D._____ An independent person
E._____ Licensed architect

30. Which **TWO** of the following are true in regards of the commissioning authority in EA-Prerequisite 1, FUNDEMENTAL Commissioning of The Building Energy Systems ? (The building area is less than 50,000 square feet)

A._____ Can NOT be part of the design team
B._____ Can NOT be part of the construction team
C._____ Can be part of the design team
D._____ Can be part of the construction team
E._____ Can NOT be part of the investment group

31. Which **THREE** of the following may apply to EA-Prerequisite 2 Minimum Energy Performance?

A._____ ASTM
B._____ ASHRAE 90.1, 2004
C._____ Local codes
D._____ DOE
E._____ NPDES

32. Which **THREE** of the following are included in the load calculation of EA- Prerequisite 2 Minimum Energy Performance?

A._____ Electrical panel dimension
B._____ Cooling loads
C._____ Window area
D._____ Skylight area
E._____ Landscape area

33. Which **THREE** of the following may apply to EA- Prerequisite 2 Minimum Energy Performance?

A._____ Underground utilities
B._____ Building envelope
C._____ HVAC system
D._____ Lighting system
E._____ Structural framing

34. Which **TWO** of the following are referenced in EA Prerequisite 3, FUNDEMENTAL Refrigerant Management?

A._____ CFR
B._____ ESC
C._____ ODP
D._____ GWP
E._____ DOE

35. Which **THREE** of the following may apply to EA P3, Fundamental Refrigerant Management?

A._____ Existing buildings- Implement zero use of CFC
B._____ Existing buildings- Replace HVAC system designed with CFC refrigerant
C._____ New buildings- Implement zero use of CFC
D._____ Existing buildings – Replace fire suppression system designed with CFC refrigerant
E._____ New building- Use zero HFC

36. Which **THREE** of the following may apply to EA Credit 4, Enhanced Refrigerant Management credit?

A._____ Do not install fire suppression system with CFR
B._____ Do not install fire suppression system with CFC
C._____ Do not install fire suppression system with HCFC
D._____ Do not install fire suppression system with Halon
E._____ Do not install fire suppression system with CFM

37. Which **TWO** of the following may apply to EA Credit 4, Enhanced Refrigerant Management credit?

A._____ Select systems with low ODP
B._____ Select systems with low SIR
C._____ Select systems with short life units
D._____ Select systems with low GWP
E._____ Select systems with low CIR

38. Which **TWO** of the following IPMVP options may apply to EA Credit 5, Measurement & Verification credit?

A._____ Option B
B._____ Option C
C._____ Option A
D._____ Option D
E._____ Option E

39. Which **ONE** of the following IPMVP options may apply to the SMALLER projects in EA Credit 5, Measurement & Verification credit?

A._____ Option A
B._____ Option C
C._____ Option B
D._____ Option D
E._____ None of above

40. Which **ONE** of the following IPMVP options may apply to the LARGER and COMPLEX projects in EA Credit 5, Measurement & Verification credit?

A._____ Option A
B._____ Option D
C._____ Option C
D._____ Option B
E._____ None of above

41. Which **TWO** of the following methods apply to EA Credit 6, Green Power? (In Open Market)

A._____ Sign a contract to purchase for 1 year
B._____ Obtain 35 percent of the annual load from green power source
C._____ Obtain 50 percent of the annual load from green power source
D._____ Sign a contract to purchase for 2 years
E._____ Obtain 25 percent of the annual load from green power source

42. Which **THREE** of the following recycled materials may apply to MR P-1, Storage & Collection of recyclables credit?

A._____ Paper
B._____ Cardboard
C._____ Concrete blocks
D._____ Metal
E._____ Grass

43. Which **THREE** of the following elements shall NOT be included in calculation of building material in MR Credit 1.1, Building Reuse and Maintain 75 percent of Existing Walls, Floors & Roof credit?

A._____ Non-structural items
B._____ Structural items
C._____ Electrical panel boards
D._____ Doors
E._____ Floor joist

44. Which **THREE** of the following elements shall be NOT be included for calculation of building material in MR Credit 1.3, Building Reuse, maintain 50 percent of Interior Non-Structural Elements credit?

A._____ Hardwood floor
B._____ Heat pump unit
C._____ Wiring control panel
D._____ Elevator machine
E._____ Gypsum wall

45. Which **ONE** of the following options is NOT applicable for MR Credit 1.1, Building Reuse, Maintain 75 percent of Existing Walls, Floors & Roof credit?

A._____ Where addition area is 50 percent of original floor area
B._____ Where original floor area is 60 percent of addition area
C._____ Where addition area is more than twice the size of original floor area
D._____ Where original floor area is 55 percent larger than addition area
E._____ None of above

46. Which **TWO** of the following statements are true for MR Credit 1.1, Building Reuse, Maintain 75 percent of Existing Walls, Floors & Roof credit?

A._____ Calculate structural items in square ft
B._____ Calculate structural items in cubic. ft.
C._____ Calculate shell items in cubic. ft.
D._____ Calculate shell items in square ft.
E._____ Calculate shell items in linear ft.

47. Which **THREE** of the following may NOT be considered as DIVERTING materials for MR Credit 2.1 & 2.2, Construction Waste Management credit?

A._____ Rocks
B._____ Metal
C._____ Soil
D._____ Vegetation elements
E._____ Timber

48. Which **THREE** of the following percentages may apply to MR Credit 3.1, 3.2, Material Reuse credits (including Exemplary Performance- EXTRA credit)?

A._____5 percent
B._____15 percent
C._____10 percent
D._____20 percent
E._____25 percent

49. Which **ONE** of the following percentages represents the ratio of the total cost of building materials to the total cost of building construction?

A._____35 percent
B._____50 percent
C._____45 percent
D._____ 75 percent
E._____ 65 percent

50. Which **THREE** of the following percentages may apply to MR Credit 4.1 , 4.2 , Recycled Content credits (including exemplary Performance – EXTRA credit)?

A._____ 30 percent
B._____ 40 percent
C._____ 10 percent
D._____ 20 percent
E._____ 25 percent

51. What is the rate of total building cost to the total material cost in MR Credit 6, Rapidly Renewable Materials credit?

A._____ 2 percent
B._____ 1.5 percent
C._____ 2.5 percent
D._____ 0.5 percent
E._____ 3 percent

52. Which **THREE** of the following may apply to MR Credit 6, Rapidly Renewable Materials credit?

A._____ Wool carpeting
B._____ Light bulbs
C._____ Bamboo flooring
D._____ Cotton batt insulation
E._____ HVAC units

53. What percentage of timber needs to be certified by FSC in MR Credit 7, Certified Wood credit?

A._____ 35 percent
B._____ 75 percent
C._____ 50 percent
D._____ 65 percent
E._____ 40 percent

54. Which **ONE** of the following is true for MR Credit 7, Certified Wood credit?

A._____ The supplier does not need to obtain a certification number in any transaction
B._____ The supplier needs to obtain a certification number, if the assembly is packaged as certified item
C._____ The contractor does NOT need to obtain a certification number
D._____ The contractor needs to obtain a certification number
E._____ None of above

55. Which ASHRAE standards may apply to EQ-P1, Minimum IAQ Performance?

A._____ 90.1, 2004
B._____ 55, 1999
C._____ 52.2, 2004
D._____ 62.1, 2004
E._____ 90.1, 2001

56. Which **ONE** of the following may be utilized for EQ Credit 2, Increased Ventilation credit?

A._____ Cogeneration design
B._____ Heat recovery
C._____ Double duct system
D._____ Multi-zone system
E._____ None of above

57. Which **TWO** of the following are true statements for breathing zone in EQ Credit 2, Increased Ventilation credit?

A._____ Areas within 2 ft from the exterior walls
B._____ Areas within 5 ft from the exterior walls
C._____ Areas within 3 to 6 ft above the finish floor
D._____ Areas within 3 ft from a fixed air conditioning unit
E._____ Areas within 3 ft from the exterior walls

58. Which **TWO** of the following standards may apply to EQ Credit 3.1, Construction IAQ Management Plan- During Construction credit?

A._____ ASTM 3525
B._____ CFR
C._____ SMACNA
D._____ ASHRAE 52.2, 1999
E._____ DOE

59. Which **TWO** of the following may apply to EQ Credit 3.1, Construction IAQ Management Plan- During Construction credit?

A._____ Use MERV-8 filter at return air duct
B._____ Comply with ASHRAE 62.1, 2004
C._____ Meet local code standards
D._____ Meet and exceed SMACNA standards
E._____ Comply with ASTM standards

60. Which **THREE** of the following shall be performed for EQ Credit 3.1, Construction IAQ Management Plan- During Construction credit?

A.____ Protect on-site material from moisture damage
B._____ Replace air filter prior of occupancy
C._____ Provide commissioning
D._____ Avoid contamination
E._____ Complete the final punch list process

61. Which **THREE** of the following may apply to EQ Credit 3.2, Construction IAQ Management Plan- Before Construction credit?

A._____ Flush-out 10000 cubic feet per minute of air circulation
B._____ Flush-out 14000 cubic feet per square feet of air circulation
C._____ Set control room humidity no greater than 60 percent relative humidity
D._____ Set control room temperature higher than 60 F degree
E._____ Set control room temperature lower than 60 F degree

62. Which **TWO** of the following standards are related to EQ Credit 4.1, Low-Emitting Materials, Adhesives and Sealants and EQ Credit 4.2, Low-Emitting Materials, Paints and Coatings credits?

A._____ SCAQMD
B._____ ASTM
C._____ Green Seal, GS-36
D._____ ASHRAE 52.2, 1999
E._____ DOE

63. Which **THREE** of the following may apply to EQ Credit 4.3, Carpet Systems credit?

A._____ CRI
B._____ ASTM
C._____ Green label Plus
D._____ California Department of Health Services
E._____ SCAQMD

64. Which **ONE** of the following statements is true for EQ Credit 4.4, Low-Emitting Materials, Composite Wood & Agrifiber Products credit?

A._____ Use materials with 50 percent added Urea-formaldehyde resins
B._____ Use materials to comply with ASHRAE 62.1, 2004
C._____ Use materials with no added Urea-formaldehyde resins
D._____ Use materials with added Urea-formaldehyde resins
E._____ None of above

65. Which **THREE** of the following building materials may be considered as COMPOSITE WOOD for EQ Credit 4.4, Low-Emitting Materials Composite Wood & Agrifiber Products credit?

A._____ Wheat board
B._____ Particle board
C._____ Walnut shell
D._____ Plywood
E._____ Sugarcane

66. Which **THREE** of the following may be considered as AGRIFIBER BOARD for EQ Credit 4.4, Low-Emitting materials Composite Wood & Agrifiber Products credit?

A._____ Walnut shell
B._____ Plywood
C._____ Cereal straw
D._____ Coconut husk
E._____ Strawboard panel

67. Which **TWO** of the following designs are required for EQ Credit 5, Indoor Chemical & Pollutant Source Control credit?

A._____ Install grates and grilles
B._____ Install separate air conditioning unit
C._____ Provide 5 ft of entryway from the building entrance
D._____ Provide 6 ft of entryway from the building entrance
E._____ Install heat recovery panel

68. Which **THREE** of the following may apply to EQ Credit 5, Indoor Chemical & Pollutant Source Control credit?

A._____ Provide MERV 8 filters for mechanical system
B._____ Provide MERV 13 filters for mechanical system
C._____ Provide filtration system to comply with ASHRAE 52.2,1999 standards
D._____ Provide hard lid ceiling for chemical gas area
E._____ Provide filtration for relief air system

69. Which **ONE** of the following may apply to EQ Credit 6.1, Controllability of Systems-Lighting credit?

A._____ 75 percent
B._____ 80 percent
C._____ 95 percent
D._____ 90 percent
E._____ None of above

70. Which **ONE** of the following percentages may apply to EQ Credit 6.2, Controllability of Systems- Thermal Comfort credit?

A._____ 45 percent
B._____ 75 percent
C._____ 50 percent
D._____ 65 percent
E._____ None of above

71. Which **ONE** of the following standards may apply to EQ Credit 7.1, Thermal Comfort-Design credit?

A._____ ASHRAE 52-2004
B._____ ASTM
C._____ ASHRAE 55-2004
D._____ EPA
E._____ None of above

72. Which **TWO** of the following tasks may apply to EQ Credit 7.2, Thermal Comfort-Verification credit?

A._____ Survey within 6 to 18 months
B._____ Survey within 2 years
C._____ If more than 25 percent of occupants complain about the system then the responsible party shall perform another verification process
D._____ If more than 20 percent of occupants complain about the system then the responsible party shall perform another verification process
E._____ If more than 30 percent of occupants complain then perform another verification process

73. Which **THREE** of the following may apply to EQ Credit 8.1, Daylight & Views credit?

A._____ Floor plan
B._____ Building material
C._____ Window's geometry
D._____ Window's area
E._____ Energy management systems

74. Which **THREE** of the following may apply to EQ Credit 8.2, Daylight & View credit?

A._____ Achieve the sight line to outdoor via windows
B._____ The sight line shall pass through windows with glazing
C._____ The design area should be located within the sight lines
D._____ The occupied space shall be designed with 95 percent lighting factor
E._____ The occupied space shall be designed with 75 percent lighting factor

75. What should be the elevation of glazing area in the EQ Credit 8.2, Daylight & View credit?

A._____ 32 to 90 inches above finish floor
B._____ 30 to 90 inches above finish floor
C._____ 30 to 92 inches above finish floor
D._____ 36 to 90 inches above finish floor
E._____ 24 to 90 inches above finish floor

76. What is the elevation for the seated area in EQ Credit 8.2, Daylight & View credit?

A._____ 40 inches above finish floor
B._____ 48 inches above finish floor
C._____ 42 inches above finish floor
D._____ 36 inches above finish floor
E._____ 30 inches above finish floor

77. Which **ONE** of the following may be considered as FIXED item in EQ Credit 8.2, Daylight & View credit?

A._____ Kitchen appliances
B._____ Lamp stands
C._____ Movable partitions
D._____ Ceiling fans
E._____ None of above

78. Which **ONE** of the following credits will require the LENGTHIEST technical and managerial analysis?

A._____ EQ Prerequisite 1, Minimum IAQ Performance
B._____ EA Credit 2, Renewable Energy
C._____ EA Credit 1, Optimize Energy Performance
D._____ EQ Prerequisite 2, Environmental Tobacco Smoke (ETS) Control
E._____ EQ Credit 4.1, Low-Emitting Material

79. Which **THREE** of the following credits are the responsibility of the MEP Engineer?

A._____ EQ Credit 2, Increase Ventilation
B._____ WE Credit 2, Innovative Wastewater Technologies
C._____ EA Credit 1, Optimize Energy Performance
D._____ EA Credit 6, Green Power
E._____ EA Credit 3, Enhanced Commissioning

80. Which **THREE** of the following are considered as prerequisites for the LEED Certified Project?

A._____ Construction Activity Pollution Prevention
B._____ Site Selection
C._____ Fundamental Refrigerant Management
D._____ Minimum Indoor Air Quality Performance
E._____ Construction Management Plan

81. Which **TWO** of the following credits may utilize ASHRAE Standards for the HVAC calculation and final design performance?

A._____ EQ Credit 2, Increased Ventilation
B._____ EQ Credit 3.1, Construction IAQ Management Plan
C._____ EQ Credit 8.2, Daylight & Views
D._____ EQ Credit 4.1, Low-Emitting Materials
E._____ EA Credit 5, Measurement and Verification

82. Which **ONE** of the following may NOT apply to SS Credit 2, Development Density & Community Connectivity credit?

A._____ Pathway for pedestrian
B._____ Location of business services
C._____ Location of properties
D._____ Location of transportation services
E._____ None of above

83. The ORGANIC material may be utilized in which **ONE** of the following credits?

A._____ EA Credit 2, On-Site Renewable Energy
B._____ MR Credit 6, Rapidly Renewable Materials
C._____ EQ Credit 4, Low-Emitting Materials
D._____ MR Credits 4.1 – 4.2, Recycled Content
E._____ SS Credit 5.1, Site development

84. Which **THREE** of the following may apply to EA Credit 5, Measurement & Verification?

A._____ Lighting System
B._____ Boiler Efficiency
C._____ Outside Air Humidity
D._____ Chiller Efficiency
E._____ Waste water factor

85. Which **THREE** of the following may apply to EA Credit 4.1,4.2,4.3, Low – Emitting Materials credits?

A._____ California Department of Health Services
B._____ Green Seal Standard
C._____ Department of Energy
D._____ Carpet and Rug Institute
E._____ IESNA standards

86. Which **ONE** of the following credits may refer to DONATION of materials?

A.______ MR Credit 2.1, Construction Waste Management
B.______ EA Credit 5, Measurement & Verification
C.______ MR Credit 6, Rapidly Renewable Materials
D.______ MR Credits 4.1 – 4.2, Recycled Content
E.______ None of above

87. Which **ONE** of the following refers to the level of temperature and humidity comfort in the occupied spaces?

A.______ EA Credit 1, Optimize Energy Performance
B.______ EQ Credit 7.1, Thermal Comfort
C.______ EQ Credit 6.1, Controllability of Systems
D.______ EA Credit 5, Measurement & Verification
E.______ None of above

88. Which **THREE** of the following may apply to SS Credit 1, Site Selection credit?

A.______ Do not develop on land within 100 feet of a wetland
B.______ Do not develop on the prime farmland
C.______ Do not develop on land within 150 feet of a wetland
D.______ Do not develop on land lower than 5 feet above the 100-year flood plane
E.______ Do not develop on land lower than 5 feet above the 150-year flood plane

89. Which **TWO** of the following credits may require sight line calculation?

A.______ EA Credit 1, Optimize Energy Performance
B.______ SS Credit 8, Light Pollution Reduction
C.______ SS Credit 1, Site Selection
D.______ EQ Credit 8.2, Daylight & Views
E.______ EA Credit 5, Measurement & Verification

90. Which **TWO** of the following may apply to ASHRAE 55, 2004 standard?

A.______ Lighting
B.______ Temperature
C.______ Humidity
D.______ Air quality effectiveness
E.______ Green power

91. Which **ONE** of the following is referenced to the FTE (Full-Time Equivalent) factor?

A._____ EQ Credit 8.2, Daylight & Views
B._____ EA Credit 1, Optimize Energy Performance
C._____ EQ Credit 2, Increased Ventilation
D._____ WE Credit 3.1, Water Use Reduction
E._____ None of above

92. Which **ONE** of the following is referenced to ASHRAE 90.1-2004 standard?

A._____ Minimum ventilation rates
B._____ Building indoor air quality management
C._____ Minimum energy performance
D._____ HVAC unit filtration system
E._____ None of above

93. Which **ONE** of the following is referenced to ASHRAE 55-2004 standard?

A._____ Minimum IAQ performance
B._____ Controllability of systems
C._____ Building energy performance
D._____ Increased ventilation
E._____ None of above

94. Which **THREE** of the following may impact the cost of registration for the LEED projects?

A._____ Membership
B._____ Location
C._____ Building square foot
D._____ Project Type
E._____ Air conditioning load

95. Which **ONE** of the following has the HIGHEST impact on the ecosystem site development?

A._____ EQ Credit 4.1, Low-Emitting Materials
B._____ WE Credit 3.1, Water Use Reduction
C._____ SS Credit 5.1, Site Development- Protect of Restore Habitat
D._____ SS Credit 5.2, Site Development- Maximize Open Space
E._____ MR Credit 4, Recycled content

96. Which **THREE** of the following shall NOT be included in the CIR forms?

A._____ Name of credits
B._____ Picture
C._____ Confidential information
D._____ Design analysis
E._____ Name of company

97. Which **ONE** of the following is NOT considered PRE-CONSUMER material ?

A._____ Grain rubber
B._____ Flyash
C._____ Pop bottles
D._____ Sawdust
E._____ None of above

98. The cost of materials has been referenced in which **TWO** of following credits?

A._____ MR Credits 4.1 – 4.2, Recycled Content
B._____ EQ Credit 4.1 – 4.2, Low-Emitting Materials
C._____ WE Credit 3.1, Water Use Reduction
D._____ MR Credits 3.1 – 3.2, Material Reused
E._____ EA Credit 5, Measurement and Verification

99. Which **THREE** of the following are NOT considered as GRAY water?

A._____ Condenser water from cooling units
B._____ Waste water from bathroom wash basin
C._____ Waste water from toilets
D._____ Waste water from kitchen sinks
E._____ Waste water from bathtubs

100. Which **THREE** of the following may be qualified for Innovation in Design credit?

A._____ The design with significant financial benefit
B._____ The design which greatly exceed the requirements set by the LEED rating systems
C._____ The design with significant environmental and occupant benefit
D._____ The design that has not been addressed by the LEED rating systems
E._____ The design that has been addressed by the LEED rating systems

101. Which **THREE** of the following are required for EA Credit 3, Enhanced Commissioning credit?

A._____ Verification of performance
B._____ Manual development
C._____ Construction document review
D._____ Submittal review
E._____ Life cycle energy analysis

102. Which **THREE** of the following may apply to EQ Credit 5, Indoor Chemical & Pollutant Source Control credit?

A._____ Entryway
B._____ Deck-to-deck partitions
C._____ Negative pressure of 7 Pascal, compared to adjacent area
D._____ Negative pressure of 5 Pascal, compared to adjacent area
E._____ Carbon monoxide sensor design parameters

103. Which **THREE** of the following may apply to EQ Credit 4.1 thru 4.3, Low-Emitting Materials credits?

A._____ Paints
B._____ Carpets
C._____ Sealants
D._____ Ceiling tiles
E._____ Cabinets

104. Which **ONE** of the following credits require the chain-of-custody document?

A._____ Minimum IAQ Performance
B._____ Construction IAQ Management Plan
C._____ MR Credit 7, Certified Wood
D._____ Indoor Chemical & Pollutant Source Control
E._____ EQ Credit 4.1, Low-Emitting Material

105. Which **TWO** of the following credits refer to the deck-to-deck partitions and exhaust system with negative pressure of 5 Pascal?

A._____ EQ Credit 5, Indoor Chemical & Pollutant Source Control
B._____ EQ Prerequisite 2, Environmental Tobacco Smoke Control
C._____ Construction IAQ Management Plan
D._____ EA Credit 6, Green Power
E._____ EA Credit 1, Optimize Energy Performance

106. Which **ONE** of the following may require the ENERGY PERFORMANCE calculation?

A._____ EA Credit 1, Optimize Energy Performance
B._____ WE Credits 3.1 & 3.2, Water Use Reduction
C._____ MR Credits 4.1 & 4.2, Recycled Content
D._____ MR Credit 6, Rapidly Renewable Materials
E._____ None of above

107. Which **ONE** of the following may require the certification of products?

A._____ MR Credit 7, Certified Wood
B._____ EQ Credits 4.1 thru 4.3, Low-Emitting Materials
C._____ EA Credit 6, Green Power
D._____ EQ Credit 6.1, Controllability of Systems
E._____ None of above

108. Which **ONE** of the following credits may require the 100-years flood plane maps?

A._____ ID Credit 1, Innovation in Design
B._____ EQ Credit 5, Indoor Chemical & Pollutant Source Control
C._____ SS Credit 1, Site Selection
D._____ SS Credit 5.1, Site development
E._____ None of above

109. Which **THREE** of the following may be utilized in EA Credit 6, Green Power credit?

A._____ Biomass
B._____ Wind power
C._____ Solar Energy
D._____ Water heat pump
E._____ Solar water heater

110. Which **THREE** of the following offer the HIGHEST points for the LEED NC 2.2 projects?

A._____ ID Innovation in Design
B._____ SS Site selection
C._____ EQ Low-Emitting Materials
D._____ SS Alternative Transportation
E._____ EQ Controllability of System

111. The MERV 13 filters may be utilized in which **ONE** of the following credits?

A._____ EQ Credit 3.1, Construction IAQ Management Plan
B._____ EQ Credit 5, Indoor Chemical & Pollutant Source Control
C._____ EQ Credit 6.1, Controllability of Systems
D._____ EA Credit 3, Enhanced Commissioning
E._____ EA Credit 1, Optimize Energy Performance

112. Which **TWO** of the following are implemented in two sections of the LEED certification process? (Consider both Prerequisite and Credit sections)

A._____ Refrigerant Management
B._____ Controllability of Systems
C._____ Building Commissioning
D._____ Construction IAQ Management Plan
E._____ Site selection

113. When the QUALITY of the air is the major concern to the owner, which **THREE** of the following shall be considered for the LEED certification process?

A._____ EQ Credit 2, Increased Ventilation
B._____ EQ Credits 4.1 thru 4.4, Low-Emitting Material
C._____ EQ Credit 6.1, Controllability of Systems
D._____ EQ Credit 3.1 and 3.2, Construction IAQ Management Plan
E._____ EQ. Credit 6.2, Controllability of Systems

114. Which **ONE** of the following ASHRAE standards is utilized for the EQ Credit 7.1, Thermal Comfort credit?

A._____ 55-2004
B._____ 129-2001
C._____ 90.1-2001
D._____ 62-2001
E._____ 52-2001

115. Which **ONE** of the following may be utilized for projects located FAR from developed and urban areas?

A._____ MR Credit 5.1, 5.2, Regional Materials
B._____ MR Credit 2.1, 2.2, Construction Waste Management
C._____ MR Credit 3.1, 3.2, Material Reuse
D._____ EA Credit 2, On-Site Renewable Energy
E._____ SS Credit 6, Stormwater Design

116. Which **ONE** of the following may apply to the Energy Policy Act of 1992?

A._____ WE Credit 3.1, Water Use Reduction
B._____ EQ Credit 3.2, Construction IAQ Management Plan- Restore Occupancy
C._____ WE Credit 2, Innovative Wastewater Technology
D._____ MR Credit 2, Construction Waste Management
E._____ EA Credit 5, Measurement and Verification

117. Which **ONE** of the following may HIGHLY be utilized for projects located NEAR the developed and urban areas?

A._____ MR Credit 5.1 & 5.2, Regional Materials
B._____ WE Credit 2, Innovative Wastewater Technologies
C._____ EA Credit 2.1 On-Site Renewable Energy
D._____ EA Credit 5, Measurement & Verification
E._____ SS Credit 5.1, Site development

118. The shading factor of windows may apply in which **ONE** of the following credits?

A._____ EQ Credit 3.2, Construction IAQ Management Plan- After Occupancy
B._____ EA Credit 1, Optimize Energy Performance
C._____ EQ Prerequisite 1, Minimum IAQ Performance
D._____ EA Credit 5, Measurement & Verification
E._____ WE Credit 2, Innovative Wastewater Technologies

119. Which **ONE** of the following may be utilized for the Green Pro certification?

A._____ EPA
B._____ CRS
C._____ ASTM
D._____ ASHRAE
E._____ CIWMB

120. Which **ONE** of the following creates the LOWEST cost to the owner?

A._____ ID Credit 2, LEED Accredited Professional
B._____ EA Credit 3, Enhanced Commissioning
C._____ EQ Credit 4.2, Low Emitting Materials
D._____ WE Credit 3.1, Water Use Reduction
E._____ EQ Credit 6.1, Controllability of Systems

121. Which **THREE** of the following credits would be considered as the MOST TIME consuming credits for commercial building projects?

A._____ EA Credit 5, Measurement & Verification
B._____ EA Credit 6, Green Power
C._____ EA Credit 3, Enhanced Commissioning
D._____ EQ Credit 3.2, Construction IAQ Management Plan
E._____ EQ Credit 4.1, Low-Emitting Materials

122. Which **THREE** of the following credits are the MOST suitable choices for the LARGE development / multi-commercial building projects?

A._____ EA Credit 6, Green Power
B._____ EQ Credit 6.1, Controllability of Systems
C._____ EA Credit 5, Measurement & Verification
D._____ EQ Credit 7.2, Thermal Comfort
E._____ EQ Credit 4.1, Low-Emitting Materials

123. Which **ONE** of the following shall be completed FIRST for the LEED certification?

A._____ Communication
B._____ Membership
C._____ Registration
D._____ Documentation
E._____ Payment

124. Which **THREE** of the following groups may become a member of the USGBC organization?

A._____ Government agencies
B._____ Business investors
C._____ Educational facilities
D._____ Professional societies
E._____ Financial advisors

125. In which **TWO** of the following phases, does the coordinator pay for the LEED certification process?

A._____ Registration
B._____ Certification
C._____ Design submittal
D._____ Construction submittal
E._____ Pre-construction

126. After January 2006, which **THREE** of the following services require an EXTRA charge by the USGBC organization?

A._____ Each appeal process
B._____ Each credit interpretations ruling process
C._____ Design review at end of design phase
D._____ LEED plaque
E._____ Commissioning process

127. Which **THREE** of the following documentations might be requested by the USGBC for final review?

A._____ Contract
B._____ Calculation
C._____ Specifications
D._____ Product manual
E._____ Cost estimate

128. After January of 2006, what method of communication is accepted by the USGBC ?

A._____ U.S. Mail
B._____ Telephone
C._____ Email
D._____ All the above
E._____ None of above

129. Which **THREE** of the following informational sets are required for WE Credit 3.2, Water Use Reduction credit?

A._____ Occupancy rate
B._____ Pressure of water system
C._____ Flow rate of fixtures
D._____ Daily uses
E._____ Water softness ratio

130. Which **ONE** of the following credits requires the implementation of the photoelectric daylight sensor?

A._____ MR Credit 4, Recycling Content
B._____ MR Credit 3, Resource Reuse
C._____ MR Credit 6, Rapidly Renewable Materials
D._____ EA Credit 1, Optimize Energy Performance
E._____ WE Credit 2, Innovative wastewater Technologies

131. Which **ONE** of the following definitions refers to the POST-CONSUMER recycled content?

A._____ Building materials that been used in the past and will be reused for other applications.
B._____ Building materials that been used in the past and will not be reused for other applications.
C._____ Building materials that been not used in the past and will be used for other applications.
D._____ Building materials that been not used in the past and will not be used for other applications.
E._____ None of above

132. Which **ONE** of the following factors refers to the ASHRAE 55-2004 standard?

A._____ Temperature and humidity
B._____ Temperature and lighting
C._____ Humidity and lighting
D._____ Humidity and filtration
E._____ None of above

133. Which **THREE** of the following documents can be found on the USGBC web site?

A._____ List of LEED-AP members
B._____ List of CIR forms
C._____ LEED specification
D._____ List of all green products
E._____ List of LEED certified projects

134. Which **TWO** of the following factors will be utilized for SS Credit 2, Development Density & Community Connectivity credit?

A._____ Site area
B._____ Parking structure area
C._____ Number of FTE
D._____ Landscape area
E._____ Alternative surface area

135. Which **ONE** of the following may apply to Energy Act of 1992?

A._____ Outside air quality
B._____ Humidity ratio of indoor air
C._____ Plumbing fixtures
D._____ Efficiency of chillers
E._____ Sensible heat ratio

136. Which **ONE** of the following sources can NOT be utilized as ALTERNATIVE fuel for commercial projects?

A._____ Diesel
B._____ Coal
C._____ Petroleum gas
D._____ Natural Gas
E._____ None of above

137. In which **TWO** of the following credits can you earn point(s) by using the post-consumer material and post-development discharge rate?

A._____ SS Credit 6.1, Stormwater Design
B._____ MR Credit 5.1 Regional Materials
C._____ MR Credit 4.1, Recycled Content
D._____ SS Credit 5.2, Site Development
E._____ EA Credit 5, Measurement and Verification

138. Which **ONE** of the following methods should be implemented for the project registration?

A._____ Call USGBC staff
B._____ Meet with USGBC staff
C._____ Complete the application on-line
D._____ Mail your documents to USGBC office
E._____ None of above

139. Which **ONE** of the following may apply to EA Credit 2, On-Site Renewable Energy credit?

A._____ Solar hot water system
B._____ Daylighting and building orientation system
C._____ Photovoltaic panel design
D._____ Underground water source heat pump system
E._____ None of above

140. Which **THREE** of the following may be utilized in EA, Credit 5, Measurement & Verification credit?

A._____ Irrigation system
B._____ Boiler efficiency
C._____ lighting dimming factor
D._____ Daylight factor
E._____ Rainfall factor

141. Which **THREE** of the following credits are the responsibilities of the MEP Engineer?

A._____ EQ Credit 1, Outdoor Air Delivery Monitoring
B._____ EA Credit 4, Enhanced Refrigerant Management
C._____ EA Credit 5, Measurement & Verification
D._____ EA Credit 3, Enhanced Commissioning
E._____ EQ. Credit 4.1, Low-Emitting Material

142. Which **ONE** of the following may apply to MR Credit 6, Rapidly Renewable Material credit?

A._____ 7 year cycle
B._____ 20 year cycle
C._____ 15 year cycle
D._____ 10 year cycle
E._____ 5 year cycle

143. Which **TWO** of the following credits are the responsibility of the Civil Engineer?

A._____ SS Credit 6.2, Stormwater Management
B._____ EA Credit 3, Enhanced Commissioning
C._____ SS Credit 5.2, Site Development
D._____ EA Credit 5, Measurement & Verification
E._____ EQ. Credit 4.1, Low-Emitting Material

144. Which **THREE** of the following credits are the responsibility of the General Contractor?

A._____ SS Credit 5.2, Site Development
B._____ MR. Credit 2.1, Construction Waste Management- Divert
C._____ EQ Credit 4.2, Low-Emitting Material , Paints & Coatings
D._____ EQ. Credit 3.1, Construction Indoor Air Quality Management Plan
E._____ WE Credit 2, Innovative wastewater Technologies

145. Which **ONE** of the following positions is the minimum requirement for the LEED AP in ID Credit 2, LEED Accredited Professional credit?

A._____ Owner of company
B._____ Project Manager of team
C._____ Primary member of team
D._____ Senior Principal of design
E._____ None of above

146. Which **ONE** of the following may apply to SS Prerequisite 1, Erosion and Sedimentation Control?

A._____ ASHRAE
B._____ ASTM
C._____ EPA
D._____ USDA
E._____ CRS

147. Which **TWO** of the following professionals can practice as COMMISSIONING AGENT in EA Prerequisites 1, Fundamental Commissioning of The Building Energy Systems (the building area is 60.000 sq. ft)?

A._____ Mechanical Engineer from contractor office
B._____ Owner's staff
C._____ Construction Manager from contractor office
D._____ Project Manager Consultant for owner's firm
E._____ Electrical Engineer from contractor office

148. Which **TWO** of the following standards may apply to EQ Credit 4.1 thru 4.3, Low Emitting Materials credit?

A._____ SMACNA
B._____ ASHRAE
C._____ Green Seal standard
D._____ SCAQMD
E._____ BMP

149. Which **ONE** of the following systems may apply to the ASHRAE 62.1-2004 standard?

A._____ Ventilation
B._____ Heating / cooling
C._____ Lighting
D._____ Filtration
E._____ None of above

150. Which **TWO** of the following elements may be utilized in SS Credit 6.2, Storm Water Design-Quality Control credit?

A._____ Non-vegetated roof
B._____ Vegetated roof
C._____ Rain garden
D._____ Non-grid pavement
E._____ Structural alternative surface

151. Which **THREE** of the following elements may be used in WE Credit 2, Innovative Wastewater Technologies credit?

A._____ FTE
B._____ Plumbing fixture flow rate
C._____ Working days
D._____ Percentage of Occupancy
E._____ Hot water pressure range

152. Which **ONE** of the following can NOT be considered as STRUCTURAL CONTROL in SS prerequisite 1, Construction Activity Pollution Prevention?

A._____ Mulching
B._____ Earth dikes
C._____ Silt fencing
D._____ Sediment basin
E._____ None of above

153. Which **TWO** of the following are the responsibility of the Civil Engineer in SS Prerequisite 1, Construction Activity Pollution Prevention?

A._____ Identify stabilization methods
B._____ Identify slope rate
C._____ Identify underground piping design
D._____ Identify soil stability
E._____ Identify heat island areas

154. What is the minimum requirement for bicycle racks within 200 yards of building in SS Credit 4.2, Alternative transportation, Bicycle Storage and Changing Rooms credit (for non-residential buildings)?

A._____ 10 percent of FTE
B._____ 5 percent of FTE
C._____ 15 percent of FTE
D._____ 20 percent of FTE
E._____ 25 percent of FTE

155. Which **TWO** of the following statements are true for the GREENFIELD sites in SS Credit 1, Site Selection credit?

A._____ Not previously been a landfill
B._____ Not previously developed
C._____ Not previously graded
D._____ Not previously vegetated
E._____ Previously leveled

156. What is the minimum requirement for the storm water runoff discharge rate, when the impervious surface is greater than 50 percent of the total site area in SS Credit 6.1, Stormwater Design, Quality Control credit?

A._____ The post development shall be 30 percent more than pre-development
B._____ The post development shall be 30 percent less than pre-development
C._____ The post development shall be 25 percent less than pre-development
D._____ The post development shall be 25 percent more than pre-development
E._____ The post development shall be 20 percent less than pre-development

157. Which **THREE** of the following may be utilized as the quality control, NON-STRUCTURAL surface method in SS Credit 6.2, Stormwater Design, Quality Control credit?

A._____ Cisterns
B._____ Pervious pavement
C._____ Vegetation roof
D._____ Rain garden
E._____ Vegetated swales

158. Which **THREE** of the following may be utilized as the quality control, for the NON-STRUCTURAL alternative surface method in SS Credit 6.2, Stormwater Design, Quality Control Management credit?

A._____ Vegetated swales
B._____ Rainwater recycling
C._____ Rain garden
D._____ Manhole devices
E._____ Grid pavers

159. Which **ONE** of the following statements is true for material with solar reflectance index of 100?

A._____ Zero percent of solar radiation is reflected back to the atmosphere
B._____ 100 percent of solar radiation is observed by the element
C._____ 100 percent of solar radiation is reflected back to the atmosphere
D._____ Zero percent of solar radiation is observed by the element
E._____ None of above

160. Which **TWO** of the following may apply to SS Credit 8, Light Pollution Reduction credit?
A._____ The exterior lighting shall not exceed over 45 percent of the landscape lighting guideline published by ASHRAE 90.1,2004 standard
B._____ Use Title 24, Energy calculation method
C._____ The exterior lighting shall not exceed over 80 percent of the landscape lighting guideline published by ASHRAE 90.1,2004 standard
D._____ Use computer program
E._____ Use 2.5 W per square foot for the total building load

161. Which **THREE** of the following may apply to SS Credit 8, Light Pollution Reduction credit?

A._____ Occupancy sensors
B._____ Light current detector
C._____ Manual override design
D._____ Sweep timers
E._____ Candle light sensor

162. Which **ONE** of the following may apply to EVAPOTRANSPIRATION rate testing in WE Credit 1.1, Water Efficient Landscaping credit?

A._____ June
B._____ March
C._____ July
D._____ December
E._____ September

163. Which **THREE** of the following shall be subtracted from the site area in WE Credit 1.1, Water Efficient Landscaping credit?

A._____ Building footprint
B._____ Green yard
C._____ Paved surface area
D._____ Water bodies
E._____ Non-grid surface areas

164. Which **ONE** of the following may apply to daily use of WATER CLOSET in WE Credit 3.1, Water Use Reduction credit?

A.____ 3 times for Female / 1 time for Male
B._____ 3 times for Male / 1 time for Female
C._____ 2 times for Female / 1 time for Male
D.____ 3 times for Female / 2 times for Male
E._____ None of above

165. Which **THREE** of the following may apply to WE Credit 3.1, Water Use Reduction credit?

A._____ Daily use rate
B._____ Number of workdays
C._____ Occupancy rate
D._____ Hardware fixture units
E._____ Treated water

166. Which **THREE** of the following documents shall be included in EA Prerequisite 1, Fundamental Commissioning of the Building Energy Systems?

A._____ Basis of design
B._____ Manual
C._____ Specification
D._____ Commissioning report
E._____ Training

167. Which **ONE** of the following ASHRAE standards refer to EA Prerequisites 2, Minimum Energy Performance?

A._____62.1-2004
B._____ 52.2- 2004
C._____ 90.1-2004
D._____ 55-1999
E._____ 55-2004

168. What is the maximum size of the building that can be used in the PRESCRIPTIVE method of EA credit 1, Optimize Energy Performance credit?

A._____ 45,000 square feet
B._____ 25,000 square feet
C._____ 20,000 square feet
D._____ 30,000 square feet
E._____ 35.000 square feet

169. How many points may be achieved by the PRESCRIPTIVE method, option # 2, in EA credit 1, Optimize Energy Performance credit?

A._____ 3
B._____ 1
C._____ 4
D._____ 2
E._____ 5

170. Which **ONE** of the following may regulate the ENERGY STAR rating for EA credit 1, Optimize Energy Performance credit?

A.____ ASHRAE
B._____ ASTM
C._____ EPA
D._____ USDA
E._____ FSC

171. Which **ONE** of the following buildings may require Building Benchmark 1.1 calculations in EA credit 1, Optimize Energy Performance credit?

A._____ Existing commercial building
B._____ Remodel building
C._____ New commercial building
D._____ Existing Church
E._____ None of above

172. Which **THREE** of the following may apply to EA credit 1, Optimize Energy Performance credit?

A._____ Quantity of floors
B._____ Building type
C._____ Plumbing fixture units
D._____ Building area
E._____ Solar heating for hot water system

173. How many baseline simulations are required for EA credit 1, Optimize Energy Performance credit?

A.____ 2
B._____ 1
C._____ 4
D._____ 3
E._____ 5

174. Which **THREE** of the following sources may be utilized for EA Credit 2, On-Site Renewable Energy credit?

A._____ Photovoltaic panels
B._____ Wind Turbines
C._____ Water source heat pumps
D._____ Solar panels
E._____ Hot water solar heating units

175. Which **TWO** of the following standards may apply to EA Credit 2, On-Site Renewable Energy credit?

A._____ National electrical code-2001
B._____ IPMVP
C._____ ASHRAE 90.1- 2004
D._____ CBECS
E._____ ANSI

176. Which **ONE** of the following refers to the VIRTUAL ENERGY rate in EA Credit 2, On-Site Renewable Energy credit?

A._____ Annual energy cost minus annual energy consumption (for specified fuel)
B._____ Annual energy cost divided by annual energy consumption (for specified fuel)
C._____ Annual energy costs multiplied by annual energy consumption (for specified fuel)
D._____ Annual energy consumption divided by annual energy cost (for specified fuel)
E._____ None of above

177. Which **TWO** of the following apply to the commissioning process?

A._____ EA Prerequisite 2
B._____ EA Prerequisite 1
C._____ EA Credit 4
D._____ EA Credit 3
E._____ EA Credit 6

178. Which **TWO** of the following shall be considered for the selection of HVAC units?

A._____ Refrigerant charge
B._____ Energy Efficiency Ratio
C._____ Coefficient of performance
D._____ Equipment life
E._____ Life cost analysis

179. Which **THREE** of the following can NOT be utilized for MR Credit 4.1, Recycled Content credit?

A._____ Floor joist
B._____ Elevator machines
C._____ HVAC units
D._____ Plumbing fixtures
E._____ Roof decking

180. Which **THREE** of the following elements are considered as URBAN MAINTENANCE in MR Credit 4.1, Recycled Content credit?

A._____ Leaves
B._____ Soil
C._____ Grass clipping
D._____ Tree trimming
E._____ Seeds

181. Which **THREE** of the following are included in the LEED- New Construction portfolio?

A._____ Laboratory
B._____ Homes
C._____ Schools
D._____ Retails
E._____ Residential building, less than 4 stories.

182. Which **TWO** of the following statements are true in regards to CIR forms?

A._____ Use CIR form when USGBC requires additional information
B._____ Use CIR form when USGBC guideline does not address a specific issue
C._____ Use CIR form when there is a conflict of compliance that needs resolution
D._____ Use CIR form when there is a conflict between design and material specification
E._____ Use CIR form for the cost benefit analysis report

183. Which **THREE** of the following statements are true in regards of CIR forms?

A._____ Maximum 800 words
B._____ Be Brief but explicit
C._____ Project team shall read other posted CIR forms that may answer their question
D._____ Submit CIR thru web site
E._____ Format it as a letter

184. Which **THREE** of the following can impact the registration fee?

A._____ Building area
B._____ Type of building
C._____ Membership to USGBC
D._____ Address of building
E._____ Owner type

185. Which **THREE** of the following informational sets are included in the project registration template?

A._____ Primary contact information
B._____ Project type
C._____ Project details
D._____ Construction schedule
E._____ Cost of project

186. What is the minimum required savings for NEW buildings, registered after 08/26/07, in EA Credit 1, Optimize Energy Performance credit?

A.______ 2.5 percent
B.______ 14 percent
C.______ 12.5 percent
D.______ 7.5 percent
E.______ 5 percent

187. What is the minimum required savings for the EXISTING buildings, registered after 08/26/07, in EA Credit 1, Optimize Energy Performance credit?

A.______ 10.5 percent
B.______ 7.5 percent
C.______ 12.5 percent
D.______ 7 percent
E.______ 5 percent

188. What is the minimum required savings for BOTH new and existing buildings in EA Credit 2, On-Site Renewable Energy credit?

A.______ 1.5 percent
B.______ 2.5 percent
C.______ 3.5 percent
D.______ 1 percent
E.______ 5 percent

189. Which **THREE** of the following sources can be utilized, if the building area is LESS than 50,000 square feet and you want to select the commissioning agent for EA Prerequisites 1, Fundamental Commissioning of the Building Energy System?

A.______ Employee with the general contracting responsibility
B.______ Employee with the project construction responsibility
C.______ Employee with the project design responsibility
D.______ Experienced person with one similar project experience
E.______ Independent person with no commissioning experience

190. Which **ONE** of the following represents the thermal emittance factor of building material?

A.______ 0.70
B.______ 0.65
C.______ 0.90
D.______ 0.80
E.______ 0.60

191. Which **ONE** of the following represents the average building performance (ENERGY STAR) in EA Credit 1, Optimize Energy Performance credit?

A._____ 60
B._____ 90
C._____ 50
D._____ 75
E._____ 80

192. Which **THREE** of the following areas shall be EXCLUDED from the building footprint for SS Credit 5.1, Site Development, Protect of Restore Habitat credits?

A._____ Parking lots
B._____ Patio
C._____ landscape
D._____ Wetlands
E._____ parking garage

193. Which **ONE** of the following ASHRAE standards refers to the BASELINE building performance in EA Credit 1, Optimize Energy Performance Credit?

A._____ 62.1-2004
B._____ 52.2-2004
C._____ 90.1-2004
D._____ 55-1999
E._____ 55-2001

194. Which **THREE** of the following informational sets are required for ID Credit 2, LEED Accredited Professional credit?

A._____ Name of LEED AP's local chapter
B._____ Name of LEED AP
C._____ Name of LEED AP's company
D._____ Copy of LEED AP certificate
E._____ Copy of membership

195. How many sets of submittal are required in ID Credit 1.1 thru 1.4, Innovation in Design credit?

A._____ One set for all four points
B._____ One set for each two points
C._____ One set for each point
D._____ One set for all Prerequisites and One set for other credits
E._____ None of above

196. Which **THREE** of the following may apply to ID Credit 1.1 thru 1.4, Innovation in Design credit?

A._____ Improvement for environmental benefit
B._____ Process must be comprehensive
C._____ Improvement for financial benefit
D._____ Must be applicable to other projects

197. Which **THREE** of the following statements are true for ID Credit 1.1 thru 1.4, Innovation in Design credit?

A._____ Exceptional performance
B._____ Innovative performance
C._____ Exceeds the requirements of existing LEED credits
D._____ Exceeds local codes
E._____ Comprehensive cost variance performance

198. In which **ONE** of the following stages, may the appeal be submitted to the USGBC office?

A._____ One at the end of design phase
B._____ One at the end of final review phase
C._____ One at the end of submittal phase
D._____ Two (one at end of design phase and one at the end of final review phase).
E._____ None of above

199. How many reviews can be offered by the USGBC office?

A._____ One at the end of design phase
B._____ None
C._____ TWO (one at end of design phase and one at the end of construction phase)
D._____ One at the end of construction phase
E._____ One at the end of inspection period

200. Which **THREE** of the following statements are true for the certification process?

A._____ Submit specification and materials cost list
B._____ Submit verification that design elements are implemented per plans
C._____ LEED credit is NOT awarded at the end of design review phase
D._____ Application shall be processed in two phases
E._____ LEED is awarded at the end of design review phase

201. Which **ONE** of the following credits is the responsibility of the Civil Engineer?

A._____ SS Credit 4.4, Alternative Transportation
B._____ WE Credit 2, Innovative Wastewater Technologies
C._____ EA Credit 5, Measurement and Verification
D._____ EQ. Credit 4.1, Low-Emitting Material
E._____ EA Credit 7.2, Thermal Comfort

202. Which **THREE** of the following credits are referenced to the ASHRAE 90.1, 2004 standards?

A._____ SS Credit 8, Light Pollution Reduction
B._____ EA Credit 1, Optimize Energy Performance
C._____ EA Credit 5, Measurement and Verification
D._____ EQ Credit 6.1, Controllability of System
E._____ EQ Prerequisite 2, Environmental Tobacco Smoke Control

203. Which **ONE** of the following credits is the responsibility of the Architect?

A._____ SS Credit 4.4, Alternative Transportation
B._____ WE Credit 2, Innovative Wastewater Technologies
C._____ EA Credit 5, Measurement and Verification
D._____ EQ. Credit 4.1, Low-Emitting Material
E._____ EA Credit 1, Optimize Energy Performance

204. Which **TWO** of the following credits are the responsibilities of the MEP engineer?

A._____ SS Credit 4.4, Alternative Transportation
B._____ MR Credit 5.1 – 5.2, Local/Regional Materials
C._____ EA Credit 5, Measurement and Verification
D._____ EQ. Credit 4.1, Low-Emitting Material
E._____ WE Credit 2, Innovative Wastewater Technologies

205. Which **TWO** of the following credits are referenced to the ASHRAE 62.1,2004 standards?

A._____ EA Credit 5, Measurement and Verification
B._____ EA Credit 1, Optimize Energy Performance
C._____ SS Credit 8, Light Pollution Reduction
D._____EQ Credit 6.2, Controllability of System
E._____ EQ Credit 1, Outdoor Air Delivery Monitoring

206. Which **ONE** of the following is referenced to the Energy Policy Act 1992 standards or regulations?

A._____ EQ Credit 6.2, Controllability of System
B._____WE Credit 3.1, Water Use Reduction
C._____EQ Credit 1, Outdoor Air Delivery Monitoring
D._____EQ Credit 7.2, Thermal Comfort
E._____ SS Credit 8, Light Pollution Reduction

207. Which **TWO** of the following percentages may apply to MR Credit 7, Certified Wood credit (including exemplary performance - Extra credit)?

A._____ 30 percent
B._____ 95 percent
C._____ 10 percent
D._____ 50 percent
E._____ 60 percent

208. Which **ONE** of the following credits is referenced to the DOE standards or regulations?

A._____ EQ Credit 6.2, Controllability of System
B._____ EA Credit 1, Optimize Energy Performance
C._____EA Credit 2, On-site Renewable Energy
D._____EQ Credit 7.2, Thermal Comfort
E._____ EQ Credit 4.1, Low-Emitting Materials

209. Which **THREE** of the following statements are accurate for the DIVERSION process in MR Credit 2.1 & 2.2, Construction waste Management credits?

A._____ Salvage of material on-site
B._____ Refurbishing of material
C._____ Recycle of Material
D._____ Treat material on-site
E._____ Donation of material

210. Which **TWO** of the following percentages may apply to SS Credit 5.1, Site Development- Protect of Restore Habitat credit (including exemplary Performance - Extra credit)?

A._____ 50 percent
B._____ 40 percent
C._____ 80 percent
D._____ 65 percent
E._____ 75 percent

211. Which **ONE** of the following may apply to pre-consumer materials in MR credit 4.1 & 4.2, recycled Content credits?

A._____ Cost
B._____ Volume
C._____ Quantity
D._____ Weight

212. Which **TWO** of the following percentages may apply to SS Credit 7.1, Heat Island Effect- Non-Roof credit (including exemplary performance - Extra credit)?

A._____ 75 percent
B._____ 60 percent
C._____ 100 percent
D._____ 80 percent
E._____ 50 percent

213. Which **THREE** of the following percentages may apply to SS Credit 7.2, Heat Island Effect- Roof credit (including exemplary performance - Extra credit)?

A._____ 95 percent
B._____ 90 percent
C._____ 100 percent
D._____ 50 percent
E._____ 75 percent

214. Which **THREE** of the following rooms shall NOT be included in final calculation of EQ Credit 8.1, Daylight & View credit?

A._____ Copy rooms
B._____ Equipment rooms
C._____ Cafeterias
D._____ Laundry rooms
E._____ Guest break rooms

215. Which **ONE** of the following credits is referenced to the CBECS (Commercial Building Energy Consumption Survey) standards or regulations?

A._____ EQ Credit 6.2, Controllability of System
B._____ EA Credit 1, Optimize Energy Performance
C._____ EA Credit 2, On-site Renewable Energy
D._____ EQ Credit 7.2, Thermal Comfort
E._____ EA Credit 5, Measurement and Verification

216. Which **ONE** of the following credits references to the Clean Air Act 1990 / Montreal Protocol 1987 standards or regulations?

A._____ EQ Credit 6.2, Controllability of System
B._____ EA Credit 4, Enhanced Refrigerant Management
C._____ EA Credit 2, On-site Renewable Energy
D._____ EQ Credit 7.2, Thermal Comfort
E._____ EQ Credit 4.1, Low-Emitting Materials

217. Which **ONE** of the following may apply to EQ Credit 8.1, 8.2, Daylight & View credit?

A._____ The glazing area located 90 inches AFF
B._____ Windows located between 30 to 90 inches AFF
C._____ The glazing area located 78 inches AFF
D._____ Windows area located between 18 to 30 inches AFF
E._____ The glazing area located 78 inches AFF

218. Which **ONE** of the following references to the SCAQMD standards or regulations?

A._____ EA Credit 1, Optimize Energy Performance
B._____ EQ Credit 4.1, Low-Emitting Materials
C._____ EA Credit 5, Measurement and Verification
D._____ EQ Prerequisite 2, Environmental Tobacco Smoke Control
E._____ SS Credit 5.1, Site Development

219. Which **ONE** of the following professionals will make the final decision for EA Credit 6, Green Power credit?

A._____ Engineer
B._____ Architect
C._____ Owner- Developer
D._____ Contractor
E._____ None of above

220. Which **TWO** of the following may apply to MR Credit 2.1 & 2.2, Construction Waste Management credits?

A._____ Weight
B._____ Area
C._____ Volume
D._____ Cost
E._____ Time

221. Which **ONE** of the following professionals will make the final decision for MR Credit 2.1, Construction Waste Management credit?

A._____ Engineer
B._____ Architect
C._____ Owner- Developer
D._____ Contractor
E._____ None of above

222. Which **TWO** of the following may NOT be utilized for MR Credit 2.2, Construction waste Management credit?

A._____ Clearing debris
B._____ Recycled concrete
C._____ Excavated soil from the site
D._____ Salvaged cabinetry
E._____ Heat pump unit

223. Which **TWO** of the following professionals will make the final decision for MR Credit 3.1, Material Reuse credit?

A._____ Engineer
B._____ Architect
C._____ Owner- Developer
D._____ Contractor
E._____ Inspector

224. Which **THREE** of the following should MOSTLY be considered for the commissioning process in EA Credit 3, Enhanced Commissioning credit?

A._____ Schedule
B._____ Cost
C._____ BOD
D._____ OPR
E._____ Environmental impact

225. Which **TWO** of the following professionals will make the final decision for MR Credit 5.1, Regional Material credit?

A._____ Engineer
B._____ Architect
C._____ Owner- Developer
D._____ Contractor
E._____ Inspector

226. Which **TWO** of the following professionals will make the final decision for MR Credit 4.1, Recycled Content credit?

A._____ Engineer
B._____ Architect
C._____ Owner- Developer
D._____ Contractor
E._____ Inspector

227. Which **ONE** of the following is related to the Green Seal standards or regulations?

A._____ EQ Credit 6.2, Controllability of System
B._____ EQ Credit 7.2, Thermal Comfort
C._____ EQ Credit 4.1, Low-Emitting Materials
D._____ EA Credit 1, Optimize Energy Performance
E._____ EA Credit 5, Measurement and Verification

228. Which **ONE** of the following is referenced to the Carpet and Rug Institute standards and regulations?

A._____ EQ Credit 6.1, Controllability of System
B._____ EQ Credit 4.1, Low-Emitting Materials
C._____ EQ Credit 4.3, Low-Emitting Materials
D._____ WE Credit 2, Innovative wastewater Technologies
E._____ EA Credit 5, Measurement and Verification

229. Which **ONE** of the following is referenced to the ISO standards and regulations?

A._____ SS Credit 4.4, Alternative transportation
B._____ EQ Credit 4.1, Low-Emitting Materials
C._____ MR Credit 4.1, Recycled Content
D._____ EQ Credit 6.2, Controllability of System
E._____ EA Credit 1, Optimize Energy Performance

230. Which **ONE** of the following is referenced to the NPDES standards and regulations?

A._____ MR Credit 4.1, Recycled content
B._____ EQ Credit 4.1, Low-Emitting Materials
C._____ SS Prerequisite 1- Construction Activity Pollution Prevention
D._____ EQ Credit 7.2, Thermal Comfort
E._____ EA Credit 5, Measurement and Verification

231. Which **ONE** of the following is referenced to the USDA standards and regulations?

A._____ SS Credit 1, Site Selection
B._____ EQ Credit 6.2, Controllability of System
C._____ WE Credit 2, Innovative wastewater Technologies
D._____ MR Credit 4.1, Recycled content
E._____ EA Credit 1, Optimize Energy Performance

232. Which **ONE** of the following is referenced to the CERCLA standards or regulations?

A._____ EA Credit 5, Measurement and Verification
B._____ WE Credit 2, Innovative wastewater Technologies
C._____ SS Credit 3, Brownfield Redevelopment
D._____ MR Credit 4.2, Recycled content
E._____ SS Credit 5.2, Reduced Site Disturbance

233. Which **ONE** of the following is referenced to the BMP standards or regulations?

A._____ EQ Credit 7.2, Thermal Comfort
B._____ SS Credit 6.1, Stormwater Design
C._____ EQ Credit 4.1, Low-Emitting Materials
D._____ WE Credit 2, Innovative wastewater Technologies
E._____ EA Credit 5, Measurement and Verification

234. Which **TWO** of the following statements are true for private office in EQ Credit 8.2, Daylight & View credit?

A._____ Include total floor area in calculation, when 75 percent or more of floor area has a view to outside
B._____ Use the percent method, when more than 65 percent of the total area has a view to outside
C._____ Use percent method, when less than 75 percent of the total area has a view to outside
D._____ Include 75 percent of the total area in calculation, when 75 percent of total area has a view to outside
E._____ When more than 75 percent of the total area has a view to outside, then implement ISO and DOE codes and standards

235. Which **ONE** of the following credits is referenced to the EIA standards or regulations?

A._____ WE Credit 2, Innovative wastewater Technologies
B._____ MR Credit 4.2, Recycled content
C._____ EA Credit 2, On-Site Renewable Energy
D._____ EQ Credit 4.1, Low-Emitting Materials
E._____ SS Credit 5.1, Site development

236. Which **ONE** of the following credits is referenced to the CBECS standards or regulations?

A._____ EA Credit 6, Green Power
B._____ MR Credit 4.1, Recycled content
C._____ EQ Credit 4.1, Low-Emitting Materials
D._____ WE Credit 2, Innovative Wastewater Technologies
E._____ EQ Credit 6.1, Controllability of System

237. Which **ONE** of the following credits is referenced to the ISO standards or regulations?

A._____ EQ Credit 4.1, Low-Emitting Materials
B._____ EQ Credit 6.2, Controllability of System
C._____ EQ Credit 7.2, Thermal Comfort
D._____ MR Credit 4.2, Recycled Content
E._____ WE Credit 2, Innovative Wastewater Technologies

238. Which **ONE** of the following credits is referenced to the CRS standards or regulations?

A._____ EQ Credit 4.1, Low-Emitting Materials
B._____ EA Credit 6, Green Power
C._____ MR Credit 4.2, Recycled Content
D._____ WE Credit 2, Innovative Wastewater Technologies
E._____ SS Credit 6, Storm Water Management

239. Which **THREE** of the following percentages may apply to WE Credit 3.1, 3.2, Water Use Reduction credits (including exemplary Performance - Extra credit)?

A._____ 30 percent
B._____ 40 percent
C._____ 10 percent
D._____ 50 percent
E._____ 20 percent

240. Which **ONE** of the following credits references to the CIBSE (Chartered Institution of Building Services Engineers) standards or regulations?

A._____ EQ Credit 7.2, Thermal Comfort
B._____ EQ Credit 2, Increased Ventilation
C._____ EQ Credit 4.1, Low-Emitting Materials
D._____ MR Credit 4.1, Recycled Content
E._____ EQ Credit 6.1, Controllability of System

241. Which **TWO** of the following credits are related to the ANSI standards and regulations?

A._____ WE Credit 2, Innovative Wastewater Technologies
B._____ SS Credit 8- Light Pollution Reduction
C._____ MR Credit 4.2, Recycled Content
D._____ EQ P2- Environmental Tobacco Smoke Control
E._____ SS Credit 5.2, Reduced Site Disturbance

242. Which **TWO** of the following may apply to EQ Credit 8.1, Daylight & Views (including exemplary performance - Extra credit)?

A._____ 75 percent
B._____ 40 percent
C._____ 85 percent
D._____ 95 percent
E._____ 55 percent

243. Which **TWO** of the following credits are referenced to the ASHRAE 55, 2004 standards?

A._____ EQ Credit 6.2, Controllability of System (Thermal Comfort)
B._____ EA Credit 1, Optimize Energy Performance
C._____ EQ Credit 1, Outdoor Air Delivery Monitoring
D._____ EQ Credit 7.2, Thermal Comfort (Verification)
E._____ EQ Credit 6.1, Controllability of System (Lighting)

244. Which **TWO** of the following may apply to MR Credit 6, Rapidly Renewable Materials credit (including exemplary performance - Extra credit)?

A._____ 2.5 percent
B._____ 4 percent
C._____ 5 percent
D._____ 3.5 percent
E._____ 7.5 percent

245. Which **TWO** of the following may be utilized for EA Credit 6, Green Power credit (including exemplary performance - Extra credit)?

A._____ 2 years
B._____ 1 year
C._____ 4 years
D._____ 5 years
E._____ 3 years

246. Which **TWO** of the following may apply to EA Credit 6, Green Power credit (including exemplary performance - Extra credit)?

A._____ 35 percent
B._____ 40 percent
C._____ 70 percent
D._____ 20 percent
E._____ 45 percent

247. Which **TWO** of the following credits are referenced to the ASHRAE 52.2, 1999 standards?

A._____EQ Credit 6.2, Controllability of System (Thermal comfort)
B._____EA Credit 1, Optimize Energy Performance
C._____EQ Credit 3.1, Construction IAQ Management Plan
D._____EQ Credit 5, Indoor chemical & Pollutant Source Control
E._____ EQ. Credit 4.1, Low-Emitting Material

248. Which **TWO** of the following percentages are referenced in WE Credit 2, Innovative Wastewater Technologies credit (including exemplary performance - Extra credit)?

A._____ 50 percent
B._____ 40 percent
C. 100 percent
D._____ 20 percent
E._____ 95 percent

249. Which **TWO** of the following credits are related to the California Title 24, 2001 standards?

A._____ SS Credit 8, Light Pollution Reduction
B._____ EA Credit 1, Optimize Energy Performance
C._____EQ Prerequisite 2, Environmental Tobacco Smoke Control
D._____EQ Credit 7.2, Thermal Comfort
E._____ EA Credit 5, Measurement and Verification

250. Which **THREE** of the following percentages are referenced in MR Credit 5.1, 5.2 Regional Materials credits (including exemplary performance - Extra credit)?

A._____ 30 percent
B._____ 40 percent
C._____ 10 percent
D._____ 20 percent
E._____ 50 percent

251. Which **TWO** of the following professionals will make the final decision for SS Credit 1, Site Selection credit?

A._____ Civil Engineer
B._____ Architect
C._____ Owner- Developer
D._____ Contractor
E._____ Inspector

252. Which **TWO** of the following professionals will make the final decision for SS Credit 4.1, Alternative Transportation credit?

A._____ Engineer
B._____ LEED AP
C._____ Owner- Developer
D._____ Contractor
E._____ Inspector

253. Which **THREE** of the following professionals will make the final decision for SS Credit 5.1, Site Development credit?

A._____ Civil Engineer
B._____ Architect
C._____ Owner- Developer
D._____ Contractor
E._____ Inspector

254. Which **TWO** of the following professionals will make the final decision for SS Credit 5.2, Site Development credit?

A._____ Civil Engineer
B._____ Contractor
C._____ Mechanical Engineer
D._____ Building Architect
E._____ Contractor

255. Which **ONE** of the following professionals will make the final decision EA Credit Prerequisite 2, Minimum Energy Performance credit?

A._____ Structural Engineer
B._____ MEP Engineer
C._____ Civil Engineer
D._____ Electrical Engineer
E._____ None of above

256. Which **THREE** of the following professionals will make the final decision for SS credit 7.1, Heat Island Effect credit?

A._____ Civil Engineer
B._____ Architect
C._____ Owner- Developer
D._____ Contractor
E._____ MEP Engineer

257. Which **ONE** of the following statements is true for the residential building design in SS Credit 2, Development Density & Community Connectivity credit?

A._____ At least 5 units per acre
B._____ At least 15 units per acre
C._____ At least 25 units per acre
D._____ At least 20 units per acre
E._____ At least 10 units per acre

258. Which **ONE** of the following professionals will make the final decision for EA Credit 2, On-site Renewable Energy credit?

A._____ Electrical Engineer
B._____ MEP Engineer
C._____ Mechanical Sub-contractor
D._____ Owner-Developer
E._____ None of above

259. Which **THREE** of the following professionals will make the final decision for EA Credit 3, Enhanced Commissioning credit?

A._____ Commissioning Authority
B._____ Electrical Engineer
C._____ Owner- Developer
D._____ Contractor
E._____ MEP Engineer

260. Which **TWO** of the following professionals will make the final decision for MR Credit 7, Certified Wood credit?

A._____ Structural Engineer
B._____ Architect
C._____ Owner- Developer
D._____ Contractor
E._____ Civil Engineer

261. Which **TWO** of the following professionals will make the final decision for EQ Credit 3.1, Construction IAQ Management Plan credit?

A._____ MEP Engineer
B._____ Architect
C._____ Owner- Developer
D._____ Contractor
E._____ None of above

262. Which **ONE** of the following credits is referenced to the FEMA (Federal Emergency Management Agency) standards and regulations?

A._____ WE Credit 2, Innovative Wastewater Technologies
B._____ EQ Credit 7.2, Thermal Comfort
C._____ SS Credit 1, Site Selection
D._____ EQ Credit 7.2, Thermal Comfort
E._____ EQ Credit 6.1, Controllability of System

263. Which **ONE** of the following credits is referenced to the CFR (Code Federal of Regulation) standards and regulations?

A._____ MR Credit 4.1, Recycled Content
B._____ WE Credit 2, Innovative Wastewater Technologies
C._____ SS Credit 1, Site Selection
D._____ EQ Credit 7.2, Thermal Comfort
E._____ EA Credit 3, Enhanced Commissioning

264. Which **TWO** of the following professionals will make the final decision for EQ credit 4.1, Low- Emitting Materials credit?

A._____ Civil Engineer
B._____ Architect
C._____ Owner- Developer
D._____ Contractor
E._____ Inspector

265. Which **ONE** of the following professionals will make the final decision for EQ Credit 6.2, Controllability of System credit?

A._____ Civil Engineer
B._____ Architect
C._____ MEP Engineer
D._____ Contractor
E._____ None of above

266. Which **TWO** of the following credits are referenced to the EPA (Environmental Protection Agency) standards and regulations?

A._____ WE Credit 2, Innovative Wastewater Technologies
B._____ EA Credit 4, Enhanced Refrigerant Management
C._____ SS Credit 4.4, Alternative Transportation
D._____ SS Credit 6.2, Stormwater Design
E._____ MR Credit 5.1 – 5.2, Local/Regional Materials

267. Which **TWO** of the following credits are referenced to the ASTM (American Society of Testing & Material) standards and regulations?

A._____ MR Credit 4.1, Recycled content
B._____ WE Credit 2, Innovative Wastewater Technologies
C._____ SS Credit 3, Brownfield Redevelopment
D._____ SS credit 7.2, Heat Island Effect
E._____ SS Credit 8, Light Pollution Reduction

268. Which **TWO** of the following professionals will make the final decision for EQ Credit 4.1, Low- Emitting Materials credit?

A._____ Structural Engineer
B._____ Architect
C._____ Owner- Developer
D._____ Contractor
E._____ Inspector

269. Which **TWO** of the following professionals will make the final decision for EQ Credit 8.1, Daylight & Views credit?

A._____ MEP Engineer
B._____ Architects
C._____ Owner- Developer
D._____ LEED AP
E._____ Contractor

270. Which **ONE** of the following conditions requires an additional verification process in EQ Credit 7.2, Verification credit?

A._____ When less than 20 percent of the occupants complain about the system
B._____ When 20 percent of the occupants complain about the system
C._____ When more than 20 percent of the occupants complain about the system
D._____ When less than 15 percent of the occupants complain about the system
E._____ When 15 percent of the occupants complain about the system

271. Which **THREE** of the following credits shall be implemented for EQ Credit 7.1, Thermal Comfort (Design section) credit?

A._____ EQ.3
B._____ EQ.P1
C._____ EQ.1
D._____ EQ.2
E._____ EQ.3

272. What percentage of occupants shall have full control of HVAC system in EQ Credit 6.2, Controllability of Systems (Thermal Comfort) credit?

A._____ 25 percent
B._____ 5 percent
C._____ 15 percent
D._____ 10 percent
E._____ 50 percent

273. Which **THREE** of the following may be considered as SHARED areas for EQ Credit 6.1, Controllability of Systems (Lighting) credit?

A._____ Conference rooms
B._____ Class rooms
C._____ Break rooms
D._____ Training rooms
E._____ Area restrooms

274. Which **ONE** of the following statements is true for EQ Credit 2, Increased Ventilation credit?

A._____ Increase the ventilation rate by 35 percent above minimum IAQ standards
B._____ Increase the ventilation rate by 25 percent above minimum SCAQMD standards
C._____ Increase the ventilation rate by 45 percent above minimum ASHRAE standards
D._____ Increase the ventilation rate by 40 percent above minimum CIBSE standards
E._____ Increase the ventilation rate by 30 percent above minimum ASHRAE standards

275. What is the minimum rate for the LIGHTING control in EQ Credit 6.1, Controllability of Systems (Lighting) credit?

A._____ 50 percent
B._____ 65 percent
C._____ 95 percent
D._____ 75 percent
E._____ 90 percent

276. Which **ONE** of the following statements is true for CO2 sensor in EQ Credit 1, Outdoor Air Delivery Monitoring credit?

A._____ Provide CO2 sensor with density factor of 25 persons per 1000 square feet
B._____ Provide CO2 sensor with density factor of 35 persons per 1000 square feet
C._____ Provide CO2 sensor with density factor of 15 persons per 1000 square feet
D._____ Provide CO2 sensor with density factor of 50 persons per 1000 square feet
E._____ Provide CO2 sensor with density factor of 20 persons per 1000 square feet

277. Which **THREE** of the following are considered a NON-REGULATED area in EQ Credit 6.1, Controllability of Systems (Lighting) credit?

A._____ Kitchens
B._____ Study rooms
C._____ Break rooms
D._____ Hallways
E._____ Conference rooms

278. What is the minimum exhaust air requirement in EQ Credit 5, Indoor Chemical & Pollutant Source Control credit?

A._____ 0.5 CFM per square foot
B._____ 1.5 CFM per square foot
C._____ 2.0 CFM per square foot
D._____ 2.5 CFM per square foot
E._____ 3.0 CFM per square foot

279. Which **ONE** of the following statements is true for EQ Credit 3.2, Construction IAQ Management Plan credit?

A._____ Collect air sample at 3 ft to 6 ft above finish floor for minimum of 4 hours
B._____ Collect air sample at 4 ft to 6 ft above finish floor for minimum of 4 hours
C._____ Collect air sample at 3 ft to 6 ft above finish floor for minimum of 6 hours
D._____ Collect air sample at 3 ft to 5 ft above finish floor for minimum of 6 hours
E._____ Collect the sampling at 4 ft to 5 ft above finish floor for minimum of 4 hours

280. Which **ONE** of the following statements applies to the natural ventilation design in EQ Credit 2, Increased Ventilation credit?

A._____ Design natural ventilation system for 95 percent of occupied space
B._____ Design natural ventilation system for 75 percent of occupied space
C._____ Design natural ventilation system for 80 percent of occupied space
D._____ Design natural ventilation system for 85 percent of occupied space
E._____ Design natural ventilation system for 90 percent of occupied space

281. What is the minimum outside air flow requirement in EQ Credit 2, Increased Ventilation credit?

A._____ 0.40 CFM per Square foot
B._____ 0.30 CFM per Square foot
C._____ 0.35 CFM per Square foot
D._____ 0.45 CFM per Square foot
E._____ 0.25 CFM per Square foot

282. Which **THREE** of the following may NOT apply to EA Credit 2, On-site Renewable Energy credit?

A._____ Daylight
B._____ Solar thermal
C._____ Passive solar
D._____ Geo-exchange
E._____ Under ground heat source

283. Which **ONE** of the following percentages may apply to the CO2 sensor ratio in the naturally ventilated occupied spaces for EQ Credit 1, Outdoor Air Monitoring credit?

A._____ 85 percent
B._____ 60 percent
C._____ 95 percent
D._____ 75 percent
E._____ 90 percent

284. Which **TWO** of the following statements may apply to the HFC refrigerant in EA Credit 4, Enhanced Refrigerant Management credit?

A._____ HFC has zero ODP.
B._____ The efficiency of HCFC is less than HFC
C._____ The efficiency of HFC is less than HCFC
D._____ The HFC will be phased out by 2020.
E._____ HCFC has zero ODP

285. Which **ONE** of the following may apply to the wall opening ratios in the naturally ventilated spaces for EQ Prerequisite 1, Minimum IAQ Performance statement?

A._____ 10 percent
B._____ 5 percent
C._____ 15 percent
D._____ 4 percent
E._____ 8 percent

286. Which **THREE** of the following materials may NOT apply to MR Credit 5.1, Regional Materials credit?

A._____ Refurbished
B._____ Rework
C._____ Reuse
D._____ Scrap
E._____ Repair

287. Which **THREE** of the following processes shall be verified by CFR in MR Credit 4.1 & 4.2 Recycled Content credits?

A._____ Material Collection
B._____ Material Storing
C._____ Material Reprocessing
D._____ Material Marketing
E._____ Material Budgeting

288. Which **ONE** of the following materials may NOT apply to MR Credit 3.1 & 3.2, Material Reuse credits?

A._____ Refurbished
B._____ Salvaged
C._____ Recycled
D._____ Reuse
E._____ Rework

289. Which **THREE** of the following systems can be considered as REGULATED systems for EA Credit 1, Optimize Energy Performance credit?

A._____ Exterior lighting system
B._____ Interior lighting system
C._____ Air conditioning system
D._____ Hot water services
E._____ Garage exhaust system

290. Which **TWO** of the following may be implemented in COST analysis of EA Credit 2, On-Site Renewable Energy credit?

A._____ ASRAHE standards
B._____ Local utility rates
C._____ Virtual energy
D._____ Star energy rating
E._____ USGBC rating

291. Which **THREE** of the following annual savings may apply to EA Credit 2, On-Site Renewable Energy credit?

A.______2.5 percent
B.______ 9.5 percent
C.______ 17.5 percent
D.______ 12.5 percent
E.______ 5.5 percent

292. Which **THREE** of the following systems are qualified for EA Credit 2, On-Site Renewable Energy credit?

A.______ Electrical system
B.______ Solar thermal system
C.______ Green power system
D.______ Geothermal system
E.______ Bio-green system

293. Which **THREE** of the following systems can be considered as NON- REGULATED systems for EA Credit 1, Optimize Energy Performance credit?

A.____ Process load
B.______ Interior lighting
C.______ Solar powered exterior lighting
D.______ Plug load
E.______ Non-process load

294. Which **THREE** of the following sources shall be EXCLUDED from the building performance calculation in EA Credit 1, Optimize Energy Performance credit?

A.______ Exhaust air waste energy
B.______ Water cooled chillers
C.______ Water heat load factor
D.______ Cogeneration system
E.______ Hot water boilers

295. Which **THREE** of the following may be considered as HARVEST energy in EA Credit 1, Optimize Energy Performance credit?

A.______ Natural ventilation
B.______ Building's heating factor
C.______ Building's orientation
D.______ Window's location
E.______ Solar roof panels

296. Which **THREE** of the following sources should be implemented in the building LOAD calculation of WE Credit 3.1, Water Use Reduction credit?

A._____ Water closet
B._____ Kitchen sink
C._____ Irrigation system
D._____ Shower heads
E._____ Trap primer

297. Which **ONE** of the following rates may be utilized for the conventional lavatory, shower heads and kitchen sink in WE Credit 3.1, Water Use Reduction credit?

A._____ 1.5 GPM
B._____ 2 GPM
C._____ 0.5 GPM
D._____ 3 GPM
E._____ 2.5 GPM

298. Which **TWO** of the following statements are true for each occupant per day in RESIDENTIAL buildings for WE Credit 3.1, Water Use Reduction credit?

A._____ Use factor of 5 for flush fixture
B._____ Use factor of 4 for kitchen sink
C._____ Use factor of 4 for flush fixture
D._____ Use factor of 5 for kitchen sink
E._____ Use factor of 3 for kitchen sink

299. Which **THREE** of the following water treatment systems may be utilized in WE Credit 2, Innovative Wastewater Technologies credit?

A._____ Store
B._____ Reprocess
C._____ Transport
D._____ Dispose
E._____ Re-treatment

300. Which **TWO** of the following rooms may require daylight design in EQ Credit 8.1, Daylight & View credit?

A._____ Copy rooms
B._____ Restrooms
C._____ Meeting rooms
D._____ Offices
E._____ Break areas

301. Which **TWO** of the following organizations manage ENERGY STAR rating for building materials in EA Credit 1, Optimize Energy Performance credit?

A._____ ASHRAE
B._____ EPA
C._____ DOE
D._____ ASTM
E._____ CFA

302. Which **TWO** of the following may NOT apply to the water treatment system in WE Credit 2, Innovative Wastewater Technologies credit?

A._____ Number of workdays
B._____ Dispose and treatment rates
C._____ Fixture units flow rates
D._____ Building occupancy types
E._____ Rate of return

303. Which **TWO** of the following infiltrated methods may apply to treated water in WE Credit 2, Innovative Wastewater Technologies credit?

A._____ Biomass
B._____ Biological
C.____ Constructed wetland
D._____ Geothermal
E._____ Bio-green thermal

304. Which **TWO** of the following statements are accurate for SS Credit 8, Light Pollution Reduction credit?

A._____ LZ 3 refers to areas with density of more than 3000 people per square mile.
B._____ LZ 1 refers to areas with density of less than 200 people per square mile.
C._____ LZ 2 refers to areas with density of 300 to 3000 people per square mile.
D._____ LZ 4 refers to areas with density of less than 100,000 people per square mile.
E._____ None of above

305. Which **THREE** types of factors may be utilized in WE 3.1, 3.2, Water Use reduction credit?

A._____ Consider 1.8 GPF for urinals
B._____ Consider 2.5 GPM for faucets
C._____ Consider 1.5 GPM for aerators
D._____ Consider 2.5 GPM for conventional kitchen sinks
E._____ Consider 2.5 GPM for conventional shower heads

306. Which **THREE** of the following designs may apply to the OPTION 1 of SS Credit 7.2, Heat Island Effect-Roof credit?

A._____ Where the roof slope is more than 3/12, use the roofing material with SRI of 29
B._____ Where the roof slope is lees equal 2/12, use the roofing material with SRI of 78
C._____ Where the roof slope is more than 1/12, use the roofing material with SRI of 29
D._____ Where the roof slope is less than 4/12, use the roofing material with SRI of 78
E._____ Where the roof slope is more than 2/12, use the roofing material with SRI of 29

307. Which **TWO** of the following designs may apply to the OPTION 2 of SS Credit 7.1, Heat Island Effect-Non Roof credit?

A._____ Locate 45 percent of parking space under roof
B._____ Locate 50 percent of parking space at underground level
C._____ Provide paving for parking space with SRI equal to or greater than 29
D._____ Provide paving for parking space with SRI equal to or greater than 78
E._____ Provide 40 percent of parking space at underground level

308. Which **THREE** of the following may apply as integrated natural and MECHANICAL TREATMENT system in SS Credit 6.2, Stormwater Design – Quality Control credit?

A._____ Constructed wetland
B._____ Grid pavers
C._____ Swales
D._____ Vegetated filtration
E._____ Open channel

309. Which **TWO** of the following may apply as NON-STRUCTRUAL SURFACE system in SS Credit 6.2, Stormwater Design – Quality Control credit?

A._____ Vegetated roofs
B._____ Grid pavers
C._____ Wetland
D._____ Cisterns
E._____ Rainwater recycling

310. Which **TWO** of the following credits may refer to the VEGETATED land or roofing?

A._____ SS Credit 5.1, Site Development
B._____ WE Credit 2, Innovative wastewater Technologies
C._____ SS Credit 2, Development Density & Connectivity
D._____ SS Credit 5.2, Site development
E._____ SS Credit 3, Brownfield Redevelopment

311. Which **THREE** of the following processes should be completed and submitted during the construction phase?

A._____ EQ Credit 3.1, Construction IAQ Management Plan
B._____ EA Credit 2.1 & 2.2, Renewable Energy
C._____ EA Credit 3, Enhanced Commissioning
D._____ EA Credit 4, Enhanced Refrigerant Management
E._____ EA Credit 6, Green Power

312. Which **ONE** of the following service areas may be counted MORE than once for SS Credit 2, Development Density & Community Connectivity credit?

A._____ School
B._____ Vegetated filtration
C._____ Retail stores
D._____ Banks
E._____ Restaurant

313. Which **THREE** of the following processes should be completed and submitted during the construction phase?

A._____ EQ Credit 4.2, Low-Emitting Material
B._____ SS Credit 1, Site Selection
C._____ MR Credit 1.1, Building Reuse
D._____ SS Credit 5.2, Maximize Open Space
E._____ EQ Credit 4.1, Low-Emitting Material

314. Which **TWO** of the following lands may qualify as GREENFIELD sites?

A._____ Not previously developed
B._____ Previously graded but not developed
C._____ Previously developed, but not graded
D._____Not previously graded
E._____ None of above

315. Which **THREE** of the following processes should be completed and submitted at the construction phase?

A._____ EA Credit 2, On-Site Renewable Energy
B._____ MR Credit 2.1, Construction Waste Management
C._____ WE Credit 2, Innovative wastewater Technologies
D._____ MR Credit 4.1, Recycled content
E._____ EQ Credit 4.4, Low-Emitting Material

316. Which **TWO** of the following should be completed and submitted during the construction phase?

A._____ SS Credit 7.1, Heat Island Effect
B._____ SS Credit 6, Storm water Management
C._____ MR P1, Storage & Collection of Recyclables
D._____ EQ Credit 7.2, Thermal Comfort
E._____ SS Credit 5.1, Site Development

317. Which **THREE** of the following materials are considered as DISCARDED material in MR Credit 4.1, 4.2, Recycled Content credits?

A._____ Interior Furniture
B._____ Wood cabinetry
C._____ Ceramic urinals
D._____ Roof decking
E._____ Air conditioning unit

318. What is the minimum requirement to achieve the LEED certified level for the NC buildings?

A._____ 34 to 51
B._____ 23 to 34
C._____ 26 to 32
D._____ 24 to 33
E._____ 36 to 49

319. Which **THREE** of the following should be completed and submitted during the construction phase?

A._____ SS P1, Construction Activity Pollution Prevention
B._____ WE Credit 2, Innovative wastewater Technologies
C._____ SS Credit 4.4, Alternative Transportation
D._____ MR Credit 6, Rapidly Renewable Materials
E._____ MR Credit 7, Certified Wood

320. What is the minimum requirement to achieve the LEED SILVER certification for the NC buildings?

A._____ 36 to 42
B._____ 34 to 45
C._____ 33 to 38
D._____ 33 to 36
E._____ 32 to 51

321. Which **THREE** of the following define the difference between Prerequisite 1, Fundamental Commissioning of the Building Energy Systems and EA Credit 3, Enhanced Commissioning credit?

A._____ Review drawings before mid-construction document phase
B._____ Staff training
C._____ Review submittal at construction phase
D._____ Preparation of project manual
E._____ Preparation of project specification

322. Which **THREE** of the following systems may be utilized for EA Credit 2, On-Site Renewable Energy credit?

A._____ Wind turbines
B._____ Solar water heater
C._____ Solar panels
D._____ Photovoltaic panels
E._____ Under ground source heat pump

323. What is the minimum requirement to achieve the LEED GOLD certified for the NC buildings?

A._____ 39 to 55
B._____ 37 to 52
C._____ 39 to 51
D._____ 36 to 50
E._____ 39 to 49

324. Which **THREE** of the following may be considered as REGULARLY occupied spaces for EQ Credit 8.2, Daylight & Views credit?

A._____ Office
B._____ Copy room
C._____ Conference room
D._____ Cafeteria
E._____ Restroom

325. What is the minimum requirement to achieve the LEED PLATINUM certified for the NC buildings?

A._____ 51 to 69
B._____ 50 to 69
C._____ 52 to 69
D._____ 53 to 69
E._____ 54 to 69

326. Which **TWO** of the following methods can be considered as NON-STRUCTURAL alternative surface methods for SS Credit 6.2, Stormwater Design, Quality Control credit?

A._____ Manhole
B._____ Rainwater cycling
C._____ Silt fencing
D._____ Sediment trap
E._____ disconnection of impervious area and pervious pavement

327. Which **TWO** of the following may apply to EA Credit 6, Green Power credit (including exemplary Performance - Extra credit)?

A._____ 35 percent
B._____ 40 percent
C._____ 70 percent
D._____ 20 percent
E._____ 10 percent

328. What are the maximum achievable points in the Energy & Atmosphere category?

A._____ 16
B._____ 14
C._____ 12
D._____ 17
E._____ 18

329. Which **THREE** of the following items may NOT be utilized for SS Credit 2, Development Density & Community Connectivity credit?

A._____ Parks
B._____ Public roads
C._____ Water bodies
D._____ Occupied office building
E._____ College campus

330. What are the maximum achievable points in the Indoor Environmental Quality category? standards?

A._____ 14
B._____ 16
C._____ 12
D._____ 10
E._____ 15

331. Which **ONE** of the following standards is true for the COMMERCIAL building in SS Credit 2, Development Density & Community Connectivity credit?

A._____ At least 10 community services within 2 ½ mile
B._____ At least 10 community services within 1 ½ mile
C._____ At least 10 community services within ¼ mile
D._____ At least 10 community services within 1 mile
E._____ At least 10 community services within ½ mile

332. Which **THREE** of the following factors can be utilized for the performance rating method in EA Credit 1, Optimize Energy Performance credit?

A._____ Type of site development
B._____ Building area
C._____ Type of low-emitting material
D._____ Building orientation
E._____ Number of floors

333. What are the maximum achievable points in the Sustainable Sites section of LEED 2.2 - NC standards?

A._____ 11
B._____ 16
C._____ 9
D._____ 8
E._____ 14

334. Which **THREE** of the following methods can be considered as the STRUCTURAL measure for SS Credit 6.2, Stormwater Design, Quality Control credit?

A._____ Manhole
B._____ Vegetation swales
C._____ Treatment devices
D._____ Sediment trap
E._____ Rainwater cisterns

335. What are the maximum achievable points in the Water Efficiency section of LEED 2.2 - NC standards?

A._____ 6
B._____ 4
C._____ 8
D._____ 9
E._____ 5

336. Which **THREE** of the following minimize the impervious surfaces for SS Credit 6.1, Stormwater Design, Quantity Control credit?

A._____ Retention ponds
B._____ Smaller footprint
C._____ Silt fencing
D._____ Sediment trap
E._____ Green roof

337. Which **THREE** of the following may apply to the selection of refrigerants in EA Prerequisite 3, Fundamental Refrigerant Management statement?

A._____ Cost
B._____ Life time
C._____ R value
D._____ GWP
E._____ ODP

338. What are the maximum achievable points in the Material and Resources section of LEED 2.2 - NC standards?

A._____ 11
B._____ 16
C._____ 13
D._____ 14
E._____ 12

339. Which **THREE** of the following may be utilized for irrigation system in WE Credit 1.2, Water Efficiency – No Potable Use credit?

A._____ Captured rainwater
B._____ Treated water
C._____ Gray water processing
D._____ Rainwater cisterns
E._____ Recycled wastewater

340. What are the maximum achievable points in the Innovation in Design section of LEED 2.2 - NC standards?

A._____ 6
B._____ 10
C._____ 8
D._____ 12
E._____ 5

341. Which **THREE** of the following control systems can be utilized for EQ Credit 6.2 Controllability of Systems credit?

A._____ Temperature sensor
B._____ Humidity sensor
C._____ Automatic sweep
D._____ Lighting sensors
E._____ Lighting control panels

342. How many days do you have for an appeal after comments have been received from the USGBC office?

A._____ 15
B._____ 8
C._____ 25
D._____ 11
E._____ 14

343. Which **THREE** of the following factors are IDENTICAL for BOTH design and baseline load calculations in EA Prerequisite 2, Minimum Energy Performance credit?

A._____ Occupancy rate
B._____ Number of workdays
C._____ Heat transfer rating for exterior walls
D._____ Lighting load
E._____ Daily use rate

344. How many working days in advance does the USGBC require a complete set of drawings and submittal , before starting the review process?

A._____ 12
B._____ 11
C._____ 8
D._____ 9
E._____ 10

345. Which **THREE** of the following statements are true for the CIR submittal process?

A._____ Use on-line services
B._____ Indicate the name of the credit
C._____ Do NOT include confidential details
D._____ Indicate the cost of material
E._____ Do NOT state the contact information

346. Which **TWO** of the following statements are true for the CIR submittal process ?

A.______ Credit will NOT be awarded through this process
B.______ Do NOT use on-line services
C.______ CIR process does NOT guarantee any credit
D.______ Credit will be awarded through this process
E.______ CIR process guarantees the credit

347. Which **ONE** of the following materials shall be EXCLUDED in MR 2.1, 2.2 Construction Waste Management credits?

A.______ Salvaged
B.______ Refurbished
C.______ Recycled
D.______ Rework
E.______ Reuse

348. Which **TWO** of the following conditions are required for SS Credit 2, Development Density & community Connectivity credit?

A.______ The density of developed site for the project site shall be 60,000 sq.ft per acre
B.______ The density of residential area shall be 10 units per acre with in ½ mile
C.______ The density of residential area shall be 10 units per acre with in ¼ mile
D.______ The density of developed site for community site shall be 60,000 sq.ft per acre
E.______ The density of developed site for the BOTH project site and community site shall be 60,000 sq.ft per acre

349. Which **ONE** of the following statements is true for SS Credit 4.1, Alternative Transportation credit?
A.______ Locate the project within ½ mile from the train station and within ¼ mile from one public bus line
B.______ Locate the project within ½ mile from the train station and within ½ mile from two (2) bus lines
C.______ Locate the project within ¼ mile from the train station and within ¼ mile from two (2) bus lines
D.______ Locate the project within ½ mile from the train station and within ¼ mile from two (2) campus bus lines
E.______ Locate the project within ¼ mile from the train station and within ½ mile from two (2) bus lines

350. How many bicycle racks are required within 200 yards of building for NON-RESIDENTIAL building with 800 FTE building, per SS 4.2, Alternative Transportation credit?

A.______ 25
B.______ 18
C.______ 35
D.______ 40
E.______ 10

351. How many showers are required within 200 yards of building for a NON-RESIDENTIAL building with 800 FTE, per SS Credit 4.2, Alternative Transportation credit?

A.______ 3
B.______ 2
C.______ 1
D.______ 4
E.______ 5

352. How many bicycle racks are required for a RESIDENTIAL building with 90 FTE , per SS Credit 4.2, Alternative Transportation credit?

A.______ 13
B.______ 12
C.______ 11
D.______ 18
E.______ 14

353. How many PREFERRED parking spaces are required for low emission cars in a COMMERCIAL building with 800 parking spaces, per SS Credit 4.3, Alternative Transportation credit?

A.______ 50
B.______ 48
C.______ 45
D.______ 44
E.______ 40

354. How many REFUEL STATIONS are required for a COMMERCIAL building with 800 parking spaces, per SS Credit 4.3 Alternative Transportation credit?

A.______ 20
B.______ 18
C.______ 65
D.______ 24
E.______ 40

355. How many times per day a FEMALE occupant is expected to use the water closet in a COMMERCIAL building per WE credit 2, Innovative Wastewater Technologies credit?

A.______ 2
B.______ 1
C.______ 6
D.______ 5
E.______ 3

356. How many times per day a MALE occupant is expected to use the water closet and urinal in the COMMERCIAL building per WE credit 2, Innovative Wastewater Technologies credit?

A._____ WC (3) & UL (2)
B._____ WC (2) & UL (2)
C._____ WC (2) & UL (2)
D._____ WC (1) & UL (2)
E._____ WC (3) & UL (1)

357. Which **TWO** of the following will be provided by the LEED Project registration?

A._____ It establishes contact between Project Administrator and USGBC
B._____ It establishes an access to the LEED online
C._____ It establishes free review process for design phase
D._____ It establishes free CIR reviews by USGBC
E._____ It establishes free access to the cost analysis data

358. How many points can be achieved by OPTION 2 (Perspective Method) in EA credit 1 , Optimize Energy Performance credit ?

A._____ 10
B._____ 2
C._____ 3
D._____ 1
E._____ 4

359. Which **THREE** of the following are the MOST important factors for EA credit 4, Enhanced Refrigerant Management credit?

A._____ Use HFC refrigerants with zero ODP
B._____ Select long life units with low ODP
C._____ Select short life units with high GWP
D._____ Innovative cooling technologies
E._____ Do not use any type of refrigeration.

360. Which **TWO** of the following statements are true for EA credit 5, Measurement and Verification credit?
A._____ Use options B for large projects
B._____ M & V period shall cover a period of not less than one year of post-construction occupancy
C._____ The result of M & V report is valid for 24 months
D._____ Install a metering device
E._____ Use options D for small projects

361. How much of regional material shall be utilized in the project to earn **THREE** points in MR Credit 5.1, 5.2, Regional Materials credits?
(total construction cost is $1,600,000 and total material cost is $800,000)

A._____ $ 320,000
B._____ $ 300,000
C._____ $ 310,000
D._____ $ 280,000
E._____ None of above

362. How much of rapidly renewable material shall be utilized in the project to earn **TWO** points in MR Credit 6, Rapidly Renewable Materials credit?
(total construction cost is $1,600,000 and total material cost is $800,000)

A._____ $ 60,000
B._____ $ 80,000
C._____ $ 30,000
D._____ $ 100,000
E._____ None of above

363. How much of recycled material shall be utilized in the project to earn **TWO** points in MR Credit 4.1,4.2 Recycled Content credits ?
(total construction cost is $ 1,600,000 and total material cost is $800,000)

A._____ $ 120,000
B._____ $ 320,000
C._____ $ 220,000
D._____ $ 160,000
E._____ None of above

364. How many points can be achieved, if the total weight of pre-consumer product is 3000 lbs and total weight of post-consumer products is 1500 lbs and the total cost of the material is 5 $ / lb ?
(total construction cost is $3,000.000 and total material cost is $1,500,000)
A._____ 2
B._____ 3
C._____ 2
D._____ 1
E._____ None of above

365. How many points can be achieved per SS Credit 5.1, Site Development credit, if the area of site is 4 acres and the owner decided to keep 3 acres of it as a vegetated land?

A._____ 1
B._____ 3
C._____ 4
D._____ 5
E._____ None of above

366. How many points can be achieved by the following approaches?

- Rebuilt building on the brown field site
- Provide open space for 25 percent more than local requirements
- Provide 50 percent of the site area as a vegetated land
- Provide daylight for 50 percent of the occupied space
- Provide charging stations based on 3 percent of the total parking space

A. 5 **B. 4** **C. 6** **D. 7** **E. None of above**

367. How many points can be achieved by the following approaches?

- Provide 10 commercial services within ½ mile
- Provide recycled material for 5 percent of the building material
- Maintain 50 percent of the non-structural elements
- Provide 75 percent of the site as a vegetated land
- Provide bicycle rack for 5 percent of FTE and shower room based on 0.5 percent of FTE within 200 yards

A. 2 **B. 6** **C. 8** **D. 4** **E. None of above**

368. How many points can be achieved by the following approaches?

- Divert 30 percent of construction waste management
- Purchase green power for 35 % of annual load and sign a contract for 2 years
- Provide 75 percent of the site as vegetated land
- Reduce water use by 20 percent
- Provide refuel station based on 3 percent of the total parking space

A. 4 **B. 2** **C. 5** **D. 3** **E. None of above**

369. How many points can be achieved by the following approaches?

- Provide preferred parking for low emission cars, based on 3 percent of FTE
- Divert 75 percent of construction waste management
- Provide 100 percent of total parking spaces at the underground level
- Purchase green power for 35 % of annual load and sign a contract for 18 months
- Provide 75 percent of site as vegetated land

A. 4 **B. 6** **C. 3** **D. 5** **E. None of above**

370. How many points can be achieved by the following approaches?

- Divert 50 percent of construction waste management
- Reduce water use by 30 percent
- Maintain 65 percent of the existing walls, floor and roof
- Purchase green power for 35 % of annual load and sign a contract for 2 years
- Provide annual energy saving of 12.5 percent buy use of renewable energy

A. 6 **B. 5** **C. 4** **D. 8** **E. None of above**

371. How many points can be achieved by the following approaches?

- Provide full shading for 100 % of the site within a period of 5 years
- Maintain 95 percent of the existing walls, floor and roof
- Maintain material reuse based on 10 percent of building material
- Locate the project half of a mile away from one train station
- Maintain material reuse based on 2.5 percent of the total building material

A. 2 **B. 8** **C. 4** **D. 7** **E. None of above**

372. How many points can be achieved by the following approaches?

- Rebuilt building on the brown field site
- Divert 95 percent of the construction waste management
- Reduce water use by 10 percent
- Locate 50 percent of the total parking spaces at underground level
- Maintain 75 percent of the existing walls, floor and roof

A. 3 **B. 4** **C. 6** **D. 2** **E. None of above**

373. How many points can be achieved by the following approaches?

- Maintain regional material for 10 percent of construction material
- Reduce water use by 40 percent
- Provide annual energy savings of 1.5 percent by use of renewable energy
- Provide daylight for 95 percent of the occupied space
- Purchase green power for 35 % of annual load and sign a contract for 4 years

A. 5 **B. 8** **C. 7** **D. 6** **E. None of above**

374. How many points can be achieved by the following approaches?

- Provide preferred parking space for low emission cars based on 5 percent of the total parking spaces
- Maintain material reuse based on 5 percent of the total building material
- Provide bicycle rack for 5 percent of FTE and shower room based on 0.5 percent of FTE within 200 yards
- Maintain regional material based on 20 percent of the total construction material
- Provide 45 percent of the site area as vegetated land

A. 4 **B. 8** **C. 3** **D. 7** **E. None of above**

375. How many points can be achieved by the following approaches?

- Provide bicycle rack for 5 percent of FTE & changing and shower room based on 0.5 percent of FTE within 200 yards
- Reduce water use by 40 percent
- Provide daylight for 95 percent of the occupied space
- Provide 40 percent of the site with full shading range of 5 years
- Maintain recycled material based on 30 percent of the total construction material

A. 9 **B. 3** **C. 8** **D. 4** **E. None of above**

376. How many points can be achieved by the following approaches for the residential buildings?

- Maintain recycled material based on 15 percent of the total construction material
- Provide 10 units per acre density within ½ mile for residential projects
- Provide daylight for 45 percent of the occupied space
- Treat 30 percent of the annual storm water runoff on the site per tertiary standards
- Provide bicycle rack for 15 percent of resident for residential buildings

A. 5 **B. 6** **C. 8** **D. 3** **E. None of above**

377. How many points can be achieved by the following approaches?

- Maintain regional material based on 20 percent of the total construction material
- Provide daylight for 95 percent of the occupied space
- Maintain material reuse based on 15 percent of the total building material
- Provide changing room for 0.05 percent of FTE within 200 yards
- Provide preferred parking spaces for low-emission cars based on 5 percent of FTE

A. 4 **B. 6** **C. 5** **D. 8** **E. None of above**

378. How many points can be achieved by the following approaches?

- Maintain material reuse based on 10 percent of the total building material
- Reduce water use by 30 percent
- Provide preferred parking spaces for low-emission vehicles based on 5 percent of the total parking spaces
- Provide 35 percent of the total parking spaces at the underground level
- Provide daylight for 75 percent of the occupied space

A. 5 **B. 4** **C. 6** **D. 7** **E. None of above**

379. How many points can be achieved by the following approaches?

- Maintain recycled material based on 20 percent of the total construction material
- Provide preferred parking spaces for low-emission cars based on 0.03 percent of FTE
- Provide certified wood for 50 percent of the timber material used in the building
- Reduce water use by 20 percent
- Provide rapidly renewable material within 2.5 percent of the total construction cost

A. 3 **B. 5** **C. 8** **D. 6** **E. None of above**

380. How many points can be achieved by the following approaches?

- Provide 50 percent of the site area as vegetated land
- Provide annual energy savings of 7.5 percent by use of renewable energy
- Provide bicycle rack for 5 percent of FTE and changing room based on 0.5 percent of FTE within 200 yards
- Provide shower rooms for 0.05 percent of FTE within 200 yards
- Maintain regional material based on 40 percent of the total construction material

A. 7 **B. 5** **C. 3** **D. 6** **E. None of above**

381. How many points can be achieved by the following approaches?

- Provide full shading for 50 % of the site within a period of 5 years
- Use green power for 35 percent of the total energy load for 2 years
- Treat 50 percent of annual waste water runoff on the site per tertiary standards
- Provide preferred parking spaces for low-emission vehicles based on 0.05 percent of the total parking spaces
- Locate the project ¼ of a mile away from two public or campus bus lines

A. 4 **B. 2** **C. 6** **D. 8** **E. None of above**

382. How many points can be achieved by the following approaches?

- Divert 50 percent of construction waste management
- Provide rapidly renewable materials as 5 percent of the total construction cost
- Provide regional material as 40 percent of construction material
- Provide annual energy saving of 12.5 percent by use of renewable energy
- Provide refuel stations based on 0.03 percent of the total parking spaces

A. 3 **B. 9** **C. 8** **D. 4** **E. None of above**

383. How many points can be achieved by the following approaches?

- Divert 95 percent of construction waste management
- Purchase green power for 35 percent of annual load and sign a contract for 2 years
- Provide open spaces as 50 percent higher than the local code requirements
- Provide certified wood as 95 percent of timber material used in the building
- Maintain 95 percent of the existing walls, floor and roof

A. 4 **B. 9** **C. 5** **D. 3** **E. None of above**

384. How many points can be achieved by the following approaches?

- Provide regional material as 10 percent of the total building material
- Purchase green power for 35 percent of annual load and sign a contract for 4 years
- Locate the project half a mile away from train station
- Maintain 40 percent of the non-structural interior elements
- Provide annual energy savings of 7.5 percent by use of renewable energy

A. 5 **B. 4** **C. 8** **D. 2** **E. None of above**

385. How many points can be achieved by the following approaches?

- Maintain recycled material based on 30 percent of the total construction material
- Provide open space for 50 percent higher than local code requirements
- Maintain material reuse as 15 percent of the total building material
- Maintain recycled material as 2.5 percent of the total building material
- Treat 100 percent of annual waste water runoff on the site per tertiary standards

A. 8 **B. 6** **C. 7** **D. 5** **E. None of above**

386. How many points can be achieved by the following approaches?

- Provide regional material for 2.5 percent of the building material
- Purchase green power for 35 percent of annual load and sign a contract for 4 years
- Provide certified wood for 35 percent of the timber material used in the building
- Provide full shading for 50 % of the site within a period of 5 years
- Provide 100 percent of the total parking spaces at the underground level

A. 5 **B. 4** **C. 2** **D. 6** **E. None of above**

387. How many points can be achieved by the following approaches?

- Purchase green power for 35 percent of annual load and sign a contract for 50 weeks
- Provide annual energy saving as 2.5 percent by use of renewable energy
- Provide preferred parking spaces for low- emission cars based on 5 percent of the total parking spaces
- Maintain regional material as 5 percent of the total building material
- Provide 50 percent of the parking spaces at the underground level

A. 4 **B. 3** **C. 2** **D. 5** **E. None of above**

388. How many points can be achieved by the following approaches?

- Provide 10 units per acre within ½ mile for residential projects on a previously developed site
- Provide bicycle rack for 5 percent of FTE and shower room based on 0.5 percent of FTE within 200 yards
- Divert 15 percent of the construction waste management
- Provide full shading for 100 % of the site within a period of 5 years.
- Provide regional material for 5 percent of the building material

A. 1 **B. 4** **C. 3** **D. 5** **E. None of above**

389. How many points can be achieved by the following approaches?

- Provide material reuse for 2.5 percent of the building material
- Provide full shading for 50 % of the site within a period of 5 years
- Purchase green power for 30 percent of annual energy load and sign a contract for 2 years
- Provide 35 percent of the total parking spaces at the underground level
- Use green power for 75 percent of the annual energy load for 28 months

A. 2 **B. 4** **C. 3** **D. 1** **E. None of above**

390. How many points can be achieved by the following approaches?

- Divert 75 percent of the construction waste management
- Reduce water use by 20 percent
- Provide recycled material for 30 percent of the total building material
- Provide rapidly renewable material base on 1.5 percent of total construction cost
- Provide certified wood for 95 percent of the timber material used in the building

A. 7 **B. 6** **C. 5** **D. 8** **E. None of above**

391. How many points can be achieved by the following approaches?

- Maintain 55 percent of the existing walls, floor and roof
- Provide 25 percent of the site with full shading range for 5 years
- Provide material reuse for 5 percent of the total building material
- Divert 75 percent of the construction waste management
- Provide 35 percent of the site area as vegetated land

A. 4 **B. 5** **C. 2** **D. 6** **E. None of above**

392. How many points can be achieved by the following approaches?

- Provide 25 percent of parking spaces at the underground level
- Divert 15 percent of construction waste management
- Provide certified wood for 50 percent of the timber material used in the building
- Provide annual energy savings of 2.5 percent by use of renewable energy
- Provide recycled material for 20 percent of the total building material

A. 5 **B. 7** **C. 2** **D. 3** **E. None of above**

393. How many points can be achieved by the following approaches?

- Provide certified wood for 35 percent of the timber material used in the building
- Provide 100 percent of the total parking spaces at the underground level
- Provide 100 percent of the site with full shading range for 2.5 years
- Provide bicycle rack for 5 percent of FTE and shower room based on 0.5 percent of FTE within 200 yards
- Use green power for 75 percent of the annual energy load for 2 years

A. 6 **B. 4** **C. 5** **D.2** **E. None of above**

394. How many points can be achieved by the following approaches?

- Provide recycled material for 10 percent of the building material
- Provide daylight for 55 percent of the occupied space
- Maintain 50 percent of interior non-structural elements
- Treat 100 percent of waste water on the site per tertiary standards
- Provide 35 percent of the site area as vegetated land

A. 4 **B. 5** **C. 3** **D. 1** **E. None of above**

395. How many points can be achieved by the following approaches?

- Provide material reuse for 10 percent of the building material
- Provide certified wood for 95 percent of the timber material used in the building
- Provide daylight for 75 percent of the occupied space
- Provide recycled material for 2.5 percent of the building material
- Provide rapidly renewable material base on 1.5 percent of total construction cost

A. 3 **B. 4** **C. 7** **D. 5** **E. None of above**

396. How many points can be achieved by the following approaches?

- Provide daylight for 95 percent of the occupied space
- Maintain 75 percent of the existing walls, floor and roof
- Purchase green power for 25 percent of annual energy load and sign a contract for 18 months
- Provide regional material for 40 percent of the building material
- Provide annual energy saving of 1.5 percent on the site

A. 7 **B. 8** **C. 5** **D. 6** **E. None of above**

397. How many points can be achieved by the following approaches?

- Reduce water use by 20 percent
- Provide preferred parking for low-emission vehicles per 5 percent of the total parking spaces
- Maintain 25 percent of the interior non-structural elements
- Treat 25 percent of the annual storm water runoff on the site per tertiary standards
- Divert 50 percent of the construction waste management

A. 3 **B. 4** **C. 5** **D. 2** **E. None of above**

398. How many points can be achieved by the following approaches?

- Provide preferred parking spaces for low-emission cars based on 3 percent of FTE
- Provide recycled material for 3.5 percent of the building material
- Purchase green power for 45 percent of annual energy load and sign a contract for 4 years
- Maintain 35 percent of the existing walls, floor and roof
- Provide daylight for 45 percent of occupied space

A. 4 **B. 5** **C. 2** **D. 3** **E. None of above**

399. How many points can be achieved by the following approaches?

- Provide daylight for 65 percent of the occupied space
- Provide bicycle rack for 5 percent of FTE& changing and shower rooms based on 0.5 percent of FTE within 200 yards
- Provide certified wood for 45 percent of the timber material used in the building
- Provide refuel station based on 3 percent of the total parking space
- Reduce water use by 30 percent

A. 5 **B. 2** **C. 7** **D. 3** **E. None of above**

400. How many points can be achieved by the following approaches?

- Purchase green power for 35 percent of annual energy load and sign a contract for 2 years
- Provide open space for 50 percent more than local code requirements
- Provide 50 percent of the site area as vegetated land
- Locate the project half of a mile away from two (2) train stations
- Provide daylight for 55 percent of the occupied space

A. 5 **B. 4** **C. 6** **D. 7** **E. None of above**

401. Which **THREE** of the following may be considered as REGULARLY occupied space for the commercial projects?

A._____ Office
B._____ Conference room
C._____ Cafeteria
D._____ Restroom
E._____ Copy room

402. Which **THREE** of the following may NOT be considered as REGULARLY occupied space for the commercial projects?

A._____ Restroom
B._____ Cafeteria
C._____ Mechanical room
D._____ Storage room
E._____ Conference room

403. Which **THREE** of the following may be considered as NON- REGULATED areas for the commercial projects?

A._____ Corridors
B._____ Break rooms
C._____ Kitchens
D._____ Cafeterias
E._____ Offices

404. Which **THREE** of the following may be considered a REGULARLY occupied space for RESIDENTIAL projects?

A._____ Dinning rooms
B._____ Storage rooms
C._____ Bathrooms
D._____ Media rooms
E._____ Kitchens

405. Green or vegetated roofs are normally being used in which **TWO** of the following credits?

A._____ SS Credit 6.1, Storm Water Design
B._____ SS Credit 7.1, Heat Island Effect
C._____ EA Credit 1, Optimize Energy Performance
D._____ SS Credit 5.3, Brownfield Redevelopment
E._____ EA Credit 5, Measurement & Verification

406. The project site boundary is normally being used in which **THREE** of the following?

A._____ SS Credit 2, Development Density & Community Connectivity
B._____ SS credit 8, Light Pollution Reduction
C._____ SS Credit 5.2, Site Development
D._____ SS Credit 6.2, Storm Water Design
E._____ EA Credit 5, Measurement & Verification

407. Which **THREE** of the following may be considered as PROCESS ENERGY in EA Credit 1, Optimize Energy Performance credit?

A._____ Elevator machines
B._____ Washers and dryers
C._____ Water pumps
D._____ Outdoor lighting
E._____ Space heating

408. Which **THREE** of the following systems may apply to EA Prerequisite 1, Fundamental Commissioning of the Building Energy Systems?

A._____ Occupant control system
B._____ HVAC systems
C._____ Domestic hot water system
D._____ Lighting system
E._____ Building envelope system

409. How many PREREQUISITES are included in the Material & Resource category?

A._____ 2
B._____ 1
C._____ 3
D._____ 4
E._____ None of above

410. How many PREREQUISITES are included in the Indoor Environmental Quality category?

A._____ 3
B._____ 4
C._____ 2
D._____ 1
E._____ None of above

411. How many PREREQUISITES are included in the Sustainable Sites category?

A._____ 1
B._____ 2
C._____ 3
D._____ 5
E._____ None of above

412. How many PREREQUISITES are included in the Water Efficiency category?

A._____ 4
B._____ 2
C._____ 1
D._____ 3
E._____ None of above

413. How many EXEMPLARY POINTS can be achieved in the Sustainable Sites category?

A._____ 6
B._____ 4
C._____ 3
D._____ 5
E._____ None of above

414. How many EXEMPLARY POINTS can be achieved in the Water Efficiency category?

A._____ 2
B._____ 3
C._____ 4
D._____ 5
E._____ None of above

415. How many EXEMPLARY POINTS can be achieved in the Energy & Atmosphere category?

A._____ 1
B._____ 5
C._____ 4
D._____ 6
E._____ None of above

416. How many EXEMPLARY POINTS can be achieved in the Material & Resources category?

A._____ 6
B._____ 8
C._____ 7
D._____ 5
E._____ None of above

417. How many EXEMPLARY POINTS can be achieved in the Indoor Environmental Quality category?

A._____ 2
B._____ 3
C._____ 2
D._____ 1
E._____ None of above

418. Which **THREE** of the following credits are qualified for EXEMPLARY points in the Sustainable Sites category?

A._____ SS Credit 5.1, Site Development
B._____ SS Credit 2, Development Density & Community Connectivity
C._____ SS Credits 6.1, 6.2, Storm Water Design
D. SS Credit 1, Site Selection
E._____ SS Credit 4.1, Alternative Transportation

419. Which **TWO** of the following credits are qualified for EXEMPLARY points in the Water Efficient category?

A._____ WE Credit 1.1 & 1.2 Water Efficient Landscaping
B._____ WE Credit 2, Innovative Wastewater Technologies
C._____ WE credit 3.1 & 3.2 Water Use reduction

420. Which **THREE** of the following credits are qualified for EXEMPLARY points in the Energy & Atmosphere category?

A._____ EA Credit 1,Optimize Energy Performance
B._____ EA Credit 6, Green Power
C._____ EA Credit 4, Enhanced Refrigerant Management
D._____ EA Credit 3, Enhanced Commissioning
E._____ EA Credit 2, On-Site Renewable Energy

421. Which **THREE** of the following credits are qualified for EXEMPLARY points in the Material & Resources category?

A._____ MR Credits 2.1 , 2.2, Construction Waste Management
B._____ MR Credits 3.1, 3.2, Material Reuse
C._____ MR Credits 4.1, 4.2, Recycled Materials
D._____ MR Credits 1.1, 1.2, 1.3, Building Reuse

422. Which **THREE** of the following may apply to SS Prerequisite 1, Construction Activity Pollution Prevention?

A._____ Silt fencing
B._____ Ecosystem
C._____ Earth dikes
D._____ Flood plain
E._____ Sediment traps

423. Which **THREE** of the following may apply to SS Credit 1, Site Selection credit?

A._____ Threatened species
B._____ Mulching
C._____ Flood level
D._____ Sedimentation
E._____ Wetland

424. Which **THREE** of the following may apply to SS Credit 2, Development Density & Community Connectivity credit?

A._____ Site area
B._____ Wetland vegetation
C._____ Pedestrian access
D._____ Erosion control plan
E._____ Building square footage

425. Which **THREE** of the following may apply to SS Credit 4.1, 4.2, 4.3, Alternative Transportation credits?

A._____ Public transportation
B._____ Development density
C._____ Emission
D._____ Basic services
E._____ Mass transit pollution

426. Which **THREE** of the following may apply to SS Credit 6.1 , Storm Water Design credit?

A._____ Post development
B._____ BMP
C._____ Impervious surfaces
D._____ Ecosystem
E._____ Discharge rate

427. Which **THREE** of the following may apply to SS Credit 7.1 & 7.2, Heat Island Effect credits?

A._____ Microclimate
B._____ Local zoning
C._____ TSS
D._____ Open-grid paving
E._____ Solar reflectance Index

428. Which **TWO** of the following may apply to SS Credit 8, Light Pollution Reduction credit?

A._____ Conductivity
B._____ Reflectance index
C._____ Glare
D._____ Illumination level
E._____ Convection factor

429. Which **THREE** of the following may apply to WE Credit 1.1 & 1.2 Water Efficiency Landscaping credits?

A._____ Irrigation system
B._____ Evapotranspriration
C._____ Tertiary treatment
D._____ Wetland
E._____ Mulching

430. Which **THREE** of the following may apply to WE Credit 2, Innovative Wastewater Technologies credit?

A._____ Drip Irrigation
B._____ Constructed wetland
C._____ Tertiary treatment
D._____ Biological system
E._____ Xeriscaping

431. Which **THREE** of the following may apply to WE Credit 3.1 , 3.2, Water Use Reduction credits?

A._____ Recovery system
B._____ Electronic faucets
C._____ Composting toilet
D._____ Dual plumbing lines
E._____ Dry Fixtures

432. Which **THREE** of the following may apply to EA Prerequisite 1, Fundamental Commissioning of the Building Energy System?

A._____ TSS
B._____ BOD
C._____ OPR
D._____ ODP
E._____ CxA

433. Which **THREE** of the following may apply to EA Prerequisite 2, Minimum Energy Performance?

A._____CFC
B._____ Building envelope
C._____ HVAC systems
D._____ Lighting systems
E._____ OPR

434. Which **THREE** of the following may apply to EA Prerequisite 3, Fundamental Refrigerant Management?

A._____ CFC
B._____ HVAC
C._____ OPR
D._____ ODP
E._____ Building envelope

435. Which **THREE** of the following may apply to EA Credit 1, Optimize Energy Performance credit?

A._____ Bio-green Thermal Method
B._____ Performance Rating Method
C._____ Thermal mass
D._____ Energy simulation
E._____ Photo-thermal analysis

436. Which **THREE** of the following may apply to EA Credit 2, On-site Renewable Energy credit?

A._____ Hydrofluoro carbons
B._____ Passive cooling
C._____ Photovoltaic
D._____ Geothermal
E._____ Biomass

437. Which **THREE** of the following may apply to EA Credit 3, Enhanced Commissioning credit?

A._____ Utility billing analysis
B._____ Independent agent authorization
C._____ Design review
D._____ Submittal review
E._____ DOE energy measurement

438. Which **THREE** of the following may apply to EA Credit 4, Enhanced Refrigerant Management credit?

A._____ ECM
B._____ CEBS
C._____ HFC
D._____ HCFC
E._____ HVAC

439. Which **THREE** of the following may apply to EA Credit 5, Measurement & Verification credit?

A._____ CBES
B._____ EVO
C._____ ECM
D._____ DOE
E._____ Energy consumption rating

440. Which **THREE** of the following may apply to EA Credit 6, Green Power credit?

A._____ Net-zero pollution
B._____ Green Pro certificate
C._____ CRS
D._____ CBECS
E._____ IPMVP

441. Which **THREE** of the following may apply to MR Prerequisite 1, Storage & Collection of Recyclables?

A._____ Recycling chutes
B._____ Salvaged
C._____ Separation approach
D._____ Material life cycle
E._____ CIWMB

442. Which **THREE** of the following may apply to MR Credit 1.1, 1.2, 1.3, Building Reuse credits?

A._____ Structure component
B._____ Shell component
C._____ Non-structural elements
D._____ Recyclable component
E._____ Salvaged component

443. Which **THREE** of the following may apply to MR Credit 2.1, 2.2, Construction Waste Management credits?

A._____ Recyclable material
B._____ Salvaged materials
C._____ Refurbished material
D._____ Life cycle of materials
E._____ Donation of materials

444. Which **THREE** of the following may apply to MR Credit 3.1, 3.2, Material Reuse credits?

A._____ Salvaged material
B._____ Recyclable material
C._____ Refurbished material
D._____ Post-consumer material
E._____ Replacement cost of material

445. Which **THREE** of the following may apply to MR Credit 4.1, 4.2, Recycled Content credits?

A._____ Material life cycle
B._____ Tipping fee
C._____ Post-consumer material
D._____ Collection cost
E._____ Pre-consumer material

446. Which **THREE** of the following may apply to MR Credit 5.1, 5.2, Regional Materials credits?

A._____ Harvested
B._____ Manufactured
C._____ Consumption
D._____ Transportation
E._____ Reused

447. Which **ONE** of the following may apply to MR Credit 6, Rapidly Renewable Materials credit?

A._____ Chain-of custody
B._____ Manufactured
C._____ Consumption
D._____ Salvaged
E._____ Material life cycle

448. Which **THREE** of the following may apply to MR Credit 7, Certified Wood credit?

A._____ Chain-of Custody
B._____ Ecosystem
C._____ FSC
D._____ ETS
E._____ ISO

449. Which **THREE** of the following may apply to EQ Prerequisite 1, Minimum IAQ Performance?

A._____ ETS
B._____ IAQ
C._____ CO2
D._____ ASHRAE
E._____ ANSI

450. Which **THREE** of the following may apply to EQ Prerequisite 2, Environmental Tobacco Smoke (ETS) Control credit?

A._____ ANSI
B._____ DOE
C._____ IAQ
D._____ ETS
E._____ ASTM

451. Which **THREE** of the following may apply to EQ Credit 1, Outdoor Air Delivery Monitoring credit?

A._____ The location of CO2 sensors
B._____ Building pressurization
C._____ Particulate filtration
D._____ Number of people
E._____ Alarm system

452. Which **THREE** of the following may apply to EQ Credit 2, Increased Ventilation credit?

A._____ Ventilation rate
B._____ The location of CO2 sensors
C._____ Breathing zone
D._____ The building pressurization
E._____ Air change effectiveness

453. Which **THREE** of the following may apply to EQ Credit 3.1, 3.2, Construction IAQ Management Plan credits?

A._____ MERV
B._____ EPA
C._____ MSDS
D._____ ETS
E._____ SMACNA

454. Which **THREE** of the following may apply to EQ Credit 4.1, 4.2, 4.3, Low Emitting Materials credits?

A._____ SMACNA
B._____ SCAQMD
C._____ ASHRAE
D._____ VOC
E._____ CRI

455. Which **THREE** of the following may apply to EQ Credit 5, Indoor Chemical & Pollutant Source Control credit?

A._____ Cross-contamination
B._____ IAQ management plan
C._____ Building pressurization
D._____ Building flush-out
E._____ Entryway design and planning

456. Which **THREE** of the following may apply to EQ Credit 6.1, 6.2, Controllability of Systems credits?

A._____ IAQ management plan
B._____ Building flush-out
C._____ Zone occupancy
D._____ Task lights
E._____ Operable window

457. Which **THREE** of the following may apply to EQ Credit 7.1, 7.2, Thermal Comfort credits?

A._____ Relative humidity
B._____ Occupancy period
C._____ Predicated mean Value
D._____ Cross contamination
E._____ Natural ventilation

458. Which **THREE** of the following may apply to EQ Credit 8.1, 8.2, Daylight & Views credits?

A._____ Conduction factor
B._____ Sightline
C._____ Building shell area
D._____ Glass area
E._____ Window's geometry

459. Which **TWO** of the following may apply to EA Prerequisite 3, Fundamental Refrigerant Management?

A._____ HVAC system
B._____ Plumbing system
C._____ Ventilation system
D._____ Hot water system
E._____ Fire suppression systems

460. Which **ONE** of the following is true statement for visible transmittance factor in EQ Credit 8.1, Daylight & Views credit?

A._____ The ratio of the total visible transmitted light divided by the total light through the surface
B._____ The ratio of the total light thru surface divided by the total visible transmitted light
C._____ The ratio of the total light reflected by the surface divided by total light through the surface
D._____ The ratio of the total light thru the surface divided by the total light reflected by the surface
E._____ None of the above

461. The total site area shall be implemented in which **ONE** of the following credit?

A._____ SS Credit 5.1
B._____ SS Credit 3.2
C._____ SS Credit 5.2
D._____ SS Credit 4.1
E._____ SS Credit 6.1

462. Which **THREE** of the following may apply to EQ Credit 8.1, Daylight & Views credit?

A._____ SRI
B._____ Solar emittance
C._____ Visible transmittance
D._____ Floor area
E._____ Window's geometry

463. Which **TWO** of the following are considered as PRE-CONSUMER material in MR Credit 4.1 & 4.2, Recycled Content credits?

A._____ Metal scrap which is not being reclaimed within the same process
B._____ Salvaged material
C._____ Seed hulls
D._____ Plastic
E._____ Paper

464. The green or vegetated roofing may earn points in which **THREE** of the following credits?

A._____ SS Credit 7.2, Heat Island Effect
B._____ SS Credit 5.1, Site Development
C._____ SS Credit 6.2, Storm Water Management
D._____ SS Credit 1, Site Selection
E._____ EQ Credit 4.2, Low- Emitting Materials

465. Which **ONE** of the following may apply to emissivity of materials?

A._____ Light transmittance
B._____ Heat radiation
C._____ Heat absorption
D._____ Solar gain
E._____ Light reflective

466. Which **ONE** of the following is true statement for a window's glazing factors?

A._____ The amount of transmitted load compared to the space illumination factor
B._____ The amount of space illumination factor compared to the exterior illumination factor
C._____ The amount of transmitted load compared to the ASHRAE lighting standards
D._____ The amount of space illumination factor compared to the ISENA lighting standards
E._____ The amounts of the exterior illumination factor compared to the local lighting standards

467. The boundary of the project may be utilized in which **THREE** of the following?

A._____ SS credit 8.1, Light Pollution Reduction
B._____ SS Credit 7.1 & 7.2 , Heat Island Effect
C._____ SS credit 2, Development Density & Community Connectivity
D._____ SS Credit 3, Brownfield Redevelopment
E._____ SS credit 5.2, Site Development

468. The salvaged materials may be utilized in which **TWO** of the following?

A._____ MR credit 3.1, Material Reuse
B._____ MR credit 4.1, Recycled Content
C._____ MR Credit 1.1, Building Reuse
D._____ MR Credit 2.1, Construction Waste Management
E._____ MR credit 5.1, Regional Materials

469. Which **THREE** of the following may apply to WE Credit 1, Water Efficient Landscaping credit?

A._____ Use native plants
B._____ Use turf grass
C._____ Use vegetated swales
D._____ Use adapted plants
E._____ Reduce the landscape area

470. Which **THREE** of the following may apply to SS Credit 7.1, Heat Island Effect credit?

A._____ Deciduous tress
B._____ Xeriscaping
C._____ Aledo materials
D._____ Absorption
E._____ Evapotranspoiration

471. Which **ONE** of the following may apply to ASHRAE 90.1,2004 standards?

A._____ Lighting Design
B._____ Ventilation effectiveness
C._____ Energy consumption
D._____ Ozone layer
E._____ C02 Monitoring system

472. Which **TWO** of the following may apply to the South Coast Air Quality Management District Rule # 1168 standards in EQ Credit 4.1,4.2, Low-Emitting Materials credits?

A._____ VOC in sealants
B._____ VOC in paints
C._____ VOC in primer
D._____ VOC in adhesives
E._____ VOC in coatings

473. Which **THREE** of the following may be considered as PROCESS load in EA Credit 1.1, 1.2, 1.3, Optimize Energy Performance credits?

A._____ Air handling units
B._____ Chillers
C._____ Elevator machines
D._____ Laundry washers
E._____ Office Equipment

474. Which **THREE** of the following calculations may be utilized for MR Credit 1, Building Reuse credits?

A._____ Area of walls
B._____ Area of roofing material
C._____ Area of doors
D._____ Area of structural items
E._____ Volume of structural items

475. Which **THREE** of the following statements may apply to REVIEW process?

A._____ Credits marked a " D " can be submitted at the end of the design phase
B._____ Credits marked as " C " can be submitted at the end of the construction phase
C._____ 1/3 of overall certification fee is due @ " C " phase
D._____ 1/3 of overall certification fee is due @ " D " phase
E._____ 2/3 of overall certification fee is due @ " C " phase

476. How many days after the receipt of the preliminary review, shall the team submit corrections or additional supporting documents to the USGBC office?

A._____ 25
B._____ 20
C._____ 27
D._____ 35
E._____ 30

477. Which **THREE** of the following statements may apply to preferred parking spaces in SS credit 4.4, Alternative Transportation credit?

A._____ The nearest spot to the main entrance of the building
B._____ The handicap parking spaces
C._____ The parking space provided at a discounted rate
D._____ The parking space designated for ride share group
E._____ The parking space designated for low emission vehicle

478. How many points can be achieved when 11 % of the total energy cost is produced by renewable energy in EA Credit 2, On-Site Renewable Energy credit?

A._____ 1
B._____ 3
C._____ 4
D._____ 2
E._____ None of above

479. Which **ONE** of the following methods may apply to option # 1 in EA Credit 1, Optimize Energy Performance credit?

A._____ Energy Budget Cost
B._____ Energy Conservation Cost
C._____ Performance Calculation Rating
D._____ Advanced Energy Method
E._____ Green-e Energy Standards

480. For the project planning process, which **ONE** of the following should be addressed during the schematic phase of the project?

A._____ SS Prerequisite 1, Construction Activity Pollution Prevention
B._____ EQ Prerequisite 2, Environmental Tobacco Smoke (ETS) Control
C._____ MR Credits 2.1, 2.2, Construction Waste Management
D._____ EA Credit 4, Enhanced Refrigerant Management
E._____ None of above

481. For the project planning process, which **ONE** of the following should be addressed during the schematic phase of the project?

A._____ SS Credits 6.1, 6.2, Stormwater Design
B._____ EA Credit 5, Measurement & Verification
C._____ SS Credit 1, Site Selection
D._____ MR Credits 2.1, 2.2, Construction Waste Management
E._____ None of above

482. For the project planning process, which **ONE** of the following should be addressed during the schematic phase of the project?

A._____ WE Credits 1.1, 1.2, Water Efficient Landscaping
B._____ MR Credits 2.1, 2.2, Construction Waste Management
C._____ MR Credits 3.1, 3.2, Material Reuse
D._____ EA Prerequisite 3, Fundamental Refrigerant Management
E._____ None of above

483. For the project planning process, which **ONE** of the following should be addressed during the schematic phase of the project?

A._____ WE Credits 3.1, 3.2, Water Use Reduction
B._____ MR Credits 3.1, 3.2, Material Reuse
C._____ MR Credits 2.1, 2.2, Construction Waste Management
D._____ EA Credit 4, Enhanced Refrigerant Management
E._____ None of above

484. For the project planning process, which **ONE** of the following should be addressed during the schematic phase of the project?

A._____ EA Credit 3, Enhanced Commissioning
B._____ SS Credit 2, Development Density & Community Connectivity
C._____ EA Credit 4, Enhanced Refrigerant Management
D._____ EQ prerequisite 2, Environmental Tobacco Smoke (ETS) Control
E._____ None of above

485. Which **THREE** of the following may have an opportunity to earn exemplary performance point(s) in the Sustainable Site category?

A._____ SS Credit 5.1 & 5.2, Site Development
B._____ SS Credit 1, Site Selection
C._____ SS Credit 6.1 & 6.2, Strom Water Design
D._____ SS Credit 2, Development Density & Community Connectivity
E._____ SS Credit 4.1 thru 4.4, Alternative Transportation

486. Which **THREE** of the following may have an opportunity to earn exemplary performance point(s) in the Energy & Atmosphere category?

A._____ EA Credit 6, Green Power
B._____ EA Credit 1, Optimize Energy Performance
C._____ EA Credit 3, Enhanced Refrigerant Management
D._____ EA Credit 5, Measurement & Verification
E._____ EA Credit 2, On-site Renewable Energy

487. Which **THREE** of the following may have an opportunity to earn exemplary performance point(s) in the Material & Resources category?

A._____ MR Credit 2.1, 2.2 , Construction Waste Management Divert
B._____ MR Credit 1.1, 1,2, 1.3, Building Reuse
C._____ MR Credit 3.1, 3.2, Material Reuse
D._____ MR Credit 4.1, 4.2 , Recycled Content

488. Which **ONE** of the following has an opportunity to earn exemplary performance points in the Indoor Environmental Quality category?

A._____ EQ Credit 6.1 Controllability of Systems
B._____ EQ Credit 3.1, 3.2, Construction IAQ Management Plan
C._____ EQ Credit 6.2, Controllability of Systems
D._____ EQ Credit 7.1, 7.2, Thermal Comfort
E. EQ Credit 8.1, 8.2, Daylight & Views

489. Which **THREE** of the following statements are true for the parking structures in SS Credit 2, Development Density & Community Connectivity credit?

A._____ For the multi- story parking structure, the area of two (2) parking levels shall be added to the building footprint
B._____ The area of both structure and stacked parking area shall be added to the building footprint
C._____ The area of stacked parking shall only be added to the building footprint
D._____ For multi- story parking structure, the area of only one (1) parking level shall be added to the building footprint
E._____ For one story parking structure, the area of one story (1) parking level shall not be added to the building footprint

490. Which **TWO** of the following may be earn additional points in SS credit 4.1, Alternative Transportation credit?

A._____ Locate the project within ½ mile from TWO train stations
B._____ Locate the project within ½ mile from ONE train stations
C._____ Locate the project within ¼ mile from TWO train stations
D._____ Locate the project within ¼ mile from TWO public or campus bus lines
E._____ Locate the project within ¼ mile from FOUR public or campus bus lines

491. Which **TWO** of the following statements are true for SS Credit 4.4, Alternative Transportation credit?

A._____ Meet the minimum requirement set by the Portland Oregon Zoning standards
B._____ Meet the minimum requirement set by the DOE , part 2.1300, Zoning section 4
C._____ Obtain 20 percent less than minimum requirement set by the Institute of Transportation Engineers.
D._____ Obtain 25 percent less than minimum requirement set by the Institute of Transportation Engineers.
E._____ Meet the minimum requirement set by the DOE , part 2.1100, Zoning section

492. Which **TWO** of the following statements are true for open area calculation in SS Credit 5.2, Site Development credit?

A._____ Follow the local code requirement
B._____ Follow the SMACNA code requirement
C._____ If there is no local code requirement, then the open space area is equal to: (the area of developed site - the area of property)
D._____ If there is no local code requirement, then the open space area is equal to: (the area of undeveloped site – the area of property)
E._____ Follow the ASHRAE code requirement

493. Which **ONE** of the following statements is accurate for selection of air conditioning units in EA Prerequisite 3, Fundamental Refrigerant Management?

A._____ Units with less than 1.50 lbs of refrigerant are excluded from this requirement.
B._____ Units with less than 0.50 lbs of refrigerant are excluded from this requirement.
C._____ Units with less than 0.25 lbs of refrigerant are excluded from this requirement.
D._____ Units with less than 1.00 lbs of refrigerant are excluded from this requirement.
E._____ None of above

494. Which **TWO** of the following statements are true for earning exemplary points in option # 1 of EA Credit 1, Optimize Energy Performance credit?

A._____ Obtain 45.5 percent of energy saving for new buildings
B._____ Obtain 43.0 percent of energy saving for new buildings
C._____ Obtain 35.0 percent of energy saving for existing buildings
D._____ Obtain 38.5 percent of energy saving for existing buildings
E._____ Obtain 45.5 percent of energy saving for existing buildings

495. How many point(s) may be achieved in EA Credit 1, Optimize Energy Performance credit?

A._____ 1
B._____ 3
C._____ 5
D._____ 2
E._____ None of above

496. How many points may be achieved in the option 3 of EA credit 1, Optimize Energy Performance credit?

A._____ 2
B._____ 1
C._____ 5
D._____ 4
E._____ 3

497. Which **THREE** of the following statements are true in option # 3 of EA Credit 1, Optimize Energy Performance credit?

A._____ It shall comply with the Core Performance Guideline published by the New Building Institute
B._____ It applies to buildings under 75,000 sq. ft of floor space
C._____ It does NOT apply to warehouse, health care buildings
D._____ It shall comply with the core performance requirement published by ASHRAE 55, 2004
E._____ It shall apply to the building under 100,000 sq.ft of floor space

498. Which **ONE** of the following may earn an extra point in EA credit 2, On-Site Renewable Energy credit?

A._____ 12.5
B._____ 17.5
C._____ 15
D._____ 2.5
E._____ None of above

499. Which **TWO** of the following statements are true for calculation of DIVERT materials for MR credit 2.2, Construction Waste Management credit?

A._____ Include reused material, if it is not included in credit MR Credit 3
B._____ Do NOT include reused material, if it is not included in MR Credit 3
C._____ Do NOT include salvaged material, if it is not included in MR Credit 3
D._____ Include salvaged material, if it is not included in credit MR Credit 3
E._____ Include reused material, if it is included in credit MR Credit 3

500. Which **THREE** of the following may apply to EQ credit 4.2, Low-Emitting Material credit?

A._____ Paints must meet the VOC limit
B._____ Adhesives must meet the VOC limit
C._____ Coating must meet the VOC limit
D._____ Sealants must meet the VOC limit
E._____ Primers must meet the VOC limit

501. Which **TWO** of the following factors may be utilized for MR Credit 6, Rapidly Renewable Material credit?

A._____ Cost of rapidly renewable material
B._____ Volume of rapidly renewable material
C._____ Combined weight of all rapidly renewable materials used in the project
D._____ Total construction cost of project
E._____ Partial weight of rapidly renewable material used in the project

502. Which **TWO** of the following tasks may apply to MR Credit Prerequisite 1, Storage & Collection of Recyclables credit?

A._____ Provide accessible area for the separation, collection and storage of materials
B._____ Method of approaches includes separation, collection and storage
C._____ Method of approaches includes separation and registration
D._____ Provide collection and storage areas for newspaper
E._____ Provide minimum access as required by UBC codes for collection and storage areas

503. Which **TWO** of the following may NOT apply to EQ Credit 6.2, Controllability of System credit?

A._____ Thermal control system
B._____ Air change ratio
C._____ Daylight factor
D._____ Relative humidity
E._____ Ventilation rate

504. The salvaged material from nearby buildings may be utilized in which **TWO** of the following credits?

A._____ MR Credit 2.1, 2.2, Construction Waste Management
B._____ MR Credit 4.1, 4.2, 4.3, Recycled Content
C._____ MR Credit 3.1, 3.2, Material Reuse
D._____ MR Credit 1.1, 1.2, 1.3, Building Reuse
E._____ MR Credit 5.1, 5.2, Regional Materials

505. Which **THREE** of the following may apply to the daylight factor in EQ Credit 8.1, Daylight & View credit?

A._____ Space floor area
B._____ Window area
C._____ Solar orientation
D._____ Visible light transmittance
E._____ Wall reflectance

506. Which **THREE** of the following may be utilized in MR Credit 4.1, 4.2, Recyclable Content credits?

A._____ Concrete
B._____ Brick
C._____ Metal wall stud
D._____ In-house industrial scrap
E._____ Cotton wall insulation

507. Which **TWO** of the following statements are true for SS Credit 8, Light Pollution Reduction credit?

A._____ It shall not exceed over 50 % of the landscape lighting guideline published by ASHRAE/ IESNA standards
B._____ The interior lighting shall stay within the building perimeters
C._____ It shall comply with pre-curfew standards
D._____ It shall comply with Uniform Building Code and IESNA standards
E._____ It shall comply with illumination ratios established by National Electrical Code

508. Which **ONE** of the following may refer to the DEMAND-CONTROLLED ventilation design of HVAC systems?

A._____ EA Credit 5, Measurement and Verification
B._____ EA Credit 3, Enhanced Commissioning
C._____ EA Credit 1, Optimize Energy Performance
D._____ EQ Credit 1, Outdoor Air Delivery Monitoring
E._____ None of above

509. Which **ONE** of the following may apply to SS Prerequisite 1, Construction Activity Pollution Prevention?

A._____ Loss of soil
B._____ Sedimentation
C._____ Condensation
D._____ Erosion
E._____ Site Imperviousness

510. Which **THREE** of the following may apply to EA Credit 5, Measurement & Verification credit?

A._____ Air effectiveness
B._____ Whole-building computer simulation
C._____ Heat recovery cycle
D._____ Occupancy period
E._____ Energy conservation and measurement

511. Which **THREE** of the following may apply to EA Prerequisite 3, Fundamental Refrigerant Management?

A._____ HVAC air handling units
B._____ Chillers
C._____ Fan motors
D._____ Variable frequency motors
E._____ Ozone-deleting potential

512. Which **THREE** of the following may apply to WE Credit 1.1, 1.2, Water Efficient Landscaping credit?

A._____ Vegetated swales
B._____ Turf grass
C._____ Impervious surfaces
D._____ Native plants
E._____ Adapted plant

513. Which **THREE** of the following may apply to SS Credit 7.1, 7.2 Heat Island credits?

A._____ SRI
B._____ Absorption
C._____ Xeiscaping
D._____ Deciduous trees
E._____ Open grid area

514. Which **TWO** of the following are the main responsibilities for the General Contractor in EQ Credit 4.3, Low-Emitting Materials credit?

A._____ Prepare energy modeling calculation
B._____ Prepare evidence for waste management plan
C._____ Prepare material safety data sheet
D._____ Prepare site photometric plans
E._____ Prepare documents for the basis of design

515. Which **THREE** of the following may apply to SS Credit 3, Brownfield Redevelopment credit?

A._____ Contaminated site location
B._____ Contaminated risks
C._____ Mitigation costs
D._____ Removal costs
E._____ Remedial measures

516. Which **THREE** of the following statements are true for EA Prerequisite 1, Fundamental Commissioning of the Building Energy system?

A._____ The commissioning agent should be an independent person
B._____ The commissioning agent should be part of the design team
C._____ The commissioning agent should verify the performance of the building after the construction phase
D._____ The commissioning agent should verify the performance of HVAC units
E._____ The commissioning agent should be a certified or registered building commissioner

517. Which **THREE** of the following statements are true for EQ Credit 3.2, Construction IAQ Management plan credit?

A._____ Supply specific volume of air into the building before occupancy period
B._____ Supply specific volume of air into the building for 3 hours during the occupancy period till specific volume of flushing is accomplished
C._____ Exhaust specific volume of air for 8 hours before the occupancy period
D._____ Exhaust specific volume of air from the building for 2 hours before the occupancy period
E._____ Test the quality of the air in occupied space during the flush-out period

518. Which **TWO** of the following statements are true for the CIR (Credit Interpretation Ruling) forms?

A._____ CIR can be submitted on-line
B._____ CIR can be reviewed by USGBC members
C._____ CIR can only be submitted and reviewed by any USGBC members
D._____ CIR can not be submitted on-line
E._____ CIR can be reviewed by non-registered team members

519. Which **THREE** of the following factors may be considered for SS Credit 8, Light Pollution Reduction credit?
A._____ Exterior Lighting shall not exceed over 80 % of ASHRAE / IENSA standards
B._____ IESNA zoning classification of LZ 2 covers density of 200 to 3000 people per sq. mile.
C._____ IESNA zoning classification of LZ 4 covers density of more than 100,000 people per sq. mile.
D._____ Exterior lighting shall not exceed over 30% of specific ASHRAE standards.
E._____ NEC zoning classification

520. Which **THREE** of the following may be utilized for MR Credit 1.1, 1.2, 1.3, Building Reuse credits?
A._____ Area of foundation
B._____ Area of roof
C._____ Area of floor
D._____ Volume of electrical units
E._____ Volume of mechanical units

521. Which **ONE** of the following LEED certificates may apply to projects that will lease spaces to retails and offices?

A._____ LEED-NC
B._____ LEED- CS
C._____ LEED-CI
D._____ LEED-EB
E._____ None of above

522. Which **THREE** of the following shall be considered for the life cycle cost analysis in EA credit1, Optimize Energy Performance credit?

A._____ First cost
B._____ Installation cost
C._____ Maintenance cost
D._____ Replacement cost
E._____ Life expectancy cost

523. Which **TWO** of the following have been referenced in ASHRAE 55-2004 standards?

A._____ Humidity ratio
B._____ Lighting level
C._____ Thermal comfort level
D._____ Ventilation level
E._____ None of above

524. The cost of material plays a major role in which **THREE** of the following credits?

A._____ MR Credit 7, Certified Wood
B._____ MR Credit 1.1,1.2,1.3, Building Reuse
C._____ MR Credit 3.1,3.2, Material Reuse
D._____ MR Credit 5.1, 5.2, Regional Materials
E._____ MR Credit 2.1, 2.2, Construction Waste Management

525. Which **ONE** of the following credits has been referenced to the Energy Policy Act of 1992 standard?

A._____ WE Credit 3, Water Use Reduction
B._____ EQ Credit 2, Increased Ventilation
C._____ EQ Credit 1, Outdoor Air Delivery Performance
D._____ EA Prerequisite 2, Minimum Energy Performance
E._____ None of above

526. Which **THREE** of the following may apply to MR Credit 4.1, 4.2, Recycled Content credits?

A._____ Cost of construction material
B._____ Cost of post-consumer material
C._____ Cost of pre-consumer material
D._____ Weight of post-consumer material
E._____ Weight of pre-consumer material

527. Which **THREE** of the following materials shall be excluded in calculation of MR credit 1.1, Building Reuse credit?

A._____ Windows
B._____ Roof decking
C._____ Hazards materials
D._____ Structural Floor
E._____ Non-structural materials

528. The full time occupant number is implemented in which **THREE** of the following credits?

A._____ WE Credit 2, Innovative Wastewater Technologies
B._____ EA Credit 5, Measurement & Verification
C._____ SS Credit 4.2, 4.3, 4.4, Alternative Transportation
D. SS credit 2, Development Density & Community Connectivity
E._____ WE Credit 3.1,3.2, Water Use Reduction

529. Which **TWO** of the following informational sets are required for MR credit 7, Certified Wood credit?

A._____ The cost of certified wood compared to the cost of new wood materials
B._____ The cost of certified wood compared to the total cost of wood used in the building
C._____ The chain -of custody documents for wood materials
D._____ The chain-of custody documents for building materials
E._____ The weight ratio of certified wood compared to the weight of material used in the building

530. Which **THREE** of the following may apply to SS Credit 7.1, Heat Island Effect credit?

A._____ The emissivity of building materials
B._____ The run-off coefficient factor for impervious paving material
C._____ The solar reflectance of materials
D._____ The percentage of shading area
E._____ The SRI of open-grid paving materials

531. Which **THREE** of the following are required for achieving WE Credit 2, Innovative Wastewater Technologies credit?

A._____ The condensate water flow rate
B._____ The annual working days
C._____ The volume of waste water generated per day
D._____ The volume of process water generated per day
E._____ The number of FTE per day

532. Which **THREE** of the following may apply to MR Credit 1.3, Building Reuse credits?

A._____ The area of floor covering
B._____ The area of structural materials
C._____ The volume of roof decks
D._____ The area of partitions
E._____ The area of doors

533. Which **THREE** of the following may apply to EA Credit 4, Enhanced Refrigerant Management credit?

A._____ The type of refrigerant for HVAC units
B._____ The fire suppression system
C._____ The refrigerant detection system
D._____ The energy efficiency rating for HVAC system
E._____ The life of HVAC units

534. Which **THREE** of the following may NOT apply to SS credit 6.1, Storm Water Design, Quality Control credit?

A._____ Impervious ratio by ASTM
B._____ Impervious surface area
C._____ The pre-development discharge rate
D._____ Rainfall factor of 4 years
E._____ Semi-humid watershed

535. Which **THREE** of the following are considered as PROCESS load in EA Credit 1, Optimize Energy Performance credit?

A._____ Landscape water pumps
B._____ Parking garage lighting
C._____ Office equipment
D._____ Elevator machine
E._____ Solar heating system

536. Which **THREE** of the following documents are required for SS Credit 7.1, Heat Island Effect credit?

A._____ Total number of covered parking spaces
B._____ The location of open grid paving
C._____ The selection method for paving materials on roof
D._____ The area of vegetated roof
E._____ The Solar Reflectance Index of paving materials

537. The owner of the project is planning to use cogeneration units for the building mechanical system. The owner is interested earning points in which **ONE** of the following credits?

A._____ EA Credit 4, Enhanced Refrigerant Management
B._____ EA credit 1, Optimize Energy Performance
C._____ EA Credit 3, Enhanced Commissioning
D._____ EA Credit 2, On-site Renewable Energy
E._____ None of above

538. The owner of the project is planning to implement the following tasks:

- Maintaining existing building material
- Replacing single glare glasses to reused double glare glasses
- Purchasing new windows that are manufactured, extracted and processed within 500 miles of the site
- Installing doors that were donated from different sources

The owner wants to earn points in which **THREE** of the following credits?

A._____ MR Credit 3.1, 3.2, Material Reuse
B._____ MR Credit 5.1, 5.2, Regional Materials
C._____ MR Credit 2.1, 2.2, Construction Waste Management
D._____ MR Credit 1, Building Reuse
E._____ MR Credit 4.1, Recycled Content

539. The owner of the project is planning to implement the following tasks:

- Providing shallow floor plate
- Installing heat recovery system
- Installing operable windows
- Installing task-ambient lighting with photocell

The owner wants to earn points in which **THREE** of the following credits?
A._____ EQ credit 6.2, Controllability of Systems- Thermal comfort
B._____ EQ Credit 2, Increased ventilation
C._____ EA Credit 5, Measurement & Verification
D._____ EQ Credit 3.1,Construction IAQ Management Plan
E._____ EA credit 1, Optimize Energy Performance

540. The owner of the project is planning to implement the following tasks:

- Providing drain heat recovery system
- Utilizing treated water for plumbing fixtures
- Installing water-efficient shower head
- Installing metered faucets

The owner wants to earn points in which **THREE** of the following credits?

A._____ EA credit 1, Optimize Energy Performance
B._____ WE Credit 3.1, 3.2, Water Use Reduction
C._____ WE credit 2, Innovative Wastewater Technologies
D._____ EA Credit 5, Measurement and Verification
E._____ WE Credit 1, Water Efficient Landscaping

541. The owner of the project is planning to implement the following tasks:

- Installing 60 % of parking space under roof
- Locating the main entrance area within the direction of natural wind
- Installing flow sensors for plumbing fixtures
- Installing vegetated filtration system

The owner wants to earn points in which **THREE** of the following credits?

A._____ SS Credit 7.1, Heat Island Effect – non roof
B._____ EA Credit 1, Optimize Energy Performance
C._____ SS Credit 6.1, Storm Water Management Quality Control
D._____ SS Credit 5.1, Reduced Site Disturbance
E._____ SS Prerequisite 1, Erosion & Sedimentation

542. The project coordinator is investigating erosion and sedimentation control, stabilization standards, EPA standards, and planning to submit the result to the USGBC @ construction phase. The project coordinator is planning to earn point(s) in which **ONE** of the following credits?

A._____ SS Credit 4.1, Alternative Transportation
B._____ SS Credit 3, Brownfield Redevelopment
C._____ SS Credit 4.3, Alternative Transportation
D._____ Not to earn a point - Comply with the SS Prerequisite 1, Construction Activity Pollution Prevention
E._____ None of above

543. The project coordinator is investigating the flood level, wetland areas, prime farmland, parking structure floor plan, the FEMA standards, and planning to submit the result to the USGBC @ design phase. The project coordinator is planning to earn point(s) in which **ONE** of the following credits?

A._____ SS Credit 2, Development Density & Community Connectivity
B._____ SS Credit 6.2, Storm Water Design
C._____ SS Credit 4.4, Alternative Transportation
D._____ SS Credit 7.2, Heat Island Effect
E._____ None of above

544. The project coordinator is investigating contaminated sites, ASTM standards, EPA regulations, and planning to submit the result to the USGBC @ design phase. The project coordinator is planning to earn point(s) in which **ONE** of the following credits?

A._____ SS Credit 5.1, Site Development
B._____ SS Credit 3, Brownfield Redevelopment
C._____ SS Credit 7.2, Heat Island Effect
D._____ SS Credit 6.1, Storm water Design
E._____ None of above

545. The project coordinator is investigating on the location of train stations, and planning to submit the result to the USGBC @ design phase. The project coordinator is planning to earn point(s) in which **ONE** of the following credits?

A._____ SS Credit 4.2, Alternative Transportation
B._____ SS Credit 4.4, Alternative Transportation
C._____ SS Credit 6.1, Strom Water Design
D._____ SS Credit 4.1, Alternative Transportation
E._____ None of above

546. The project coordinator is investigating the number of bicycle racks, design of changing rooms, and planning to submit the result to the USGBC @ design phase. The project coordinator is planning to earn point(s) in which **ONE** of the following credits?

A._____ SS Credit 5.2, Site Development
B._____ SS Credit 4.2, Alternative Transportation
C._____ SS Credit 4.3, Alternative Transportation
D._____ SS Credit 4.1, Alternative Transportation
E._____ None of above

547. The project coordinator is investigating the design of preferred parking for the low emission cars, and planning to submit the result to the USGBC @ design phase. The project coordinator is planning to earn point(s) in which **ONE** of the following credits?

A._____ SS Credit 4.2, Alternative Transportation
B._____ SS Credit 4.1, Alternative Transportation
C._____ SS Credit 4.4, Alternative Transportation
D._____ SS Credit 4.3, Alternative Transportation
E._____ None of above

548. The project coordinator is investigating the design of preferred parking for the carpool parking spaces, and planning to submit the result to the USGBC @ design phase. The project coordinator is planning to earn point(s) in which **ONE** of the following credits?

A._____ SS Credit 5.2, Site Development
B._____ SS Credit 4.1, Alternative Transportation
C._____ SS Credit 4.2, Alternative Transportation
D._____ SS Credit 4.4, Alternative Transportation
E._____ None of above

549. The project coordinator is investigating Greenfield area, previously developed land with the project boundary, and planning to submit the result to the USGBC @ construction phase. The project coordinator is planning to earn point(s) in which **ONE** of the following credits?

A._____ SS Credit 5.1, Site Development
B._____ SS Credit 5.2, Site Development
C._____ SS Credit 3, Brownfield Redevelopment
D._____ SS Credit 6.2, Storm Water Design
E._____ None of above

550. The project coordinator is investigating the design of open space and wetland areas within the project boundaries, and planning to submit the result to the USGBC @ design phase. The project coordinator is planning to earn point(s) in which **ONE** of the following credits?

A._____ SS Credit 3, Brownfield Redevelopment
B._____ SS Credit 6.1, Strom Water Design
C._____ SS Credit 5.2, Site Development
D._____ SS Credit 5.1, Site Development
E._____ None of above

551. The project coordinator is investigating impervious surfaces, pre-development and post development areas for the project, the EPA standards, and planning to submit the result to the USGBC @ design phase. The project coordinator is planning to earn point(s) in which **ONE** of the following credits?

A._____ SS credit 7.1, Heat Island Effect
B._____ SS Credit 3, Brownfield Redevelopment
C._____ SS Credit 6.2, Storm Water Design
D._____ SS Credit 6.1, Strom Water Design
E._____ None of above

552. The project coordinator is investigating constructed wetland, vegetated filtration system, grid pavers, BMP standards, and planning to submit the result to the USGBC @ design phase. The project coordinator is planning to earn point(s) in which **ONE** of the following credits?

A._____ SS credit 6.2, Storm water Design
B._____ SS Credit 6.1, Strom Water Design
C._____ SS Credit 4.4, Alternative Transportation
D._____ SS Credit 7.2, Heat Island Effect
E._____ None of above

553. The project coordinator is investigating open grid area, shading area, paving for parking, ASTM standards, and planning to submit the result to the USGBC @ construction phase. The project coordinator is planning to earn point(s) in which **ONE** of the following credits?

A._____ SS Credit 7.2, Heat Island Effect
B._____ SS Credit 6.1, Strom Water Design
C._____ SS Credit 7.1, Heat Island Effect
D._____ SS Credit 3, Brownfield Redevelopment
E._____ None of above

554. The project coordinator is investigating roof material, solar reflectance index, ASTM standards, and planning to submit the result to the USGBC @ design phase. The project coordinator is planning to earn point(s) in which **ONE** of the following credits?

A._____ SS Credit 5.2, Site Development
B._____ SS Credit 6.2, Storm water Design
C._____ SS credit 7.1, Heat Island Effect
D._____ SS Credit 7.2, Heat Island Effect
E._____ None of above

555. The project coordinator is investigating plant spices factors, captured rainwater, treated water, and planning to submit the result to the USGBC @ design phase. The project coordinator is planning to earn point(s) in which **ONE** of the following credits?

A._____ EA Credit 1, Optimize Energy Performance
B._____ EQ Credit 6.2, Controllability of Systems
C._____ WE Credit 2, Innovative Wastewater Technologies
D._____ WE Credit 1.1, 1.2 Water Efficient landscaping
E._____ None of above

556. The project coordinator is investigating roof collection system, waterless urinals, constructed wetlands, water treatment system and planning to submit the result to the USGBC @ design phase. The project coordinator is planning to earn point(s) in which **ONE** of the following credits?

A._____ WE Credit 1, Water Efficient Landscaping
B._____ EA Credit 5, Measurement & Verification
C._____ EA Credit 1, Optimize Energy Performance
D._____ WE Credit 2, Innovative Wastewater Technologies
E._____ None of above

557. The project coordinator is investigating the selection of water closet, plumbing fixtures, shower heads, the energy policy act of 1992, and planning to submit the result to the USGBC @ design phase. The project coordinator is planning to earn point(s) in which **ONE** of the following credits?

A._____ WE credit 2, Innovative Wastewater Technologies
B._____ WE Credit 1, Water Efficient Landscaping
C._____ WE Credit 3.1,3.2 ,Water Use Reduction
D._____ EA Credit 5, Measurement & Verification
E._____ None of above

558. The project coordinator is investigating the installation of building systems and its performance comparison to the original design, and planning to submit the result to the USGBC @ construction phase. The project coordinator is planning to earn point(s) in which **ONE** of the following credits?

A._____ EA Credit 4, Enhanced Refrigerant Management
B._____ EA Credit 5, Measurement & Verification
C._____ No to earn a point - Comply with EA Prerequisite 1, Fundamental Commissioning of The Building Energy System
D._____ EA Credit 3, Enhanced Commissioning
E._____ None of above

559. The project coordinator is investigating HVAC systems, window areas, skylight areas and wants to ensure the building energy design comply with the ASHRAE and DOE standard. The result will be submitted to the USGBC @ design phase. The project coordinator is planning to earn point(s) in which **ONE** of the following credits?

A.______ EA Credit 5, Measurement and Verification
B.______ EA Credit 1, Optimize Energy Performance
C.______ EA Credit 4, Enhanced Refrigerant Management
D.______ Not to earn a point - Comply with EA prerequisite 2, Minimum energy Performance
E.______ None of above

560. The project coordinator is investigating the zero use of CFC products in HVAC system, EPA standards, and planning to submit the result to the USGBC @ design phase. The project coordinator is planning to earn point(s) in which **ONE** of the following credits?

A.______ EA Credit 4, Enhanced Refrigerant Management
B.______ Not to earn a point- comply with EA Prerequisite 3, Fundamental Refrigerant Management
C.______ EA Credit 3, Enhanced Commissioning
D.______ EA Credit 1, Optimize Energy Performance
E.______ None of above

561. The project coordinator is investigating building energy simulation design, the prescriptive method of energy analysis, the ASHRAE 90.1 standards, and planning to submit the result to the USGBC @ design phase. The project coordinator is planning to earn point(s) in which **ONE** of the following credits?

A.______ EA Credit 3, Enhanced Commissioning
B.______ EA Credit 5, Measurement & Verification
C.______ EA Credit 2, On-site Renewable Energy
D.______ EA Credit 1, Optimize Energy Performance
E.______ None of above

562. The project coordinator is investigating local utility rates, building solar design, DOE standards, virtual energy rating, and planning to submit the result to the USGBC @ design phase. The project coordinator is planning to earn point(s) in which **ONE** of the following credits?

A.______ EA Credit 4, Enhanced Refrigerant Management
B.______ EA credit 1, Optimize Energy Performance
C.______ EA Credit 5, Measurement and Verification
D.______ EA Credit 2, On-site Renewable Energy
E.______ None of above

563. The project coordinator is investigating a submittal review and training processes, manual preparation, and planning to submit the result to the USGBC @ construction phase. The project coordinator is planning to earn point(s) in which **ONE** of the following credits?

A._____ EA Credit 5, Measurement & Verification
B._____ EA credit 1, Optimize Energy Performance
C._____ EA Credit 3, Enhanced Commissioning
D._____ EA Credit 2, On-site Renewable Energy
E._____ None of above

564. The project coordinator is investigating ODP, GWP and efficiency of HVAC units, and planning to submit the result to the USGBC @ design phase. The project coordinator is planning to earn point(s) in which **ONE** of the following credits?

A._____ EA Credit 2, On-site Renewable Energy
B._____ EA Credit 3, Enhanced Commissioning
C._____ EA Credit 5, Measurement & Verification
D._____ EA Credit 4, Enhanced Refrigerant Management
E._____ None of above

565. The project coordinator is investigating calibrated energy simulation methods, energy conservation systems, EVO standards, and planning to submit the result to the USGBC @ construction phase. The project coordinator is planning to earn point(s) in which **ONE** of the following credits?

A._____ EA Credit 4, Enhanced Refrigerant Management
B._____ EA Credit 5, Measurement & Verification
C._____ EA Credit 3, Enhanced Commissioning
D._____ EA Credit 1, Optimize Energy Performance
E._____ None of above

566. The project coordinator is investigating various renewable resources, DOE regulations, CBECS standards, and planning to submit the result to the USGBC @ construction phase. The project coordinator is planning to earn point(s) in which **ONE** of the following credits?

A._____ EA Credit 2, On-Site Renewable Energy
B._____ EA Credit 5, Measurement & Verification
C._____ EA Credit 4, Enhanced Refrigerant
D._____ EA Credit 6, Green Power
E._____ None of above

567. The project coordinator is investigating various procedures for collection and storage of building materials, the CIWMB standards, and planning to submit the result to the USGBC @ construction phase. The project coordinator is planning to earn point(s) in which **ONE** of the following credits?

A._____ MR Credit 5.1 Regional Materials
B._____ MR Credit 4.2, Recycled Content
C._____ Not to earn a point – Comply with MR Prerequisite 1
D._____ MR Credit 6, Rapidly Renewable Materials
E._____ None of above

568. The project coordinator is investigating the volume of structural elements, the area of building shell items, and planning to submit the result to the USGBC @ construction phase. The project coordinator is planning to earn point(s) in which **ONE** of the following credits?

A._____ MR Credit 2.1, Construction Waste Management
B._____ MR credit 4.1, Recycled Content
C._____ MR Credit 1.1, Building Reuse
D._____ MR Credit 5.2, Regional Materials
E._____ None of above

569. The project coordinator is investigating the weight of salvaged materials, the volume of recycled materials, the weight of reuse materials, and planning to submit the result to the USGBC @ construction phase. The project coordinator is planning to earn point(s) in which **ONE** of the following credits?

A._____ MR Credit 4.1, Recycled Content
B._____ MR Credit 5.1 Regional Materials
C._____ MR Credit 6, Rapidly Renewable Materials
D._____ MR Credit 2.1, Construction Waste Management
E._____ None of above

570. The project coordinator is investigating the weight of post-consumer and pre-consumer materials, total cost of materials, the ISO standards, and planning to submit the result to the USGBC @ construction phase. The project coordinator is planning to earn point(s) in which **ONE** of the following credits?

A._____ MR Credit 4.1, Recycled Content
B._____ MR Credit 2.1, Construction Waste Management
C._____ MR Credit 5.1 Regional Materials
D._____ MR Credit 1.1, Building Reuse
E._____ None of above

571. The project coordinator is investigating the cost of extracted materials within 500 mile radius, and planning to submit the result to the USGBC @ construction phase. The project coordinator is planning to earn point(s) in which **ONE** of the following credits?

A._____ MR Credit 2.1, Construction Waste Management
B._____ MR Credit 5.2, Regional Materials
C._____ MR Credit 6, Rapidly Renewable Materials
D._____ MR Credit 4.1, Recycled Content
E._____ None of above

572. The project coordinator is investigating the cost of bamboo flooring, wool carpeting, cork flooring, and planning to submit the result to the USGBC @ construction phase. The project coordinator is planning to earn point(s) in which **ONE** of the following credits?

A._____ MR credit 5.2, Regional Materials
B._____ MR Credit 4.2, Recycled Content
C._____ MR Credit 1.1, Building Reuse
D._____ MR Credit 6, Rapidly Renewable Materials
E._____ None of above

573. The project coordinator is investigating ventilation design, the quality of indoor, ASHRAE 62.1 standards, and planning to submit the result to the USGBC @ design phase. The project coordinator is planning to earn point(s) in which **ONE** of the following credits?

A._____ EQ Credit 4.1, Low-Emitting Material
B._____ EQ Credit 1, Outdoor Air Delivery Monitoring
C._____ EQ Credit 6.2, Controllability of Systems
D._____ Not to earn a point – Comply with EQ Prerequisite 1, Minimum IAQ performance
E._____ None of above

574. The project coordinator is investigating the air sampling processes, room pressurization, ANSI standard, and planning to submit the result to the USGBC @ design phase. The project coordinator is planning to earn point(s) in which **ONE** of the following credits?

A._____ EQ Credit 7.2, Thermal Comfort
B._____ EQ Credit 6.2, Controllability of System
C._____ Not to earn point- Comply with EQ Prerequisite 2, Environmental Tobacco Smoke Control
D._____ EQ Credit 3.1, Construction IAQ Management Plan
E._____ None of above

575. The project coordinator is investigating the location of CO2 sensor for both mechanical and natural ventilation systems, ASHRAE 62.1-2004 standards, and planning to submit the result to the USGBC @ design phase. The project coordinator is planning to earn point(s) in which **ONE** of the following credits?

A._____ EQ Credit 7.2, Thermal Comfort
B._____ EQ Credit 1, Outdoor Air Delivery Monitoring
C._____ EQ Credit 2, Increased Ventilation
D._____ EQ Credit 6.2, Controllability of System
E._____ None of above

576. The project coordinator is investigating heat recovery design, the breathing zone, air change effectiveness, ASHRAE 62.1,2004 standards, and planning to submit the result to the USGBC @ design phase. The project coordinator is planning to earn point(s) in which **ONE** of the following credits?

A._____ EQ Credit 5, Indoor Chemical & Pollutant Source Control
B._____ EQ Credit 2, Increased Ventilation
C._____ EQ Credit 6.2, Controllability of Systems
D._____ EQ Credit 3.1, Construction IAQ Management Plan
E._____ None of above

577. The project coordinator is investigating selection of air filters for HVAC system, ASHRAE 52.2 standards, and planning to submit the result to the USGBC @ construction phase. The project coordinator is planning to earn point(s) in which **ONE** of the following credits?

A._____ EQ Credit 3.2, Construction IAQ Management Plan
B._____ EQ Credit 4.1, Low-Emitting Materials
C._____ EQ Credit 3.1, Construction IAQ Management Plan
D._____ EQ Credit 7.2, Thermal Comfort
E._____ None of above

578. The project coordinator is investigating flush-out design, air sample testing, and planning to submit the result to the USGBC in construction phase. The project coordinator is planning to earn point(s) in which **ONE** of the following credits?

A._____ EQ Credit 1, Outdoor Air Delivery Monitoring
B._____ EQ Credit 3.1, Construction IAQ Management Plan
C._____ EQ Credit 7.2, Thermal Comfort
D._____ EQ Credit 3.2, Construction IAQ Management Plan
E._____ None of above

579. The project coordinator is investigating the VOC limit for adhesives, sealants materials, and planning to submit the result to the USGBC @ construction phase. The project coordinator is planning to earn point(s) in which **ONE** of the following credits?

A._____ EQ Credit 4.1
B._____ EQ Credit 4.2
C._____ EQ Credit 4.3
D._____ EQ Credit 4.4
E._____ None of above

580. The project coordinator is investigating the VOC limit for paints, primers, coating materials, and planning to submit the result to the USGBC @ construction phase. The project coordinator is planning to earn point(s) in which **ONE** of the following credits?

A._____ EQ credit 4.1
B._____ EQ Credit 4.2
C._____ EQ Credit 4.3
D._____ EQ Credit 4.4
E._____ None of above

581. The project coordinator is investigating the VOC limit for carpets, and planning to submit the result to the USGBC @ construction phase. The project coordinator is planning to earn point(s) in which **ONE** of the following credits?

A._____ EQ credit 4.1
B._____ EQ Credit 4.2
C._____ EQ Credit 4.3
D._____ EQ Credit 4.4
E._____ None of above

582. The project coordinator is investigating urea-formaldehyde resins in composite woods, agrifiber board, and planning to submit the result to the USGBC @ construction phase. The project coordinator is planning to earn point(s) in which **ONE** of the following credits?

A._____ EQ credit 4.1
B._____ EQ Credit 4.2
C._____ EQ Credit 4.3
D._____ EQ Credit 4.4
E._____ None of above

583. The project coordinator is investigating the design of HVAC systems in the occupied space, the final design of deck to deck partition, ASHRAE 52.2,1999 standards, and planning to submit the result to the USGBC @ design phase. The project coordinator is planning to earn point(s) in which **ONE** of the following credits?

A._____ EQ credit 5, Indoor Chemical & Pollutant Source Control
B._____ EQ Credit 7.2, Thermal Comfort
C._____ EQ Credit 6.2, Controllability of Systems
D._____ EQ Credit 3.1, Construction IAQ Management Plan
E._____ None of above

584. The project coordinator is investigating the size and location of the operable windows, the ASHRAE 62.1-2004 standards, and planning to submit the result to the USGBC @ design phase. The project coordinator is planning to earn point(s) in which **ONE** of the following credits?

A._____ EQ Credit 3.2, Construction IAQ Management Plan
B._____ EQ Credit 6.1, Controllability of Systems
C._____ EQ Credit 4.1, Low-Emitting Materials
D._____ EQ Credit 7.2, Thermal Comfort
E._____ None of above

585. The project coordinator is investigating the relative humidity ratio control, zone radiant temperature, ASHRAE 55-2004, and planning to submit the result to the USGBC @ design phase. The project coordinator is planning to earn point(s) in which **ONE** of the following credits?

A._____ EQ Credit 1, Outdoor Air Delivery Monitoring
B._____ EQ. Credit 4.1, Low-Emitting Material
C._____ EQ Credit 7.2, Thermal Comfort
D._____ EQ credit 7.1, Thermal Comfort
E._____ None of above

586. The project coordinator is investigating the survey process, ASHRAE 55-2004, and planning to submit the result to the USGBC @ design phase. The project coordinator is planning to earn point(s) in which **ONE** of the following credits?

A._____ EQ Credit 6.2, Controllability of System
B._____ EQ Credit 7.1 Thermal Comfort
C._____ EQ credit 5, Indoor Chemical & Pollutant Source Control
D._____ EQ Credit 2, Increased Ventilation
E._____ None of above

587. The project coordinator is investigating the geometry of building, glazing factor and elevation of exterior window, light shelves, and planning to submit the result to the USGBC @ design phase. The project coordinator is planning to earn point(s) in which **ONE** of the following credits?

A._____ EQ Credit 7.1
B._____ EQ Credit 7.2
C._____ EQ Credit 8.2
D._____ EQ Credit 8.1
E._____ None of above

588. The project coordinator is investigating sight line of building to outdoor, and planning to submit the result to the USGBC @ design phase. The project coordinator is planning to earn point(s) in which **ONE** of the following credits?

A._____ EQ credit 8.1
B._____ EQ Credit 7.2
C._____ EQ Credit 7.1
D._____ EQ Credit 8.2
E._____ None of above

589. For the project planning process, which **TWO** of the following should be addressed during the schematic phase of the project?

A._____ EQ Credits 7.1, 7.2, Thermal Comfort
B._____ EQ Prerequisite 2, Environmental Tobacco Smoke (ETS) Control
C._____ SS Credits 4.2, 4.3, 4.4, Alternative Transportation
D._____ EA Credit 4, Enhanced Refrigerant Management
E._____ SS Credits 5.1, 5.2, Site Development

590. For the project planning process, which **THREE** of the following should be addressed during the schematic phase of the project?

A._____ WE Credits 3.1, 3.2, Water Use Reduction
B._____ EA Credit 5, Measurement & Verification
C._____ SS Credits 7.1, 7.2, Heat Island Effect
D._____ MR Credits 2.1, 2.2, Construction Waste Management
E._____ SS Credit 8, Light Pollution Reduction

591. For the project planning process, which **TWO** of the following should be addressed during the schematic phase of the project?

A._____ EQ Credits 6.1, 6.2, Controllability of Systems
B._____ MR Credits 2.1, 2.2, Construction Waste Management
C._____ WE Credit 2, Innovative Wastewater Technologies
D._____ EA Prerequisite 3, Fundamental Refrigerant Management
E._____ EQ Prerequisite 1, Minimum IAQ Performance

592. For the project planning process, which **THREE** of the following should be addressed during the schematic phase of the project?

A._____ EQ Credits 8.1, 8.2, Daylight & Views
B._____ MR Credits 3.1, 3.2, Material Reuse
C._____ EA Credit 1, Optimize Energy Performance
D._____ EA Credit 4, Enhanced Refrigerant Management
E._____ EA Credit 2, On-Site Renewable Energy

593. For the project planning process, which **TWO** of the following should be addressed during the schematic phase of the project?

A._____ EQ Credit 5, Indoor Chemical & Pollutant Source Control
B._____ SS Credit 2, Development Density & Community Connectivity
C._____ MR Prerequisite 1, Storage & Collection of Recyclables
D._____ EQ prerequisite 2, Environmental Tobacco Smoke (ETS) Control
E._____ MR Credits 4.1, 4.2, 4.3, Recycled Content

594. For the project planning process, which **THREE** of the following should be addressed during the schematic phase of the project?

A._____ EQ Credit 1, Outdoor Air Delivery Monitoring
B._____ EQ Prerequisite 2, Environmental Tobacco Smoke (ETS) Control
C._____ EQ Credit 2, Increased Ventilation
D._____ MR Credits 3.1, 3.2, Material Reuse
E._____ EQ Credits 8.1, 8.2, Daylight & Views

595. For the project planning process, which **THREE** of the following should be addressed during the pre-design phase of the project?

A._____ SS Credit 1, Site Selection
B._____ SS Credits 7.1, 7.2, Heat Island Effect
C._____ SS Credit 2, Development Density & Community Connectivity
D._____ SS Credits 5.1, 5.2, Site Development
E._____ SS Credit 3, Brownfield Redevelopment

596. For the project planning process, which **THREE** of the following should be addressed during the pre-design phase of the project?

A._____ SS Credit 4.1, Alternative Transportation
B._____ EQ Credits 3.1, 3.2, Construction IAQ Management Plan
C._____ MR Credits 1.1, 1.2, 1.3, Building Reuse
D._____ EA Prerequisite 1, Fundamental Commissioning of the Building Energy Systems
E._____ EQ prerequisite 2, Environmental Tobacco Smoke (ETS) Control

597. For the project planning process, which **THREE** of the following should be addressed during the design development phase of the project?

A._____ EA Prerequisite 2, Minimum Energy Performance
B._____ SS Credits 5.1, 5.2, Site Development
C._____ EA Prerequisite 3, Fundamental Refrigerant Management
D._____ WE Credits 3.1, 3.2, Water Use Reduction
E._____ EA Credit 4, Enhanced Refrigerant Management

598. For the project planning process, which **THREE** of the following should be addressed during the design development phase of the project?

A._____ EA Credit 5, Measurement & Verification
B._____ SS Credits 5.1, 5.2, Site Development
C._____ EQ Credits 4.1, 4.3, Low –Emitting Materials
D._____ EQ Credits 8.1, 8.2, Daylight & Views
E._____ EQ Credits 4.2, 4.4, Low-Emitting Materials

599. For the project planning process, which **THREE** of the following should be addressed during the design development phase of the project?

A._____ EQ Credit 5, Indoor Chemical & Pollutant Source Control
B._____ EQ Credits 8.1, 8.2, Daylight & Views
C._____ EQ Credits 6.1, 6.2, Controllability of Systems
D._____ WE Credits 3.1, 3.2, Water Use Reduction
E._____ EQ Credits 7.1, 7.2, Thermal Comfort

600. For the project planning process, which **TWO** of the following should be addressed during the construction document phase of the project?

A._____ MR Credits 2.1, 2.2, Construction Waste Management
B._____ EQ Credits 3.1, 3.2, Construction IAQ Management Plan
C._____ SS Credits 7.1, 7.2, Heat Island Effect
D._____ EA Credit 1, Optimize Energy Performance
E._____ MR Credits 3.1, 3.2, Material Reuse

601. The project coordinator is investigating mulching, temporary seeding, earth dikes, silt fencing, and planning to submit the result to the USGBC @ construction phase. The project coordinator is planning to earn point(s) in which **ONE** of the following credits?

A._____ SS Credit 4.1, Alternative transportation
B._____ SS Credit 3, Brownfield Redevelopment
C._____ SS Credit 4.3, Alternative Transportation
D._____ Not to earn a point - Comply with the SS Prerequisite 1, Construction Activity Pollution Prevention
E._____ None of above

602. The project coordinator is investigating ecosystem, flood plan, delineation, CFR standards, and planning to submit the result to the USGBC @ design phase. The project coordinator is planning to earn point(s) in which **ONE** of the following credits?

A._____ SS Credit 2, Development Density & Community Connectivity
B._____ SS Credit 6.2, Storm Water Design
C._____ SS Credit 4.4, Alternative Transportation
D._____ SS Credit 1, Site Selection
E._____ None of above

603. The project coordinator is investigating channel development to urban areas, property area, parking structures, building services, landfill development, and planning to submit the result to the USGBC @ design phase. The project coordinator is planning to earn point(s) in which **ONE** of the following credits?

A._____ SS Credit 2, Development Density & Community Connectivity
B._____ SS Credit 6.2, Storm Water Design
C._____ SS Credit 4.4, Alternative Transportation
D._____ SS Credit 1, Site Selection
E._____ None of above

604. The project coordinator is investigating site assessment planning, remediation process. CERCLA standards and planning to submit the result to the USGBC @ design phase. The project coordinator is planning to earn point(s) in which **ONE** of the following credits?

A._____ SS Credit 5.1, Site Development
B._____ SS Credit 3, Brownfield Redevelopment
C._____ SS Credit 7.2, Heat Island Effect
D._____ SS Credit 6.1, Strom water Design
E._____ None of above

605. The project coordinator is investigating location of bicycle storages, mass transit, hybrid vehicles, and planning to submit the result to the USGBC @ design phase. The project coordinator is planning to earn point(s) in which **ONE** of the following credits?

A._____ SS Credit 4.4, Alternative Transportation
B._____ SS Credit 7.2, Heat Island Effect
C._____ SS Credit 1, Site Selection
D._____ SS Credit 4.1, 4.2, 4.3, Alternative Transportation
E._____ None of above

606. The project coordinator is investigating number of carpool parking spaces, shared vehicle program, low-emission vehicles, number of building users, and planning to submit the result to the USGBC @ design phase. The project coordinator is planning to earn point(s) in which **ONE** of the following credits?

A._____ SS Credit 4.2, Alternative Transportation
B._____ SS Credit 7.2, Heat Island Effect
C._____ SS Credit 4.4, Alternative Transportation
D._____ SS Credit 7.1, Heat Island Effect
E._____ None of above

607. The project coordinator is investigating site survey, Greenfield sites, building foot print, vegetated roofs, and planning to submit the result to the USGBC @ construction phase. The project coordinator is planning to earn point(s) in which **ONE** of the following credits?

A._____ SS credit 7.1, Heat Island Effect
B._____ SS Credit 5.1, Site Development
C._____ SS Credit 3, Brownfield Redevelopment
D._____ SS Credit 5.2, Site Development
E._____ None of above

608. The project coordinator is investigating project development footprint, courtyards, open space area, local zoning requirements, and planning to submit the result to the USGBC @ design phase. The project coordinator is planning to earn point(s) in which **ONE** of the following credits?

A._____ SS Credit 3, Brownfield Redevelopment
B._____ SS Credit 5.1, Site Development
C._____ EA Credit 2, On-site Renewable Energy
D._____ SS Credit 5.2, Site Development
E._____ None of above

609. The project coordinator is investigating discharge rain factors, impervious surface, watershed, riparian buffers, TRAP standards, and planning to submit the result to the USGBC @ design phase. The project coordinator is planning to earn point(s) in which **ONE** of the following credits?

A._____ SS credit 7.1, Heat Island Effect
B._____ SS Credit 3, Brownfield Redevelopment
C._____ SS Credit 6.2, Storm Water Design
D._____ SS Credit 6.1, Storm Water Design
E._____ None of above

610. The project coordinator is investigating constructed wetland, vegetated infiltration basins, open channels, TSS standards, and planning to submit the result to the USGBC @ design phase. The project coordinator is planning to earn point(s) in which **ONE** of the following credits?

A._____ SS credit 6.2, Storm water Design
B._____ SS Credit 6.1, Strom Water Design
C._____ SS Credit 4.4, Alternative Transportation
D._____ SS Credit 7.2, Heat Island Effect
E._____ None of above

611. The project coordinator is investigating shading factors of glazing areas, Solar Reflectance Index of roofing materials, ASTM standards, and planning to submit the result to the USGBC @ construction phase. The project coordinator is planning to earn point(s) in which **ONE** of the following credits?

A._____ SS Credit 8, Light Pollution Reduction
B._____ SS Credit 6.1, Strom Water Design
C._____ SS Credit 7.1, Heat Island Effect
D._____ SS Credit 3, Brownfield Redevelopment
E._____ None of above

612. The project coordinator is investigating curfew hours, nocturnal environments, tradable surfaces, ASHARE / IESNA standards, and planning to submit the result to the USGBC @ design phase. The project coordinator is planning to earn point(s) in which **ONE** of the following credits?

A._____ SS Credit 7.1, Heat Island Effect
B._____ SS Credit 6.1, Strom Water Design
C._____ SS Credit 7.2, Heat Island Effect
D._____ SS Credit 3, Brownfield Redevelopment
E._____ None of above

613. The project coordinator is investigating adapted plants, reduction of potable water consumption, evapotranspiration rate, micro-irrigation systems, and planning to submit the result to the USGBC @ design phase. the project coordinator is planning to earn point(s) in which **ONE** of the following credits?

A._____ EA Credit 1, Optimize Energy Performance
B._____ EQ Credit 6.2, Controllability of Systems
C._____ WE Credit 2, Innovative Wastewater Technologies
D._____ WE Credit 1, Water Efficient landscaping
E._____ None of above

614. The project coordinator is investigating recovery systems, various treatment methods, biological systems, dry fixtures, rainwater harvesting, and planning to submit the result to the USGBC @ design phase. The project coordinator is planning to earn point(s) in which **ONE** of the following credits?

A._____ WE Credit 1, Water Efficient Landscaping
B._____ EA Credit 5, Measurement & Verification
C._____ EA Credit 1, Optimize Energy Performance
D._____ WE Credit 2, Innovative Wastewater Technologies
E._____ None of above

615. The project coordinator is investigating metering devices, kitchen sink capacity, replacement aerators, energy policy act of 1992, and planning to submit the result to the USGBC @ design phase. The project coordinator is planning to earn point(s) in which **ONE** of the following credits?

A._____ WE credit 2, Innovative Wastewater Technologies
B._____ WE Credit 1, Water Efficient Landscaping
C._____ WE Credit 3.1, Water Use Reduction
D._____ EA Credit 5, Measurement & Verification
E._____ None of above

616. The project coordinator is investigating OPR, BOD, building elements, CxA qualification, and planning to submit the result to the USGBC @ construction phase. The project coordinator is planning to earn point(s) in which **ONE** of the following credits?

A._____ EA Credit 4, Enhanced Refrigerant Management
B._____ EA Credit 5, Measurement & Verification
C._____ No to earn a point - Comply with EA Prerequisite 1, Fundamental Commissioning of The Building Energy System
D._____ EA Credit 3, Enhanced Commissioning
E._____ None of above

617. The project coordinator is investigating building envelope, lighting systems, occupancy rate, performance rating method, and DOE standard. The result will be submitted to the USGBC @ design phase. The project coordinator is planning to earn point(s) in which **ONE** of the following credits?

A._____ EA Credit 5, Measurement and Verification
B._____ EA Credit 1, Optimize Energy Performance
C._____ EA Credit 4, Enhanced Refrigerant Management
D._____ Not to earn a point - Comply with EA prerequisite 2, Minimum energy Performance
E._____ None of above

618. The project coordinator is investigating HVAC equipments, fire suppression system, ultraviolet radiation, ODP, GWP, EPA standards, and planning to submit the result to the USGBC @ design phase. The project coordinator is planning to earn point(s) in which **ONE** of the following credits?

A._____ EA Credit 5, Measurement and Verification
B._____ Not to earn a point- comply with EA Prerequisite 3, Fundamental Refrigerant Management
C._____ EA Credit 3, Enhanced Commissioning
D._____ EA Credit 1, Optimize Energy Performance
E. None of above

619. The project coordinator is investigating baseline models, process energy loads, thermal mass, climate zone standards, ECB regulations, simulation methods, and planning to submit the result to the USGBC @ design phase. The project coordinator is planning to earn point(s) in which **ONE** of the following credits?

A._____ EA Credit 3, Enhanced Commissioning
B._____ EA Credit 5, Measurement & Verification
C._____ EA Credit 2, On-site Renewable Energy
D._____ EA Credit 1, Optimize Energy Performance
E._____ None of above

620. The project coordinator is investigating air leakage factors, air filtration systems, EER, COP, waste heat load factors, Core Performance guidelines, ASHRAE 90.1 standards, and planning to submit the result to the USGBC @ design phase. The project coordinator is planning to earn point(s) in which **ONE** of the following credits?

A._____ EA Credit 3, Enhanced Commissioning
B._____ EA Credit 5, Measurement & Verification
C._____ EA Credit 2, On-site Renewable Energy
D._____ EA Credit 1, Optimize Energy Performance
E._____ None of above

621. The project coordinator investigating regulated energy load, plug loads, SHGC, SC, building orientation, New Building Institute, and planning to submit the result to the USGBC @ design phase. The project coordinator is planning to earn point(s) in which **ONE** of the following credits?

A._____ EA Credit 4, Enhanced Refrigerant Management
B._____ EA credit 1, Optimize Energy Performance
C._____ EA Credit 5, Measurement and Verification
D._____ EA Credit 2, On-site Renewable Energy
E._____ None of above

622. The project coordinator is investigating cogeneration systems, gasification, geo-exchange systems, wind turbines, REC regulations, DOE standards, virtual energy, and planning to submit the result to the USGBC @ design phase. The project coordinator is planning to earn point(s) in which **ONE** of the following credits?

A._____ EA Credit 4, Enhanced Refrigerant Management
B._____ EA credit 1, Optimize Energy Performance
C._____ EA Credit 5, Measurement and Verification
D._____ EA Credit 2, On-site Renewable Energy
E._____ None of above

623. The project coordinator is investigating post-occupancy progress, warranty–end review, independent authority, contractor submittal, and planning to submit the result to the USGBC @ construction phase. The project coordinator is planning to earn point(s) in which **ONE** of the following credits?

A._____ EA Credit 5, Measurement & Verification
B._____ EA credit 1, Optimize Energy Performance
C._____ EA Credit 3, Enhanced Commissioning
D._____ EA Credit 2, On-site Renewable Energy
E._____ None of above

624. The project coordinator is investigating HFC, HCFC. HVAC equipment specifications, life of ice thermal storage units, and planning to submit the result to the USGBC @ design phase. The project coordinator is planning to earn point(s) in which **ONE** of the following credits?

A._____ EA Credit 2, On-site Renewable Energy
B._____ EA Credit 3, Enhanced Commissioning
C._____ EA Credit 5, Measurement & Verification
D._____ EA Credit 4, Enhanced Refrigerant Management
E._____ None of above

625. The project coordinator is investigating utility bills, ECM, statistical sampling, EVO standards, metering device, performance factor, and planning to submit the result to the USGBC @ construction phase. The project coordinator is planning to earn point(s) in which **ONE** of the following credits?

A._____ EA Credit 4, Enhanced Refrigerant Management
B._____ EA Credit 5, Measurement & Verification
C._____ EA Credit 3, Enhanced Commissioning
D._____ EA Credit 1, Optimize Energy Performance
E._____ None of above

626. The project coordinator is investigating solar energy systems, net-zero pollution, geothermal design, electricity bills, CRS standards, and planning to submit the result to the USGBC @ construction phase. The project coordinator is planning to earn point(s) in which **ONE** of the following credits?

A._____ EA Credit 2, On-Site Renewable Energy
B._____ EA Credit 5, Measurement & Verification
C._____ EA Credit 4, Enhanced Refrigerant
D._____ EA Credit 6, Green Power
E._____ None of above

627. The project coordinator is investigating solid waste materials, separation of materials, collection bins, can crusher, and planning to submit the result to the USGBC @ construction phase. The project coordinator is planning to earn point(s) in which **ONE** of the following credits?

A._____ MR Credit 5.1 Regional Materials
B._____ MR Credit 4.2, Recycled Content
C._____ Not to earn a point – Comply with MR Prerequisite 1
D._____ MR Credit 6, Rapidly Renewable Materials
E._____ None of above

628. The project coordinator investigating the volume of non-shell elements, the area of shell elements, the building renovation methods, and planning to submit the result to the USGBC @ construction phase. The project coordinator is planning to earn point(s) in which **ONE** of the following credits?

A._____ MR Credit 2.1, Construction Waste Management
B._____ MR credit 4.1, Recycled Content
C._____ MR Credit 1.1, Building Reuse
D._____ MR Credit 5.2, Regional Materials
E._____ None of above

629. The project coordinator is investigating different construction technologies, tipping fees, solid waste factors, diversion process, salvage systems, and planning to submit the result to the USGBC @ construction phase. The project coordinator is planning to earn point(s) in which **ONE** of the following credits?

A._____ MR Credit 4.1, Recycled Content
B._____ MR Credit 5.1 Regional Materials
C._____ MR Credit 6, Rapidly Renewable Materials
D._____ MR Credit 2.2, Construction Waste Management
E._____ None of above

630. The project coordinator is investigating refurbished materials, LCA, salvaged material life cycle, replacement cost, UBC standards, and planning to submit the result to the USGBC @ construction phase. The project coordinator is planning to earn point(s) in which **ONE** of the following credits?

A._____ MR Credit 5.1 Regional Materials
B._____ MR Credit 4.2, Recycled Content
C._____ MR Credit 3.1, Material Reuse
D._____ MR Credit 6, Rapidly Renewable Materials
E._____ None of above

631. The project coordinator is investigating building life cycle costs, the area of addition to the building, construction cost, salvaged materials, and planning to submit the result to the USGBC @ construction phase. The project coordinator is planning to earn point(s) in which **ONE** of the following credits?

A._____ MR Credit 5.1 Regional Materials
B._____ MR Credit 4.2, Recycled Content
C._____ MR Credit 1.1, Building Reuse
D._____ MR Credit 6, Rapidly Renewable Materials
E._____ None of above

632. The project coordinator is investigating reclaimed materials, cost of materials, on-site processing, post consumer materials, ISO standards, and planning to submit the result to the USGBC @ construction phase. The project coordinator is planning to earn point(s) in which **ONE** of the following credits?

A._____ MR Credit 4.2, Recycled Content
B._____ MR Credit 2.1, Construction Waste Management
C._____ MR Credit 5.1 Regional Materials
D._____ MR Credit 1.1, Building Reuse
E._____ None of above

633. The project coordinator is investigating the cost of recovered materials, the location of final assembly for building materials, the methods of transportation for building materials, pre-consumer products, and planning to submit the result to the USGBC @ construction phase. The project coordinator is planning to earn point(s) in which **ONE** of the following credits?

A._____ MR Credit 2.1, Construction Waste Management
B._____ MR Credit 5.1, Regional Materials
C._____ MR Credit 6, Rapidly Renewable Materials
D._____ MR Credit 4.1, Recycled Content
E._____ None of above

634. The project coordinator is investigating the life cycle of building materials, cotton batt insulation, fine raw materials, wheat board cabinets, and planning to submit the result to the USGBC @ construction phase. The project coordinator is planning to earn point(s) in which **ONE** of the following credits?

A._____ MR credit 5.2, Regional Materials
B._____ MR Credit 4.2, Recycled Content
C._____ MR Credit 1.1, Building Reuse
D._____ MR Credit 6, Rapidly Renewable Materials
E._____ None of above

635. The project coordinator is investigating different land use rights, cost of materials, FSC standards, and planning to submit the result to the USGBC @ construction phase. The project coordinator is planning to earn point(s) in which **ONE** of the following credits?

A._____ MR Credit 7, Certified Wood
B._____ MR Credit 4.2, Recycled Content
C._____ MR Credit 3.2, Material Reuse
D._____ MR Credit 6, Rapidly Renewable Materials
E._____ None of above

636. The project coordinator is investigating flooring materials, supplier certification, the chain-of-custody standards, and planning to submit the result to the USGBC @ construction phase. The project coordinator is planning to earn point(s) in which **ONE** of the following credits?

A._____ MR Credit 5.1 Regional Materials
B._____ MR Credit 4.2, Recycled Content
C._____ MR Credit 7, Certified Wood
D._____ MR Credit 6, Rapidly Renewable Materials
E._____ None of above

637. The project coordinator is investigating passive and active ventilation systems, building pressurization, air filtration system, ASHRAE 62.1 standards, and planning to submit the result to the USGBC @ design phase. The project coordinator is planning to earn point(s) in which **ONE** of the following credits?

A._____ EQ Credit 4.1, Low-Emitting Material
B._____ EQ Credit 1, Outdoor Air Delivery Monitoring
C._____ EQ Credit 6.2, Controllability of Systems
D._____ Not to earn a point – Comply with EQ Prerequisite 1, Minimum IAQ performance
E._____ None of above

638. The project coordinator is investigating fan pressurization test, the negative pressure design for HVAC system, Title 24, 2001 regulation, sampling process, and planning to submit the result to the USGBC @ design phase. The project coordinator is planning to earn point(s) in which **ONE** of the following credits?

A._____ EQ Credit 7.2, Thermal Comfort
B._____ EQ Credit 6.2, Controllability of System
C._____ Not to earn point- Comply with EQ Prerequisite 2, Environmental Tobacco Smoke Control
D._____ EQ Credit 3.1, Construction IAQ Management Plan
E._____ None of above

639. The project coordinator is investigating breathing zones, displacement ventilation design, age of air, CDVR regulations, CIBSE standards, and planning to submit the result to the USGBC @ design phase. The project coordinator is planning to earn point(s) in which **ONE** of the following credits?

A._____ EQ Credit 7.2, Thermal Comfort
B._____ EQ Credit 1, Outdoor Air Delivery Monitoring
C._____ EQ Credit 2, Increased Ventilation
D._____ EQ Credit 6.2, Controllability of System
E._____ None of above

640. The project coordinator is investigating methods of protection for building materials, MERV numbers for air filters, SMACNA standards, and planning to submit the result to the USGBC @ construction phase. The project coordinator is planning to earn point(s) in which **ONE** of the following credits?

A._____ EQ Credit 3.2, Construction IAQ Management Plan
B._____ EQ Credit 4.1, Low-Emitting Materials
C._____ EQ Credit 3.1, Construction IAQ Management Plan
D._____ EQ Credit 7.2, Thermal Comfort
E._____ None of above

641. The project coordinator is investigating house keeping approaches for building materials, final punch list methods, air testing procedures, EPA standards, and planning to submit the result to the USGBC in construction phase. The project coordinator is planning to earn point(s) in which **ONE** of the following credits?

A._____ EQ Credit 1, Outdoor Air Delivery Monitoring
B._____ EQ Credit 3.1, Construction IAQ Management Plan
C._____ EQ Credit 7.2, Thermal Comfort
D._____ EQ Credit 3.2, Construction IAQ Management Plan
E._____ None of above

642. The project coordinator is investigating cross contamination, chemical pollutants, entryway design, ASHRAE 52.2, 1999 and planning to submit the result to the USGBC @ design phase. The project coordinator is planning to earn point(s) in which **ONE** of the following credits?

A._____ EQ credit 5, Indoor Chemical & Pollutant Source Control
B._____ EQ Credit 7.2, Thermal Comfort
C._____ EQ Credit 6.2, Controllability of Systems
D._____ EQ Credit 3.1, Construction IAQ Management Plan
E._____ None of above

643. The project coordinator is investigating lighting control system, non-regulated areas, building wiring system, shared areas, ASHRAE- IESNA 90.1, 2004 standards, and planning to submit the result to the USGBC @ design phase. The project coordinator is planning to earn point(s) in which **ONE** of the following credits?

A._____ EQ Credit 4.1, Low-Emitting Material
B._____ EQ Credit 1, Outdoor Air Delivery Monitoring
C._____ EQ Credit 6.2, Controllability of Systems
D._____ EQ Credit 6.1, Controllability of Systems
E._____ None of above

644. The project coordinator is investigating building dimming controls for lighting systems, occupancy controls, ASHRAE 90.1, 2004 standards, and planning to submit the result to the USGBC @ design phase. The project coordinator is planning to earn point(s) in which **ONE** of the following credits?

A._____ EQ Credit 6.1, Controllability of Systems
B._____ EQ Credit 1, Outdoor Air Delivery Monitoring
C._____ EQ Credit 6.2, Controllability of Systems
D._____ EQ Credit 7.2, Thermal Comfort
E._____ None of above

645. The project coordinator is investigating thermal system, operable windows, ventilation design, ASHARE 55-2004, and planning to submit the result to the USGBC @ design phase. The project coordinator is planning to earn point(s) in which **ONE** of the following credits?

A._____ EQ Credit 3.2, Construction IAQ Management Plan
B._____ EQ Credit 6.2, Controllability of Systems
C._____ EQ Credit 4.1, Low-Emitting Materials
D._____ EQ Credit 7.2, Thermal Comfort
E._____ None of above

646. The project coordinator is investigating PMV models, humidification process, air movement design, ASHRAE 55-2004, and planning to submit the result to the USGBC @ design phase. The project coordinator is planning to earn point(s) in which **ONE** of the following credits?

A._____ EQ Credit 1, Outdoor Air Delivery Monitoring
B._____ EQ. Credit 4.1, Low-Emitting Material
C._____ EQ Credit 7.2, Thermal Comfort
D._____ EQ credit 7.1, Thermal Comfort
E._____ None of above

647. The project coordinator is investigating post occupancy survey method, corrective action for the building systems, verification process, ASHRAE 55-2004, and planning to submit the result to the USGBC @ design phase. The project coordinator is planning to earn point(s) in which **ONE** of the following credits?

A._____ EQ Credit 6.2, Controllability of System
B._____ EQ Credit 7.2, Thermal Comfort
C._____ EQ credit 5, Indoor Chemical & Pollutant Source Control
D._____ EQ Credit 2, Increased Ventilation
E._____ None of above

648. The project coordinator is investigating diffused lighting design, visible light transmittance, illumination levels, NFRC standards, and planning to submit the result to the USGBC @ design phase. The project coordinator is planning to earn point(s) in which **ONE** of the following credits?

A._____ EQ Credit 7.1
B._____ EQ Credit 7.2
C._____ EQ Credit 8.2
D._____ EQ Credit 8.1
E._____ None of above

649. The project coordinator is investigating sloped sills, seating area elevation, section views of the building sight lines, and planning to submit the result to the USGBC @ design phase. The project coordinator is planning to earn point(s) in which **ONE** of the following credits?

A._____ EQ credit 8.1
B._____ EQ Credit 7.2
C._____ EQ Credit 7.1
D._____ EQ Credit 8.2
E._____ None of above

650. The project coordinator is investigating the following subjects:

- Certified wood
- Optimize Energy Performance
- Recycled Content

Which **THREE** of the following standards or regulations may apply to the above mentioned subjects?

A._____ FSC
B._____ DOE
C._____ New Building Institute
D._____ EPA
E._____ ISO

651. The project coordinator is investigating the following subjects:

- Optimize Energy Performance
- Controllability of System- lighting
- Light Pollution Reduction

Which **THREE** of the following standards or regulations may apply to the above mentioned subjects?

A._____ Advanced Building Bench Mark 1.1 Method
B._____ CFR
C._____ ASHRAE / IESNA 90.1, 2004
D._____ EIA
E._____ ANSI

652. The project coordinator is investigating the following subjects:

- Light Pollution Reduction
- Optimize Energy Performance
- Environmental Tobacco Smoke Control

Which **THREE** of the following standards or regulations may apply to the above mentioned subjects?

A._____ ASHRAE / IESNA 90.1, 2004
B._____ Energy Policy Act 1992
C._____ ASHRAE 2004 Prescriptive Method
D._____ FEMA
E._____ ANSI

653. The project coordinator is investigating the following subjects:

- Construction IAQ Management Plan- before occupancy
- Indoor Chemical & Pollutant Source Control
- Fundamental Refrigerant Management

Which **THREE** of the following standards or regulations may apply to the above mentioned subjects?

A._____ EPA
B._____ FSC
C._____ ASHRAE 52.2, 1999
D._____ ISO
E._____ Montreal Protocol 1987

654. The project coordinator is investigating the following subjects:

- Strom Water Design
- Recycled Content
- Construction IAQ Management Plan- during construction

Which **THREE** of the following standards or regulations may apply to the above mentioned subjects?

A._____ EPA
B._____ New Building Institute
C._____ ISO
D._____ Montreal Protocol 1987
E._____ ASHRAE 52.2, 1999

655. The project coordinator is investigating the following subjects:

- Controllability of Systems
- Measurement & Verification
- Enhanced Refrigerant Management

Which **THREE** of the following standards or regulations may apply to the above mentioned subjects?

A._____ ASHRAE 55.2004
B._____ ISO
C._____ IPMVP
D._____ CIWMB 1999
E._____ EPA

656. The project coordinator is investigating the following subjects:

- Storm Water Design
- Site Selection for flood
- Thermal Comfort - design

Which **THREE** of the following standards or regulations may apply to the above mentioned subjects?

A._____ EPA
B._____ CRS
C._____ FEMA
D._____ ASTM
E._____ ASHRAE 55.2004

657. The project coordinator is investigating the following subjects:

- Site Selection
- Certified Wood
- Fundamental Refrigerant Management

Which **THREE** of the following standards or regulations may apply to the above mentioned subjects?

A._____ CFR
B._____ Green Label
C._____ FSC
D._____ Energy Policy Act 1992
E._____ EPA

658. The project coordinator is investigating the following subjects:

- Low-Emitting Materials – Adhesives & Sealants
- Thermal Comfort (Verification)
- Measurement & Verification

Which **THREE** of the following standards or regulations may apply to the above mentioned subjects?

A._____ Green Seal
B._____ IPMVP
C._____ ASHRAE 55.2004
D._____ New Building Institute
E._____ EVO

659. The project coordinator is investigating the following subjects:

- Low-Emitting Materials- Paints & Coatings
- Outdoor Air Delivery Monitoring
- Brownfield Redevelopment

Which **THREE** of the following standards or regulations may apply to the above mentioned subjects?

A._____ Green Seal
B._____ ISO
C._____ ASHRAE 62.1, 2004
D._____ FSC
E._____ EPA

660. The project coordinator is investigating the following subjects:

- Minimum IAQ Performance
- Increased Ventilation
- Materials Reuse

Which **THREE** of the following standards or regulations may apply to the above mentioned subjects?

A._____ ASHRAE 62.1, 2004
B._____ NPDES
C._____ CIBSE
D._____ Oregon Zoning Code
E._____ LCA

661. The project coordinator is investigating the following subjects:

- Storage & Collection of Recyclables
- Minimum Energy Performance
- Increase Ventilation

Which **THREE** of the following standards or regulations may apply to the above mentioned subjects?

A._____ CIWMB 1999
B._____ Oregon Zoning Code
C._____ DOE
D._____ NPDES
E._____ ASHRAE 62.1, 2004

662. The project coordinator is investigating the following subjects:

- Controllability of Systems (thermal comfort)
- Brownfield Redevelopment
- Green Power

Which **THREE** of the following standards or regulations may apply to the above mentioned subjects?

A._____ ASHRAE 62.1, 2004
B._____ USAD
C._____ CERCLA
D._____ The Institute of transportation Engineers
E._____ CBECS

663. The project coordinator is investigating the following subjects:

- Brownfield Redevelopment
- Enhanced Refrigerant Management
- Environmental Tobacco Smoke Control

Which **THREE** of the following standards or regulations may apply to the above mentioned subjects?

A._____ ASTM
B._____ IPMVP
C._____ Clean Air Act 1990
D._____ FSC
E._____ California Energy Code, Title 24, 2001

664. The project coordinator is investigating the following subjects:

- On-Site Renewable Energy
- Green Power
- On-site Renewable Energy

Which **THREE** of the following standards or regulations may apply to the above mentioned subjects?

A._____ CBECS
B._____ FEMA
C._____ CRS
D._____ CFR
E._____ REC

665. The project coordinator is investigating the following subjects:

- Construction Activity Pollution Prevention
- Heat Island Effect (roof and no-roof)
- On-site Renewable Energy

Which **THREE** of the following standards or regulations may apply to the above mentioned subjects?

A._____ EPA
B._____ ANSI
C._____ ASTM
D._____ BMP
E._____ DOE

666. The project coordinator is investigating the following subjects:

- On-Site renewable Energy
- Light Pollution Reduction
- Water Use Reduction

Which **THREE** of the following standards or regulations may apply to the above mentioned subjects?

A._____ EIA
B._____ BMP
C._____ California Energy Code , Title 24, 2001
D._____ ASTM
E._____ Energy Policy Act 1992

667. The project coordinator is investigating the following subjects:

- Low- emitting Materials- carpet systems
- Green Power
- Environmental Tabasco Smoke Control

Which **THREE** of the following standards or regulations may apply to the above mentioned subjects?

A._____ California Department Health Services
B._____ EPA
C._____ DOE
D._____ CFR
E._____ ASTM

668. The project coordinator is investigating the following subjects:

- Storm Water Design
- Optimize Energy Performance
- Daylight & Views

Which **THREE** of the following standards or regulations may apply to the above mentioned subjects?

A._____ BMP
B._____ CFR
C._____ New Building Institute
D._____ DOE
E._____ NFRC

669. The project coordinator is investigating the following subjects:

- Optimize Energy Performance
- Construction Activity Pollution
- Alternative Transportation – Parking Capacity

Which **THREE** of the following standards or regulations may apply to the above mentioned subjects?

A._____ New Building Institute
B._____ EPA
C._____ NPDES
D._____ EIA
E._____ Oregon Zoning Code

670. The project coordinator is investigating the following subjects:

- Construction Activity Pollution
- Alternative Transportation – Parking Capacity
- Low-Emitting Materials – Adhesives & Sealants

Which **THREE** of the following standards or regulations may apply to the above mentioned subjects?

A._____ NPDES
B._____ Green Seal
C._____ The Institute of Transportation Engineers
D._____ FSC
E._____ SCAQMD

671. The project coordinator is investigating the following subjects:

- Construction IAQ Management Plan- During Construction
- Recycled Content
- Site Selection

Which **THREE** of the following standards or regulations may apply to the above mentioned subjects?

A._____ SMACNA
B._____ IPMVP
C._____ ISO
D._____ Montreal Protocol 1987
E._____ USAD

672. The owner of project is evaluating to implement the following concepts:

- Construction Activity pollution Prevention
- Site Selection
- Development Density & Community Connectivity

Which **THREE** of the following team members could help the owner to make the final decision?

A._____ Civil Engineers
B._____ Architects
C._____ Contractors
D._____ MEP Engineers
E._____ LEEP AP

673. The owner of project is evaluating to implement the following concepts:

- Brownfield Redevelopment
- Alternative Transportation, Public Transportation
- Site Development

Which **THREE** of the following team members could help the owner to make the final decision?

A._____ Civil Engineers
B._____ MEP Engineers
C._____ LEED AP
D._____ Architects
E._____ Contractors

674. The owner of project is evaluating to implement the following concepts:

- Alternative Transportation, Parking Capacity
- Heat Island Effect - Roof
- Light Pollution Reduction

Which **THREE** of the following team members could help the owner to make the final decision?

A._____ Civil Engineers
B._____ MEP Engineers
C._____ Contractors
D._____ MEP Engineers
E._____ LEEP AP

675. The owner of project is evaluating to implement the following concepts:

- Storm Water Design
- Heat Island Effect –Non roof
- Light Pollution Reduction

Which **THREE** of the following team members could help the owner to make the final decision?

A._____ Civil Engineers
B._____ MEP Engineers
C._____ Landscape Architects
D._____ Architects
E._____ LEEP AP

676. The owner of project is evaluating to implement the following concepts:

- Water Efficient Landscaping
- Innovative Wastewater Technologies
- Water Use Reduction

Which **TWO** of the following team members could help the owner to make the final decision?

A._____ Landscape Architect
B._____ Civil Engineers
C._____ MEP Engineers
D._____ Contractor
E._____ Architect

677. The owner of project is evaluating to implement the following concepts:

- Minimum Energy Performance
- Fundamental Refrigerant Management
- Optimize Energy Performance

Which **THREE** of the following team members could help the owner to make the final decision?

A._____ Mechanical Engineers
B._____ Civil Engineers
C._____ Electrical Engineers
D._____ Contractors
E._____ Plumbing Engineers

678. The owner of project is evaluating to implement the following concepts:

- On-site Renewable Energy
- Enhanced Commissioning
- Enhanced Refrigerant Management

Which **THREE** of the following team members could help the owner to make the final decision?

A._____ Mechanical Engineers
B._____ Architects
C._____ Electrical Engineers
D._____ Civil Engineers
E._____ Contractor

679. The owner of project is evaluating to implement the following concepts:

- Measurement & Verification
- Recycled Content
- Certified Wood

Which **THREE** of the following team members could help the owner to make the final decision?

A._____ MEP Engineers
B._____ Contractors
C._____ Architects
D._____ Civil Engineers
E._____ LEED AP

680. The owner of project is evaluating to implement the following concepts:

- Construction IAQ Management Plan
- Low-Emitting Materials
- Controllability of Systems

Which **THREE** of the following team members could help the owner to make the final decision?

A._____ Contractors
B._____ MEP Engineers
C._____ Civil engineers
D._____ LEED AP
E._____ Architect

681. The owner of project is evaluating to implement the following concepts:

- Increased Ventilation
- Rapidly Renewable Materials
- Low-emitting Material

Which **THREE** of the following team members could help the owner to make the final decision?

A._____ Contractors
B._____ Architects
C._____ MEP Engineers
D._____ Owner
E._____ Civil Engineers

682. The owner of project is evaluating to implement the following concepts:

- Indoor Chemical & Pollutant Source Control
- Green Power
- Construction Waste Management

Which **THREE** of the following team members could help the owner to make the final decision?

A._____ LEED AP
B._____ Contractors
C._____ Civil Engineers
D._____ MEP Engineers
E._____ Architects

683. The owner of project is evaluating to implement the following concepts:

- Building Reuse
- Storage & Collection of Recyclables
- Regional Materials

Which **TWO** of the following team members could help the owner to make the final decision?

A._____ Contractors
B._____ Architects
C._____ LEED AP
D._____ MEP Engineers
E._____ Civil Engineers

684. The owner of project is evaluating to implement the following concepts:

- Material Reuse
- Thermal Comfort
- Minimum IAQ Performance

Which **THREE** of the following team members could help the owner to make the final decision?

A._____ Contractors
B._____ LEED AP
C._____ Architects
D._____ Civil Engineers
E._____ MEP Engineers

685. The owner of project is evaluating to implement the following concepts:

- Environmental Tobacco Smoke Control
- Thermal Comfort
- Outdoor Air Delivery Monitoring

Which **THREE** of the following team members could help the owner to make the final decision?

A._____ MEP Engineers
B._____ LEED AP
C._____ Civil Engineers
D._____ Architects
E._____ Building Management

686. The owner of project is evaluating to implement the following concepts:

- Water Efficient Landscaping
- Innovative Wastewater Technologies
- Water Use Reduction

Which **TWO** of the following team members could help the owner to make the final decision?

A._____ MEP engineers
B._____ Inspector
C._____ Civil Engineers
D._____ Landscape Architect
E._____ Contractors

687. The owner of project is evaluating to implement the following concepts:

- Daylight & Views
- Building Reuse
- Green Power

Which **THREE** of the following team members could help the owner to make the final decision?

A._____ LEED AP
B._____ Contractor
C._____ Architect
D._____ MEP Engineers
E._____ Civil Engineers

688. Which **THREE** of the following may apply to SS Credit 5.1, Site Development credit?

A._____ Vegetated land
B._____ Impervious area
C._____ Annual storm water runoff
D._____ Ecosystem
E._____ Greenfield sites

689. Which **THREE** of the following may apply to SS Credit 5.2, Site Development credit?

A._____ Open space
B._____ Alternative surface
C._____ Wet land
D._____ Building footprint
E._____ Local code

690. Which **THREE** of the following may apply to SS Credit 6.2, Quality Control credit?

A._____ Mechanical treatment
B._____ Pre-development
C._____ Post development
D._____ Natural treatment
E._____ Annual storm water runoff

691. Which **THREE** of the following may apply to EQ Credit 4.4, Low-Emitting Materials credit?

A._____ Agrifiber board
B._____ SCAQMD
C._____ Composite wood
D._____ ASHRAE
E._____ Urea-formaldehyde resins

692. Which **THREE** of the following may apply to SS Credit 4.4, Alternative Transportation credit?

A._____ Low emission cars
B._____ Carpool parking spaces
C._____ Local code
D._____ Bicycle racks
E._____ Shared vehicle program

693. Which **ONE** of the following credits may apply to the Predicted Mean Vote Model?

A._____ EQ Credit 6.1, Controllability of Systems
B._____ EQ Credit 2, Increased Ventilation
C._____ EQ Credit 7.1, Thermal Comfort
D._____ EQ 8.1, Daylight & Views
E._____ None of above

694. The owner is interested to accomplish the following goals for his/ her next project:

- Reduce pollution from construction site
- Reduce environmental impact at the site
- Create high ratio of open space

Which **THREE** of the following credits and standards may assist the owner to achieve his / her sustainable goals?

A._____ SS P.1
B._____ SS 4.1
C._____ SS 1
D._____ SS 5.1
E._____ SS 5.2

695. The owner is interested to accomplish the following goals for his/ her next project:

- Avoid development of inappropriate sites
- Conserve natural areas
- Limit the disruption of natural hydrology

Which **THREE** of the following credits and standards may assist the owner to achieve his / her sustainable goals?

A._____ SS 5.1
B._____ SS 2
C._____ SS 1
D._____ SS 3
E._____ SS 6.1

696. The owner is interested to accomplish the following goals for his/ her next project:

- Promote biodiversity
- Remove pollutants from storm water runoff
- Reduce impervious cove

Which **THREE** of the following credits and standards may assist the owner to achieve his / her sustainable goals?

A._____ SS 5.1
B._____ SS 7.1
C._____ SS 6.2
D._____ SS 4.1
E._____ SS 6.1

697. The owner is interested to accomplish the following goals for his/ her next project:

- Reduce land development required fro auto use
- Reduce burden on municipal water
- Increase on-site infiltration

Which **THREE** of the following credits and standards may assist the owner to achieve his / her sustainable goals?

A._____ SS 4.1
B._____ WE 2
C._____ WE 3.2
D._____ SS 5.1
E._____ SS 6.1

698. The owner is interested to accomplish the following goals for his/ her next project:

- Provide channel development within existing infrastructure
- Reduce burden on waste water system
- Reduce heat islands

Which **THREE** of the following credits and standards may assist the owner to achieve his / her sustainable goals?

A._____ SS 2
B._____ WE 2
C._____ WE 3.1
D._____ WE 1.3
E._____ SS 7.1

699. The owner is interested to accomplish the following goals for his/ her next project:

- Reduce generation of wastewater
- Establish minimum level of energy standards
- Manage storm water runoff

Which **THREE** of the following credits and standards may assist the owner to achieve his / her sustainable goals?

A._____ WE 2
B._____ WE 1.1
C._____ EA P.2
D._____ EA P.1
E._____ SS 6.1

700. The owner is interested to accomplish the following goals for his/ her next project:

- Minimize the impact on wildlife habitat
- Rehabilitate damaged sites
- Reduce pollution generated for auto use

Which **THREE** of the following credits and standards may assist the owner to achieve his / her sustainable goals?

A._____ SS 7.2
B._____ SS 6.1
C._____ SS 3
D._____ SS 5.1
E._____ SS 4.2

701. The owner is interested to accomplish the following goals for his/ her next project:

- Maximize water efficiency
- Reduce and eliminate water pollution
- Reduce sky-glow

Which **THREE** of the following credits and standards may assist the owner to achieve his / her sustainable goals?

A._____ WE 3.1
B._____ WE 2
C._____ SS 6.1
D._____ SS 5
E._____ SS 8

702. The owner is interested to accomplish the following goals for his/ her next project:

- Reduce pollution generated for auto use
- Minimize light trespass from building and project site
- Reduce pressure on undeveloped land

Which **THREE** of the following credits and standards may assist the owner to achieve his / her sustainable goals?

A._____ SS 4.1
B._____ SS 6.1
C._____ SS 8
D._____ SS 5.1
E._____ SS 3

703. The owner is interested to accomplish the following goals for his/ her next project:

- Restore damaged sites
- Offset building energy cost
- Reduce ozone layer issues

Which **THREE** of the following credits and standards may assist the owner to achieve his / her sustainable goals?

A._____ SS 5.1
B._____ EA 1
C._____ EA 2
D._____ EA P.2
E._____ EA P.3

704. The owner is interested to accomplish the following goals for his/ her next project:

- Reduce land development required by auto use
- Verify mechanical system is installed per plan
- Use renewable energy based on net-zero pollution standards

Which **THREE** of the following credits and standards may assist the owner to achieve his / her sustainable goals?

A._____ SS 4.1
B._____ EA 2
C._____ EA P.1
D._____ SS 3.1
E._____ EA 6

705. The owner is interested to accomplish the following goals for his/ her next project:

- Increase on-site infiltration
- Obtain habitat spaces
- Reduce site development on nocturnal condition

Which **THREE** of the following credits and standards may assist the owner to achieve his / her sustainable goals?

A._____ SS 6.1
B._____ SS 4.1
C._____ SS 5.1
D._____ SS 3
E._____ SS 8

706. The owner is interested to accomplish the following goals for his/ her next project:

- Increase the level of energy performance
- Increase job demand within the region
- Reduce waste hauled in landfill

Which **THREE** of the following credits and standards may assist the owner to achieve his / her sustainable goals?

A._____ EA 1
B._____ MR 4
C._____ MR 5.1
D._____ M 6
E._____ MR P.1

707. The owner is interested to accomplish the following goals for his/ her next project:

- Reduce ODP and GWP
- Measure building energy consumption
- Reduce excessive energy use

Which **THREE** of the following credits and standards may assist the owner to achieve his / her sustainable goals?

A._____ EA 4
B._____ EA 2
C._____ EA 5
D._____ EA P.1
E._____ EA 1

708. The owner is interested to accomplish the following goals for his/ her next project:

- Reduce waste generated by occupants
- Reuse long cycle materials
- Use materials with recycled content

Which **THREE** of the following credits and standards may assist the owner to achieve his / her sustainable goals?

A._____ MR P.1
B._____ MR 1.2
C._____ MR 6
D._____ MR 3.2
E._____ MR 4.2

709. The owner is interested to accomplish the following goals for his/ her next project:

- Extend life cycle of existing buildings
- Reduce impact on fuel energy use
- Reduce waste disposed of in landfills

Which **THREE** of the following credits and standards may assist the owner to achieve his / her sustainable goals?

A._____ MR 1.1
B._____ MR 3.2
C._____ EA 2
D._____ EA 4
E._____ MR P.1

710. The owner is interested to accomplish the following goals for his/ her next project:

- Provide accessible area for collection of recyclable materials at the site
- Use indigenous resources
- Increase on-site renewable energy

Which **THREE** of the following credits and standards may assist the owner to achieve his / her sustainable goals?

A._____ MR P.1
B._____ MR 6
C._____ MR 5.2
D._____ EA 3
E._____ EA 2

711. The owner is interested to accomplish the following goals for his/ her next project:

- Reduce the use of finite raw materials
- Improve indoor air quality during construction phase
- Sustain well being for building occupants

Which **THREE** of the following credits and standards may assist the owner to achieve his / her sustainable goals?

A._____ MR 6
B._____ MR 4.1
C._____ EQ 3.1
D._____ EQ P1
E._____ EQ 1

712. The owner is interested to accomplish the following goals for his/ her next project:

- Reduce environmental impacts on new buildings
- Provide comfort zone for construction team during the construction phase
- Increase ventilation rate in the building

Which **THREE** of the following credits and standards may assist the owner to achieve his / her sustainable goals?

A._____ MR 1.2
B._____ EQ 4.2
C._____ EQ 3.1
D._____ MR 7
E._____ EQ 2

713. The owner is interested to accomplish the following goals for his/ her next project:

- Encourage forest management program
- Monitor ventilation system by CO2 sensors
- Reduce harmful airborne containments in air

Which **THREE** of the following credits and standards may assist the owner to achieve his / her sustainable goals?

A._____ MR 7
B._____ MR 5.2
C._____ EQ 1
D._____ EQ P1
E._____ EQ 4.2

714. The owner is interested to accomplish the following goals for his/ her next project:

- Provide additional outdoor air ventilation system
- Reduce odorous and irritating contaminates in air
- Protect HVAC units during the construction phase

Which **THREE** of the following credits and standards may assist the owner to achieve his / her sustainable goals?

A._____ EQ 2
B._____ EQ 6.1
C._____ EQ 4.1
D._____ EQ 7.2
E._____ EQ 3.1

715. The owner is interested to accomplish the following goals for his/ her next project:

- Avoid any constraints for transporting materials to the site
- Establish minimum requirements for indoor air quality
- Redirect recyclable materials to manufacture

Which **THREE** of the following credits and standards may assist the owner to achieve his / her sustainable goals?

A._____ MR 1.3
B._____ EQ P2
C._____ EQ P1
D._____ MR 4.2
E._____ MR 2.2

716. The owner is interested to accomplish the following goals for his/ her next project:

- Redirect reusable material to the site
- Retain Cultural resource
- Minimize the exposure of building occupants to Tobacco smoke

Which **THREE** of the following credits and standards may assist the owner to achieve his / her sustainable goals?

A._____ MR 2.2
B._____ MR 6
C._____ MR 1.2
D._____ EQ P1
E._____ EQ P2

717. The owner is interested to accomplish the following goals for his/ her next project:

- Reduce the processing of virgin materials
- Reduce impact of extraction process
- Divert debris from disposal in landfills

Which **THREE** of the following credits and standards may assist the owner to achieve his / her sustainable goals?

A._____ MR 3.2
B._____ MR 5.2
C._____ MR 4.1
D._____ MR 6
E._____ MR 2.1

718. The owner is interested to accomplish the following goals for his/ her next project:

- Provide high level of thermal comfort for each occupant
- Promote productivity in space
- Minimize the exposure of hazardous particulates and chemical pollutants

Which **THREE** of the following credits and standards may assist the owner to achieve his / her sustainable goals?

A._____ EQ 6.2
B._____ EQ 8.1
C._____ EQ 7.2
D._____ EQ 8.2
E._____ EQ 5

719. The owner is interested to accomplish the following goals for his/ her next project:

- Provide high level of lighting control for each occupant
- Introduce views into the occupied space
- Connect indoor space and outdoor space for building occupants

Which **THREE** of the following credits and standards may assist the owner to achieve his / her sustainable goals?

A._____ EQ 6.1
B._____ EQ 6.2
C._____ EQ 8.2
D._____ EQ 5
E._____ EQ 8.1

720. The owner is interested to accomplish the following goals for his/ her next project:

- Promote productivity and comfort for building occupants
- Introduce daylight into the occupied space
- Monitor ventilation system by CO2 sensors

Which **THREE** of the following credits and standards may assist the owner to achieve his / her sustainable goals?

A._____ EQ 6.1
B._____ EQ P1
C._____ EQ 8.1
D._____ EQ 7.2
E._____ EQ 1

721. Insulation of building materials is mostly linked to which **THREE** of the followings LEED categories?

A._____ Energy & Atmosphere
B._____ Materials & Resources
C._____ Innovation & Design
D._____ Indoor Environmental Quality
E._____ Sustainable Sites

722. Green roof design is mostly linked to which **THREE** of the followings LEED categories?

A._____ Materials & Resources
B._____ Energy & Atmosphere
C._____ Sustainable Sites
D._____ Water efficiency
E._____ Innovation & Design

723. Daylight zoning is mostly linked to which **TWO** of the followings LEED categories?

A._____ Innovation & Design Process
B._____ Water Efficiency
C._____ Indoor Environmental Quality
D._____ Energy & Atmosphere
E._____ Sustainable Sites

724. Light shelves are <u>mostly</u> linked to which **<u>TWO</u>** of the followings LEED categories?

A._____ Sustainable Sites
B._____ Energy & Atmosphere
C._____ Materials & Resources
D._____ Indoor Environmental Quality
E._____ Innovation & Design Process

725. Active solar energy systems are <u>mostly</u> linked to which **<u>ONE</u>** of the followings LEED categories?

A._____ Innovation & Design Process

B._____ Indoor Environmental Quality
C._____ Sustainable Sites
D._____ Energy & Environment
E._____ None of above

726. Micro-hydro turbines are <u>mostly</u> linked to which **<u>TWO</u>** of the followings LEED categories?

A._____ Innovation & Design Process
B._____ Indoor Environmental Quality
C. Energy & Atmosphere
D._____ Sustainable Sites
E._____ Water Efficiency

727. Ground source heat pumps are <u>mostly</u> linked to which **<u>TWO</u>** of the followings LEED categories?

A._____ Indoor Environmental Quality
B._____ Innovation & Design Process
C._____ Sustainable Sites
D._____ Energy & Atmosphere
E._____ Water Efficiency

728. Stack ventilation systems are <u>mostly</u> linked to which **<u>THREE</u>** of the followings LEED categories?

A._____ Energy & Atmosphere
B._____ Indoor Environmental Quality
C._____ Sustainable Sites
D._____ Water Efficiency
E._____ Innovation & Design Process

729. Plug load design and calculation are <u>mostly</u> linked to which **<u>TWO</u>** of the followings LEED categories are linked to the?

A._____ Innovation & Design Process
B._____ Water Efficiency
C._____ Indoor Environmental Quality
D._____ Energy & Atmosphere
E._____ Sustainable Sites

730. Photovoltaic systems are <u>mostly</u> linked to which **<u>TWO</u>** of the following LEED categories?

A._____ Energy & Atmosphere
B.____ Indoor Environmental Quality
C._____ Sustainable Sites
D._____ Water Efficiency
E._____ Innovation & Design Process

731. Energy recovery systems are <u>mostly</u> linked to which **<u>THREE</u>** of the followings LEED categories?

A._____ Energy & Atmosphere
B.____ Indoor Environmental Quality
C._____ Water Efficiency
D._____ Sustainable Sites
E._____ Innovation & Design Process

732. Slide lighting systems are <u>mostly</u> linked to which **<u>TWO</u>** of the following LEED categories?

A._____ Energy & Atmosphere
B._____ Materials & Resources
C._____ Innovation & Design
D._____ Indoor Environmental Quality
E._____ Sustainable Sites

733. Ground source heat pump units are <u>mostly</u> linked to which **<u>TWO</u>** of the following LEED categories?

A._____ Energy & Atmosphere
B._____ Materials & Resources
C._____ Innovation & Design
D._____ Indoor Environmental Quality
E._____ Sustainable Sites

734. Cross ventilation systems are mostly linked to which **TWO** of the following LEED categories?

A._____ Energy & Atmosphere
B._____ Materials & Resources
C._____ Innovation & Design
D._____ Indoor Environmental Quality
E._____ Sustainable Sites

735. Stack ventilation systems are mostly linked to which **THREE** of the followings LEED categories?

A._____ Energy & Atmosphere
B._____ Materials & Resources
C._____ Innovation & Design
D._____ Indoor Environmental Quality
E._____ Sustainable Sites

736. Earth sheltering systems are NOT linked to which **ONE** of the followings LEED categories?

A._____ Energy & Atmosphere
B. Materials & Resources
C._____ Water Efficiency
D._____ Indoor Environmental Quality
E._____ Sustainable Sites

737. Air to air heat exchanger units are mostly linked to which **THREE** of the followings LEED categories?

A._____ Energy & Atmosphere
B._____ Materials & Resources
C._____ Innovation & Design
D._____ Indoor Environmental Quality
E._____ Sustainable Sites

738. Wind turbines are mostly linked to which **ONE** of the followings LEED categories?

A._____ Energy & Atmosphere
B._____ Materials & Resources
C._____ Innovation & Design
D._____ Indoor Environmental Quality
E._____ Sustainable Sites

739. Compositing toilets are <u>mostly</u> linked to which **<u>ONE</u>** of the followings LEED categories?

A._____ Energy & Atmosphere
B._____ Materials & Resources
C._____ Water Efficiency
D._____ Indoor Environmental Quality
E._____ Sustainable Sites

740. Water catchments are NOT linked to which **<u>ONE</u>** of the followings LEED categories?

A._____ Energy & Atmosphere
B._____ Materials & Resources
C._____ Innovation & Design
D._____ Indoor Environmental Quality
E._____ Sustainable Sites

741. Pervious surfaces are <u>mostly</u> linked to which **<u>TWO</u>** of the followings LEED categories?

A._____ Energy & Atmosphere
B._____ Materials & Resources
C._____ Innovation & Design
D._____ Indoor Environmental Quality
E._____ Sustainable Sites

742. Bio-swales are <u>mostly</u> linked to which **<u>TWO</u>** of the followings LEED categories?

A._____ Water Efficiency
B._____ Materials & Resources
C._____ Innovation & Design
D._____ Indoor Environmental Quality
E._____ Sustainable Sites

743. Top lighting systems are <u>mostly</u> linked to which **<u>TWO</u>** of the followings LEED categories?

A._____ Energy & Atmosphere
B._____ Materials & Resources
C._____ Innovation & Design
D._____ Indoor Environmental Quality
E._____ Sustainable Sites

744. Electrical lighting fixtures are mostly linked to which **TWO** of the following LEED categories?

A._____ Energy & Atmosphere
B._____ Materials & Resources
C._____ Innovation & Design
D._____ Indoor Environmental Quality
E._____ Sustainable Sites

745. How much the implementation of commissioning process often improves the energy efficiency of buildings?

A._____ 10% to 12 %
B._____ 15 % to 18 %
C._____ 5 % to 10 %
D._____ 2 % to 5 %
E._____ None of above

746. Which **ONE** of the following is NOT included in Section 7 of ASHRAE/IESNA 60.1-2004, Section 6 component?

A._____ Parking garage ventilation
B._____ Freeze protection
C._____ Thermal storage
D._____ Service water heating
E._____ Exhaust air recovery

747. Which **ONE** of the following buildings may refer to ASHRAE/IESNA 90.1-2004 standards?

A._____ Low rise residential building
B._____ Single family home
C._____ Multi – family structures of four habitable stories
D._____ Manufactured homes
E._____ None of above

748. Which **ONE** of the following reports is required when the credit is being sought under EA Credit 1 and the owner is planning to use Performance Compliance Approach per ASHRAE/IESNA 90.1, 2004 Standards?

A._____ Performance Cast Report
B._____ Energy Rating Report
C._____ Performance Rating Report
D._____ Energy Baseline Compliance Report
E._____ Energy Cost Budget Compliance Report

749. Which **ONE** of the following is NOT required for mandatory measures of ASHRAE/IESNA 90.1, 2004 standards in EA Prerequisite 2, Minimum Energy Performance?

A._____ Building Envelope Compliance Documentation
B._____ HVAC Compliance Documentation
C._____ Lighting Compliance Documentation
D._____ Sprinkler System Compliance Documentation.
E._____ Service Water Heating Compliance Documentation

750. Which **THREE** of following documentations are required for Prescriptive Requirements of ASHRAE/IESNA 90.1 standard in EA Prerequisite 2, Minimum Energy Performance?

A._____ Building Envelope Compliance Documentation
B._____ Sprinkler System Compliance Documentation
C._____ Service Water Heating Compliance Documentation
D._____ Lighting Compliance Documentation
E._____ HVAC Compliance Documentation

751. Which **TWO** of the following are true for energy calculation of commercial buildings?

A._____ HVAC Compliance Documenting Part 1 of ASHRAE/IESNA 90.1, 2004 refers to small buildings MORE than 25,000 square feet.
B._____ In Option 2 of EA Credit 1, optimize Energy Performance, the building must be UNDER 25,000 square feet
C._____ In Option 2 of EA Credit 1, optimize Energy Performance, the building must be OVER 20 square feet.
D._____ In option 2 of EA Credit 1, optimize Energy Performance, the building must be between 20,000 to 25,000 square feet
E._____ HVAC Compliance Documenting Part 1 of ASHRAE/IESNA 90.1, 2004 refers to small buildings MORE than 25,000 square feet.

752. Which **ONE** of the following will NOT increase the energy performance in EA Credit 1, Optimize Energy Performance credit?

A._____ Reduce demand
B._____ Harvest free energy
C._____ Increase efficiency
D._____ Recover waste energy
E._____ Use of default ratios

753. Which **THREE** of the following can be used for Energy rates in EA Credit 1, Optimize Energy Performance credit?

A._____ ASHRAE/IESNA 90.1
B._____ Local utility schedules
C._____ DOE
D._____ ANSI
E._____ ASHRAE 62.2, 2004

754. Which **TWO** of the following are NOT included in the cost of Proposed Building Performance for EA Credit 1, Optimize Energy Performance credit?

A._____ The cost of on-site renewable energy
B._____ The cost of site recovered energy
C._____ The cost of process energy
D._____ The cost of non-regulated energy
E._____ The cost of lighting systems

755. Which **ONE** of the following may apply to Advanced Buildings Benchmark Version 1.1 in EA Credit 1, Optimize Energy Performance credit?

A._____ ASHRAE 90.1, 2004
B._____ ASHRAE Advanced Energy Design
C._____ ANSI
D._____ New Building Institute
E._____ None of above

756. Which **THREE** of the following items consider as on-site renewable energy systems in EA Credit 1, Optimize Energy Performance credit?

A._____ Thermal energy collected by solar panels
B._____ Power generated by photovoltaic
C._____ Geo-exchange systems
D._____ Power generated by wind turbines
E._____ Passive solar systems

757. Which **TWO** of the following consider as site recovered energy in EA Credit 1, Optimize Energy Performance credit?

A._____ Heat recovered with chiller heat recovery systems
B._____ Power generated by photovoltaic
C._____ Waste heat recovery units on distributed generation systems
D._____ Power collected buy solar panels
E._____ Power generated by wind turbines

758. Innovation of Design may earn points in which **THREE** of the following credits?

A._____ WE Credit 1.1, Water Efficient Landscaping
B._____ EA Credit 3, Enhanced Commissioning
C._____ WE Credit 3.1, Water USE Reduction
D._____ EA Credit 6, Green Power
E._____ MR credit 7, Certified Wood

759. Which **THREE** of the following can be used in EA Credit 2 ,On-Site Renewable Energy credit?

A._____ Use ECM Guideline
B._____ Use building annual energy cost calculated in EA Credit 1
C._____ Use DOE/EIA standards
D._____ Use CBECS database
E._____ Use building annual energy cost calculated in EA Credit 5

760. Which **THREE** of the following are NOT eligible on-site renewable energy systems in EA Credit 2, On-Site Renewable Energy credit?

A._____ Daylight strategies
B._____ Passive solar systems
C._____ Geothermal heating systems
D._____ Hydro electric power systems
E._____ Architectural features

761. Which **THREE** of the following are true statements for commissioning process in EA Credit 3, Enhanced Commissioning credit?

A._____ Minimize the negative environmental impact
B._____ Reduce repairs and construction change orders
C._____ Reduce energy cost and maintenance cost.
D._____ Increase energy cost and reduce operation cost
E._____ Reduce operation cost and increase repair cost

762. Which **TWO** of the followings may apply to energy calculations in EA Credit 6, Green Power credit?

A._____ Baseline energy cost
B._____ Design energy cost
C._____ Annual heat load
D._____ Default electricity consumption
E._____ Proposed electrical consumption

763. Materials qualifying as reused for MR Credit 3.1, 3.2 can be applied in which **ONE** of the following credits?

A._____ MR Credit 1
B._____ MR Credit 5
C._____ MR Credit 2
D._____ MR Credit 6
E._____ MR Credit 7

764. The project is incorporating existing building but it does NOT meet the requirements for MR Credit 1.1, Building Reuse credit. Which **ONE** of the following can be applied for reused portion of the existing material?

A._____ Apply the reused portion toward achievement of MR 2 Credit (by weight of existing elements)
B._____ Apply the reused portion toward achievement of MR 2 Credit (by surface area of existing enhancements)
C._____ Apply the reused portion toward achievement of MR 3 Credit (by weight of existing elements)
D._____ Apply the reused portion toward achievement of MR 3 Credit (by surface area of existing enhancements)
E._____ None of above

765. Which **THREE** of the following shall be excluded in calculation of MR Credit 1.1, 1.2 Building Reuse credits?

A._____ Non-structural roofing materials
B._____ Unsound material from a structural perspective
C._____ Structural materials that are considered non-hazard
D._____ Envelope materials with no contamination risks
E._____ Window assemblies

766. Which **TWO** of the following statements are true for MR 1.1, 1.2, 1.3 Building Reuse credits?

A._____ Achievement of MR Credit 1.1 is required for MR Credit 1.3
B._____ Achievement of MR Credit 1.2 is required for MR Credit 1.3
C._____ Achievement of MR Credit 1.1 is not required for MR Credit 1.3
D._____ Achievement of MR Credit 1.2 is required for MR Credit 1.3
E._____ Achievement of MR Credit 3 is required for MR Credits 1.1, 1.2

767. Which **TWO** of the following does NOT contribute to MR Credit 2.1, Construction Waste Management credit?

A._____ Demolition debris from disposal in landfills
B._____ Construction debris from disposal in incinerators
C._____ Excavated soil
D._____ Land – cleaning debris
E._____ Recyclable clean wood

768. Which **TWO** of the following are true statements for MR Credit 2.1, Construction Waste Management credit?

A._____ Materials salvaged on-site can be contributed to this credit if it is not included in MR3
B._____ Materials reused on-site can be contributed to this credit if it is not included in MR3
C._____ Materials salvaged on-site can not be contributed to this credit if it is not included in MR3
D._____ Materials reused on-site can not be contributed to this credit if it is not included in MR3
E._____ Materials refurbished on-site can be contributed to this credit if it is not included in MR3

769. Which **TWO** of the following may refer to cost of materials in MR Credit 3, Material Reuse credit?

A._____ Actual cost of the on- site materials
B._____ Replacement cost of on-site materials
C._____ Actual cost of off-site materials
D._____ Replacement cost of off-site materials

770. Which **ONE** of the following standards may apply to construction cost in MR Credit 3, Material Reuse credit?

A._____ CSI Main Format 2004 Division 2-10
B._____ CSI Main Format 1995 Division 2-10
C._____ CSI Main Format 1995 Division 2-15
D._____ CSI Main Format 2004 Division 2-10
E._____ None of the above

771. Which **THREE** of the following may be considered as POST–CONSUMER waste in MR Credit 4.1, 4.2 Recycled Content credits?

A._____ Construction debris
B._____ Discarded products
C._____ Urban maintenance
D._____ Ply trim
E._____ Chips

772. Which **THREE** of the following may be considered as PRE –CONSUMER content in MR Credit 4.1, 4.2 Recycled Content credits?

A.______ Planer shaving
B.______ Bagasse
C.______ Trimmed materials
D.______ Furniture
E.______ Leaves

773. Which **THREE** of the following apply to EQ, Prerequisite1,Minimum IAQ Performance standard?

A.______ Mechanical ventilation shall be designed based on ASHRAE 55-2004
B.______ Mechanical ventilation shall be designed by using the Ventilation Rate Procedure or local code, whichever is more stringent
C.______ Naturally ventilated building shall meet the minimum requirement of ASHRAE 62.1-2004 standards
D.______ Balance the system to optimize for energy efficiency
E.______ Balance the system to optimize for outdoor lighting distribution

774. Which **THREE** of the following may apply to SMACNA Standards?

A.______ Control measures
B.______ Construction process management
C.______ Communication with building occupant
D.______ Energy assumption standards
E.______ VOC limit of materials

775. Which **THREE** of the following may apply to flush-out procedure in MR Credit 3.2 Construction IAQ Management Plan credit?

A.______ Flush out may begin after construction work is completed
B.______ All cleaning shall be completed before flush-out
C.______ All cleaning shall be completed after flush-out
D.______ Commissioning may occur during flush-out
E.______ Commissioning may occur before flush-out

776. Which **THREE** of the following shall be in place for air sample testing in EQ Credit 3.2 Construction IAQ Management Plan credit?

A.______ Carpet
B.______ Workstations
C.______ Doors
D.______ Millwork
E.______ Partitions

777. Which **THREE** of the following may apply to design of minimum outside air rate in Credit 3.2, Construction IAQ Management Plan credit?

A._____ ASHRAE 62.1, 2004
B._____ ASHRAE 5.5, 2004
C._____ Local codes
D._____ SMACNA
E._____ EQ Prerequisite 1

778. Which **THREE** of the following are required for narrative description of LEED AP in IQ Credit 2, LEED Accredited Professional?

A._____ Name of AP
B._____ Provide a copy of the LEED AP Certificate
C._____ Name of LEED AP's Company
D._____ Signature of LEED AP
E._____ Narrative description of the LEED AP's background

779. Which **TWO** of the followings may apply to FIXED items in Credit 3.2, Material Reuse credit?

A._____ Items that can serve as its original function
B._____ Items that are no longer be able to serve their original function
C._____ Items that remain as their existing condition in new building
D._____ Items that were reconditioned and installed for different locations
E._____ Items that were not reconditioned and installed for different locations

780. Which **ONE** of the following is a true statement for Solar Reflectance Index?

A._____ Measure of material's ability to observe solar heat
B._____ Measure of material's ability to reject solar heat
C._____ Measure of material's ability to transfer solar heat
D._____ Measure of material's ability to conduct solar heat
E._____ None of above

781. Which **TWO** of the following are true statements for gray water systems in WE Credit 2, Innovative Wastewater Technology credit?

A._____ Gray water systems have fewer code requirements than rain water systems
B._____ Gray water systems have more code requirements than rain water systems
C._____ Gray water systems are less expensive than rain water systems
D._____ Gray water systems are more expensive than rain water systems

782. Which **THREE** of the following are true statements for aquatic systems in WE Credit 2, Innovative Wastewater Technologies credit?

A._____ Ecological treatment systems
B._____ Utilize a diverse community of biological organisms
C._____ Treat wastewater to advanced levels
D._____ Part of composting toilet systems
E._____ Transport wastewater volumes generated on the site

783. Which **THREE** of the followings can be considered as gray water in WE Credit 2, Innovative Wastewater Technologies credit?

A._____ Waste water from bathtubs, showers, bathroom wash basin
B._____ Waste water from clothes-washer
C._____ Waste water from laundry tubs
D._____ Waste water from kitchen sink
E._____ Waste water from dishwashers

784. Which **THREE** of the following statements are true for WE Credit 2, Innovative Wastewater Technology credit?

A._____ Tertiary treatment is the highest form of wastewater treatment system
B._____ Tertiary treatment is the lowest form of wastewater treatment system
C._____ Process water is part of chillers and cooling towers water systems.
D._____ On-site wastewater treatment systems utilize localized treatment systems to transport and dispose all wastewater
E._____ Tertiary treatment is not related to wastewater treatment systems

785. Which **ONE** of the following is a true statement for use of flow metering controllers?

A._____ Limit the flow time of air
B._____ Limit the flow time of water
C._____ Limit the flow time of humidity in the air
D._____ Limit the flow time of CO_2 in the air
E._____ None of above

786. Which **THREE** of the following are considered as PROCESS LOAD in EA Credit 1, Optimize Energy Performance credit?

A._____ Interior lighting
B._____ Garage fans
C._____ Receptacle equipment
D._____ Circulating pumps for hot water system
E._____ Compressors for refrigeration cycle

787. Which **THREE** of the following can be considered NON-HAZARDOUS materials for recycling in MR Prerequisite 1, Storage & Collection of Recyclables credit?

A._____ Paper, metal
B._____ Corrugated cardboard
C._____ Glass, plastic
D._____ Aluminum
E._____ Structural angle irons

788. What is the rate of fly ash per yard by considering the fly ash is a pre-consumer recycled content material? (The mass of Portland cement = 200 lbs , The mass of fly ash= 50 lbs, The dollar value of all cementations materials :$35)

A._____ $7
B._____ $3.50
C._____ $5
D._____ $4.25
E._____ None of the above

789. Which **TWO** of the following statements are true for residential units in Prerequisite 2, Environmental Tobacco Smoke (ETS) Control?

A._____ All doors in the residential units leading to hallways shall be weather stripped
B._____ All doors in the residential units leading to hallways shall be sound stripped
C._____ All doors in the residential units leading to hallways does not need be weather stripped if common area is pressurized with respect to the residential units
D._____ All doors in the residential units leading to hallways need to be weather stripped if common area is pressurized with respect to the residential units
E._____ All doors shall be weather and sound stripped all the time

790. Which **THREE** of the following should be included for total count of task lighting in EQ Credit 6.1 Controllability of System credit?

A._____ Conference room
B._____ Private office
C._____ Reception stations
D._____ Ticket booths
E._____ Elevator rooms

791. Which **THREE** of the following should be included for each room when daylight is used as a component of an ambient lighting system in EQ Credit 6.1 Controllability of System credit?

A._____ Room darkening shades
B._____ Glare control
C._____ Metering device
D._____ Lighting level controls
E._____ Personal environmental modular controller

792. Which **THREE** of the following designs may be incorporated to EQ credit 6.2, Controllability of Systems credit?

A._____ Operable windows
B._____ Mechanical systems
C._____ Hybrid systems
D._____ Solar panels
E._____ Natural lighting

793. Which **THREE** of the following may be incorporated to daylight in EQ Credit 8.1 Daylight and Views credit?

A._____ Floor area
B._____ Area, geometry and height of window
C._____ Visible light transmittance
D._____ Solar reflectance Index
E._____ Conduction factor

794. Which **ONE** of the following statements is true for visible light transmittance?

A._____ Ratio of total incidental light to total transmitter light
B._____ Ratio of total reflected light to total transmitter light
C._____ Ratio of total transmitted light to total incident light
D._____ Ratio of total transmitted light to total reflected light
E._____ None of the above

795. Which **FOUR** of the following shall be submitted in writing for ID Credits 1.1 through 1.4, Innovation in Design credit?

A._____ Identify the intent of you proposal
B._____ Proposed requirements for compliance
C._____ Proposed submittals to demonstrate compliance
D._____ Design strategies and approaches
E._____ Cost of proposed design

796. Which **THREE** of the following statements are true regarding Credit Interpretation Request forms?

A._____ Do not include name of credit
B._____ Include your contact information
C._____ It shall be submitted with LEED application
D._____ Do not provide detailed information about the project
E._____ Include the name of credit

797. Which **TWO** of the following statements are true regarding the appeal process?

A._____ Include LEED registration information
B._____ Include payment in the amount of $500 for each appeal
C._____ Include payment in the amount of $250 for each appeal
D._____ Include narrative information for each appeal and limit it to 600 words
E._____ Include narrative information for each appeal and limit it to 4000 words

798. What is the daily water use for female & male occupants using conventional water closet?

A._____ Female (3 uses) and male (1 use) @ 1.6 GPF
B._____ Female (3 uses) and male (1 use) @ 2.5 GPM
C._____ Female (3 uses) and male (1 use) @ 1 GPF
D._____ Female (1 uses) and male (3 uses) @ 1.8 GPF
E._____ None of the above

799. Which **THREE** of the following statements are true for adhesives and sealants in EQ Credit 4.1 Low Emitting Material credit?

A._____ Adhesives used on the exterior of the building shall comply with SCAQMD standards
B._____ Adhesives used on the interior of the building shall comply with SCAQMD standards
C._____ Sealant used on the interior of the building shall comply with SCAQMD standards
D._____ Primers used on the interior of the building shall comply with SCAQMD standards
E._____ Sealant used on the exterior of the building shall comply with SCAQMD standards

800. Which **FOUR** of the followings may apply to Performance Rating Method in EA Credit 1, Optimize Energy Performance credit?

A._____ Building type
B._____ Building area
C._____ Quantity of floors
D._____ Heating fuel source of the design
E._____ Cooling source for the design

LEEDPASS

(Chapter 12)

ANSWER SHEETS

Number	Answer	LEEDPASS Page Number	Remarks
1	B-C-D	3-14	
2	A-C-D	3-15, 3-16, 3-22	
3	A-C	3-1	
4	C	3-1	
5	A-C-D	3-1	
6	B-C-D	3-2	
7	A-C-D	3-2	
8	B-C-D	3-3	
9	B	3-2	
10	B-C	3-4	
11	A-C	3-5	
12	A-D	3-6	
13	A-C	3-7	
14	C-D	3-8	
15	B-C-D	3-9	
16	C-D	3-10	
17	A-B-D	3-11	
18	B-C	3-11	
19	B-C	3-50	
20	B-C-D	3-12	

Number	Answer	LEEDPASS Page Number	Remarks
21	C	3-12	
22	B-C-D	3-14	
23	A-B-D	3-14	
24	A-C-D	3-14	
25	A-C-D	3-14	
26	A-C-D	3-15	
27	A-B-C	3-16	
28	C	3-16	
29	C-D	3-17	
30	C-D	3-17	
31	B-C-D	3-18	
32	B-C-D	3-18	
33	B-C-D	3-19	
34	C-D	3-19	
35	B-C-D	3-19	
36	B-C-D	3-25	
37	A-D	3-25	
38	A-D	3-26	
39	C	3-26	
40	B	3-26	

Number	Answer	LEEDPASS Page Number	Remarks
41	B-D	3-27	
42	A-B-D	3-28	
43	A-C-D	3-29	
44	B-C-D	3-29	
45	C	3-29	
46	A-D	3-29	
47	A-C-D	3-30	
48	A-B-C	3-31	
49	C	3-31	
50	A-C-D	3-32	
51	C	3-34	
52	A-C-D	3-34	
53	C	3-35	
54	C	3-35	
55	D	3-36	
56	B	3-39	
57	A-C	3-39	
58	C-D	3-40	
59	A-D	3-40	
60	A-B-D	3-40	

Number	Answer	LEEDPASS Page Number	Remarks
61	B-C-D	3-41	
62	A-C	3-42	
63	A-C-D	3-42	
64	C	3-43	
65	A-B-D	3-43	
66	A-C-D	3-43	
67	A-D	3-44	
68	B-C-D	3-44	
69	D	3-45	
70	C	3-46	
71	C	3-47	
72	A-D	3-47	
73	A-C-D	3-48	
74	A-B-C	3-49	
75	B	3-49	
76	C	3-49	
77	C	3-49	
78	C	3-21	
79	A-B-C	5-1 thru 5-13	
80	A-C-D	8-1	

Number	Answer	LEEDPASS Page Number	Remarks
81	A-B	4-2	
82	D	3-3	
83	A	3-23	
84	A-B-D	3-26	
85	A-B-D	3-42	
86	A	3-30	
87	B	3-47	
88	A-B-D	3-2	
89	B-D	3-13, 3-49	
90	B-C	4-2	Thermal comfort includes both tempreture nd humidity factors
91	D	3-16	
92	C	4-1	
93	B	4-2	
94	A-C-D	2-8	
95	C	3-9	
96	A-C-E	2-4	
97	C	3-32	
98	A-D	3-32, 3-31	Refer to code / standard column on sheets 3-32, 3-31 which indicates " the cost of materials"
99	A-C-D	3-14	
100	B-C-D	3-50	

Number	Answer	LEEDPASS Page Number	Remarks
101	B-C-D	3-24	
102	A-B-D	3-44	
103	A-B-C	3-42	
104	C	3-35	
105	A-B	3-37, 3-44	
106	A	3-20	
107	A	3-35	
108	C	3-2	
109	A-B-C	3-27	Per new standard, Green Pro certificate is not required.
110	A-C-D	3-50, 3-2, 3-42, 3-43, 3-5, 3-6, 3-7, 3-8, 3-75	A= 5 points, B= 1 point, C= 4 points, D= 4 points, E= 2 points
111	B	3-44	
112	A-C	3-17, 3-19 3-24, 3-25	
113	A-B-D	3-39, 3-40 3-41, 3-42	
114	A	3-47	
115	A-D	3-23, 3-33	
116	A	3-16	
117	A	3-33	
118	B	3-20	
119	B	3-27	
120	A	3-50	

Number	Answer	LEEDPASS Page Number	Remarks
121	A-C-D	3-26, 3-24, 3-41	
122	B-C--D	3-26, 3-45, 3-47	
123	C	2-2	
124	A-C-D	2-12	
125	A-B	2-6	
126	A-B-D	2-6	
127	B-C-D	2-14	
128	C	2-2	
129	A-C-D	3-16	
130	D	3-21	
131	A	3-32	
132	A	4-2	Includes both tempreture and humidity standards
133	A-B-E	2-15	
134	A-B	3-3	
135	C	3-16	
136	B	3-22	
137	A-C	3-11, 3-32	
138	C	2-7	
139	C	3-23	
140	A-B-C	3-26	

Number	Answer	LEEDPASS Page Number	Remarks
141	A-B-C	5-1 thru 5-13	
142	D	3-34	
143	A-C	5-1 thru 5-13	
144	B-C-D	5-1 thru 5-13	
145	C	3-50	
146	C	3-1	
147	B-D	3-17	
148	C-D	3-42	
149	A	4-2	
150	B-C	3-11	
151	A-B-C	3-15	
152	A	3-1	
153	A-D	3-1	
154	B	3-6	
155	B-C	3-2	
156	C	3-11	
157	A-B-C	3-11	
158	A-B-C	3-11	
159	C	3-12	
160	C-D	3-13	

Number	Answer	LEEDPASS Page Number	Remarks
161	A-C-D	3-13	
162	C	3-14	
163	A-C-D	3-14	
164	A	3-15	
165	A-B-C	3-18	
166	A-C-D	3-17	
167	C	3-18	
168	C	3-21	
169	C	3-21	
170	C	3-21	
171	C	3-21	
172	A-B-D	3-20	
173	C	3-20	
174	A-B-D	3-23	
175	C-D	3-23	
176	B	3-23	
177	B-D	3-17, 3-24	
178	A-D	3-25	
179	B-C-D	3-32	
180	A-C-D	3-32	

Number	Answer	LEEDPASS Page Number	Remarks
181	A-C-D	2-2	
182	B-C	2-3	
183	B-C-D	2-4	
184	A-B-C	2-6	
185	A-B-C	2-10	
186	B	3-20	Minimum 2 points (10.5 %+3.5 %=14 %)
187	D	3-20	Minimum 2 points (3.5%+3.5%=7%)
188	B	3-23	
189	A-B-C	3-17	
190	C	3-12	
191	C	3-21	
192	A-C-D	3-9	
193	C	3-20	
194	B-C-D	3-50	
195	C	3-50	
196	A-B-D	3-50	
197	A-B-C	3-50	
198	D	2-9	
199	C	2-7	
200	B-C-D	2-7	

Number	Answer	LEEDPASS Page Number	Remarks
201	A	5-2	
202	A-B-D	4-1	
203	D	5-11	
204	C-E	5-4, 5-6	
205	D-E	4-2	
206	B	4-5	
207	B-D	3-35	
208	C	4-4	
209	A-C-E	3-30	
210	A-E	3-9	
211	D	3-32	
212	C-E	3-12	
213	C-D-E	3-12	
214	A-B-D	3-48	
215	C	4-3	
216	B	4-4	
217	B	3-49	
218	B	4-7	
219	C	5-6	
220	A-C	3-30	

Number	Answer	LEEDPASS Page Number	Remarks
221	D	5-7	
222	A-C	3-30	
223	B-D	5-8	
224	C-D-E	3-24	
225	B-D	5-8	
226	B-D	5-8	
227	C	4-6	
228	C	4-3	
229	C	4-6	
230	C	4-7	
231	A	4-7	
232	C	4-4	
233	B	4-3	
234	A-C	3-49	
235	C	4-5	
236	A	4-3	
237	D	4-6	
238	B	4-4	
239	A-B-E	3-16	
240	B	4-4	

Number	Answer	LEEDPASS Page Number	Remarks
241	B-D	4-1	
242	A-D	3-48	
243	A-D	4-2	
244	A-C	3-34	
245	A-C	3-27	
246	A-C	3-27	
247	C-D	4-2	
248	A-C	3-15	
249	A-C	4-3	
250	B-C-D	3-33	
251	A-C	5-1	
252	B-C	5-1	
253	A-C-D	5-2	
254	A-E	5-2	
255	B	5-5	
256	A-B-D	5-3	
257	E	3-3	
258	B	5-5	
259	A-C-D	5-5	
260	B-D	5-9	

Number	Answer	LEEDPASS Page Number	Remarks
261	A-D	5-10	
262	C	4-5	
263	C	4-4	
264	B-D	5-11	
265	C	5-11	
266	B-D	4-5	
267	C-D	4-3	
268	B-D	5-11	
269	B-D	5-12	
270	C	3-47	
271	B-C-D	3-47	
272	E	3-46	
273	A-B-D	3-45	
274	E	3-39	
275	E	3-45	
276	A	3-38	
277	A-C-D	3-45	
278	A	3-44	
279	A	3-41	
280	E	3-39	

Number	Answer	LEEDPASS Page Number	Remarks
281	B	3-39	
282	A-C-D	3-23	
283	E	3-38	
284	A-C	3-25	
285	D	3-36	
286	B-C-D	3-33	
287	A-C-D	3-32	
288	C	3-31	
289	B-C-D	3-21	
290	B-C	3-23	
291	A-C-D	3-23	
292	A-B-D	3-23	
293	A-C-D	3-21	
294	A-C-D	3-22	
295	A-C-D	3-22	
296	A-B-D	3-16	
297	E	3-16	
298	A-B	3-16	
299	A-C-D	3-15	
300	C-D	3-48	

Number	Answer	LEEDPASS Page Number	Remarks
301	B-C	3-21	
302	B-E	3-15	
303	B-C	3-15	
304	A-B	3-13	
305	B-D-E	3-16	
306	A-B-E	3-12	
307	B-C	3-12	
308	A-C-D	3-11	
309	A-D	3-11	
310	A-D	3-9	
311	A-C-E	7-1, 7-2	
312	E	3-3	
313	A-C-E	7-1	
314	A-D	3-2	
315	B-D-E	7-1, 7-2	
316	A-E	7-1, 7-2	
317	A-B-D	3-32	
318	C	2-12	
319	A-D-E	7-2	
320	C	2-12	

Number	Answer	LEEDPASS Page Number	Remarks
321	A-C-D	3-17, 3-24	
322	A-C-D	3-23	
323	C	2-12	
324	A-C-D	3-49	
325	C	2-12	
326	B-E	3-11	
327	A-C	3-27	
328	D	2-13	
329	A-B-C	3-3	
330	E	2-13	
331	E	3-3	
332	B-D-E	3-20, 3-21, 3-22	
333	E	2-13	
334	A-C-E	3-11	
335	E	2-13	
336	A-B-E	3-11	
337	B-D-E	3-19	
338	C	2-13	
339	A-B-E	3-14	
340	E	2-13	

Number	Answer	LEEDPASS Page Number	Remarks
341	A-B-C	3-45, 3-46	
342	C	2-9	
343	A-B-E	3-18	
344	E	2-9	
345	A-C-E	2-4	
346	A-C	2-5	
347	D	3-30	
348	B-E	3-3	
349	D	3-5	
350	D	3-6	800(0.05)=40
351	D	3-6	800(0.005)=4
352	E	3-6	90(0.15)=13.5
353	E	3-7	800(0.05)=40
354	D	3-7	800(0.03)=24
355	E	3-15	
356	D	3-15	
357	A-B	2-9	
358	E	3-21	
359	A-B-E	3-25	
360	B-D	3-26	

Number	Answer	LEEDPASS Page Number	Remarks
361	A	3-33	800000(0.40)=320000
362	B	3-34	1600000(.05)=80000
363	D	3-32	800000(0.20)=160000
364	E	3-32	(1500lb)+(1/2)(3000lb)=3000lb (3000lb)($5/lb)=$15000 $15000/$1500000=0.01 (1 percent earns NO point)
365	E	3-9	3/4=0.75 (75 percent earns 2 points)
366	B	3-4, 3-10, 3-9, 3-48, 3-7	1+1+1+0+1=4
367	E	3-3, 3-32, 3-29, 3-9, 3-6	1+0+1+2+1=5
368	C	3-30, 3-27, 3-9, 3-16, 3-7	0+1+2+1+1=5
369	B	3-7, 3-30, 3-12, 3-27, 3-9	0+2+2+0+2=6
370	E	3-30, 3-16, 3-29, 3-27, 3-23	1+2+0+1+3=7
371	D	3-12, 3-29, 3-31, 3-5, 3-31	2+2+2+1+0=7
372	C	3-4, 3-30, 3-16, 3-12, 3-29	1+3+0+1+1=6
373	B	3-33, 3-16, 3-23, 3-48, 3-27	1+3+0+2+2=8
374	E	3-7, 3-31, 3-6, 3-33, 3-9	1+1+1+2+0=5
375	A	3-6, 3-16, 3-48, 3-12, 3-32	1+3+2+0+3=9
376	D	3-32, 3-3, 3-48, 3-11, 3-6	1+1+0+0+1=3
377	D	3-33, 3-48, 3-31, 3-6, 3-7	2+2+3+0+1=8
378	C	3-31, 3-16, 3-7, 3-12, 3-48	2+2+1+0+1=6
379	B	3-32, 3-7, 3-35, 3-16, 3-34	2+0+1+1+1=5
380	A	3-9, 3-23, 3-6, 3-6, 3-33	1+2+1+0+3=7

Number	Answer	LEEDPASS Page Number	Remarks
381	A	3-12, 3-27, 3-11, 3-7, 3-5	1+1+1+0+1=4
382	B	3-30, 3-34, 3-33, 3-23, 3-7	1+2+3+3+0=9
383	B	3-30, 3-27, 3-10, 3-35, 3-29	3+0+2+2+2=9
384	E	3-33, 3-27, 3-5, 3-29, 3-23	1+2+1+0+2=6
385	A	3-32, 3-10, 3-31, 3-32, 3-11	3+1+3+0+1=8
386	A	3-33, 3-27, 3-35, 3-12, 3-12	0+2+0+1+2=5
387	B	3-27, 3-23, 3-7, 3-33, 3-12	0+1+1+0+1=3
388	B	3-3, 3-6, 3-30, 3-12, 3-33	1+1+0+2+0=4
389	C	3-31, 3-12, 3-27, 3-12, 3-27	0+1+0+0+2=3
390	D	3-30, 3-16, 3-32, 3-34, 3-35	2+1+3+0+2=8
391	E	3-29, 3-12, 3-31, 3-30, 3-9	0+0+1+2+0=3
392	E	3-12, 3-30, 3-35, 3-23, 3-32	0+0+1+1+2=4
393	C	3-35, 3-12, 3- 12, 3-6, 3- 27	0+2+0+1+2=5
394	A	3-32, 3-48, 3-29, 3-15, 3-9	1+0+1+2+0=4
395	D	3-31, 3-35, 3- 48, 3-32, 3-34	2+2+1+0+0=5
396	D	3-48, 3-29,3-27,3-33,3-23	2+1+0+3+0=6
397	A	3-16, 3-7, 3- 29, 3-11, 3-30	1+1+0+0+1=3
398	C	3-7, 3-32, 3-27, 3- 29, 3-48	0+0+2+0+0=2
399	E	3-48, 3-6, 3-35, 3-7, 3-16	0+1+0+1+2=4
400	A	3-27, 3-10, 3-9, 3-5, 3-48	1+1+1+2+0=5

Number	Answer	LEEDPASS Page Number	Remarks
401	A-B-C	3-45	
402	A-C-D	3-45	
403	A-B-C	3-45	
404	A-D-E	3-45	
405	A-B	3-11, 3-12	
406	A-B-C	3-3, 3-10, 3-13	
407	A-B-C	3-22	
408	B-C-D	3-17	
409	B	2-13	
410	C	2-13	
411	A	2-13	
412	E	2-13	
413	A	2-16	
414	A	2-16	
415	C	2-16	
416	A	2-16	
417	D	2-16	
418	A-B-E	3-3, 3-5, 3-9	
419	B-C	3-15, 3-16	
420	A-B-E	3-20, 3-23, 3-27	

Number	Answer	LEEDPASS Page Number	Remarks
421	A-B-C	3-30, 3-31, 3-22	
422	A-C-E	3-1	
423	A-C-E	3-2	
424	A-C-E	3-3	
425	A-C-E	3-5, 3-6, 3-7	
426	A-C-E	3-11	
427	A-D-E	3-12	
428	C-D	3-13	
429	A-B-E	3-14	
430	B-C-D	3-15	
431	B-C-E	3-16	
432	B-C-E	3-17	
433	B-C-D	3-18	
434	A-B-D	3-19	
435	B-C-D	3-20	
436	C-D-E	3-23	
437	B-C-D	3-24	
438	C-D-E	3-25	
439	B-C-E	3-26	
440	A-B-C	3-27	

Number	Answer	LEEDPASS Page Number	Remarks
441	A-C-E	3-28	
442	A-B-C	3-29	
443	A-B-E	3-30	
444	A-C-E	3-31	
445	C-D-E	3-32	
446	A-B-D	3-33	
447	E	3-34	
448	A-B-C	3-35	
449	B-D-E	3-36	
450	A-D-E	3-37	
451	A-D-E	3-38	
452	A-C-E	3-39	
453	A-B-E	3-40, 3-41	
454	B-D-E	3-42	
455	A-C-E	3-44	
456	C-D-E	3-45, 3-46	
457	A-B-C	3-47	
458	B-D-E	3-48, 3-49	
459	A-E	3-19	
460	A	3-48	

Number	Answer	LEEDPASS Page Number	Remarks
461	C	3-10	
462	C-D-E	3-48	
463	A-C	3-32	
464	A-B-C	3-9, 3-11, 3-12	
465	B	3-12	
466	B	3-48	
467	A-C-E	3-3, 3-10, 3-13	
468	A-E	3-31, 3-33	
469	A-C-D	3-14	
470	A-C-E	3-12	
471	C	4-1	
472	A-D	3-42	
473	C-D-E	3-22	
474	A-C-D	3-29	
475	A-B-C	2-15	
476	A	2-8	
477	A-D-E	3-8	
478	D	3-23	
479	C	3-21	
480	A	9-1	

Number	Answer	LEEDPASS Page Number	Remarks
481	A	9-5, 9-6	
482	A	9-8	
483	A	9-9	
484	A	9-12	
485	A-D-E	6-2	
486	A-B-E	6-1	
487	A-C-D	6-1	
488	E	6-1	
489	A-B-E	3-3	
490	A-E	3-5	
491	A-D	3-8	
492	A-C	3-10	
493	B	3-19	
494	A-D	3-20	
495	E	3-22	Option # 1: 2 points, Option # 2: 2 points, Option # 3: 5 points (Since only one option can be used for each project, then the maximum credit is 5 points)
496	C	3-22	
497	A-C-E	3-22	
498	B	3-23	
499	A-D	3-30	
500	A-C-E	3-42	

Number	Answer	LEEDPASS Page Number	Remarks
501	A-D	3-34	
502	A-B	3-28	
503	B-E	3-46	
504	C-E	3-31,3-33	
505	A-B-D	3-48	
506	A-B-C	3-32	
507	B-C	3-13	
508	C	3-20	
509	D	3-1	
510	B-D-E	3-26	
511	A-B-E	3-19	
512	A-D-E	3-14	
513	A-D-E	3-12	
514	B-C	3-42	
515	A-B-E	3-4	
516	A-C-D	3-17	
517	A-B-E	3-41	
518	A-B	2-3	
519	A-B-C	3-13	
520	A-B-C	3-29	

Number	Answer	LEEDPASS Page Number	Remarks
521	B	2-1	
522	A-B-C	3-21	
523	A-C	4-2	
524	A-C-D	3-31, 3-33, 3-35	
525	A	4-5	
526	A-D-E	3-32	
527	A-C-E	3-29	
528	A-C-E	3-6, 3-7, 3-8, 3-15, 3-16	
529	A-C	3-35	
530	C-D-E	3-12	
531	B-C-E	3-15	
532	A-D-E	3-29	
533	A-B-E	3-25	
534	A-D-E	3-11	
535	A-C-D	3-22	
536	A-B-E	3-2	
537	B	3-20	
538	A-B-D	3-30, 3-31, 3-33	
539	A-B-E	3-20, 3-39, 3-46	
540	A-B-C	3-15, 3-16, 3-20	

Number	Answer	LEEDPASS Page Number	Remarks
541	A-B-C	3-11, 3-12, 3-20	
542	D	3-1	
543	E	3-2	
544	B	3-4	
545	D	3-5	
546	B	3-6	
547	D	3-7	
548	D	3-8	
549	A	3-9	
550	C	3-10	
551	D	3-11	
552	A	3-11	
553	C	3-12	
554	D	3-12	
555	D	3-14	
556	D	3-15	
557	C	3-16	
558	C	3-17	
559	D	3-18	
560	B	3-19	

Number	Answer	LEEDPASS Page Number	Remarks
561	D	3-20	
562	D	3-23	
563	C	3-24	
564	D	3-25	
565	B	3-26	
566	D	3-27	
567	C	3-28	
568	C	3-29	
569	D	3-30	
570	A	3-32	
571	B	3-33	
572	D	3-34	
573	D	3-36	
574	C	3-37	
575	B	3-38	
576	B	3-39	
577	C	3-40	
578	D	3-41	
579	A	3-42	
580	B	3-42	

Number	Answer	LEEDPASS Page Number	Remarks
581	C	3-42	
582	D	3-43	
583	A	3-44	
584	E	3-46	
585	D	3-47	
586	E	3-47	
587	D	3-48	
588	D	3-49	
589	C-E	9-4, 9-5	
590	A-C-E	9-6, 9-7, 9-9	
591	C-E	9-9, 9-19	
592	A-C-E	9-11, 9-12, 9-22	
593	C-E	9-15, 9-17	
594	A-C-E	9-19, 9-20, 9-22	
595	A-C-E	9-2, 9-3	
596	A-C-E	9-3, 9-15, 9-19	
597	A-C-E	9-10, 9-11, 9-13	
598	A-C-E	9-13, 9-20	
599	A-C-E	9-21, 9-22	
600	A-E	9-16	

Number	Answer	LEEDPASS Page Number	Remarks
601	D	3-1	
602	D	3-2	
603	A	3-3	
604	B	3-4	
605	D	3-5, 3-6, 3-7	
606	C	3-7	
607	B	3-9	
608	D	3-10	
609	D	3-11	
610	A	3-11	
611	E	3-12	
612	E	3-13	
613	D	3-14	
614	D	3-15	
615	C	3-16	
616	C	3-17	
617	D	3-18	
618	B	3-19	
619	D	3-20, 3-21, 3-22	
620	D	3-20, 3-21, 3-22	

Number	Answer	LEEDPASS Page Number	Remarks
621	B	3-20, 3-21, 3-22	
622	D	3-23	
623	C	3-24	
624	D	3-25	
625	B	3-26	
626	D	3-27	
627	C	3-28	
628	C	3-29	
629	D	3-30	
630	C	3-31	
631	C	3-29	
632	A	3-32	
633	B	3-33	
634	D	3-34	
635	A	3-35	
636	C	3-35	
637	D	3-36	
638	C	3-37	
639	C	3-39	
640	C	3-40	

Number	Answer	LEEDPASS Page Number	Remarks
641	D	3-41	
642	A	3-44	
643	D	3-45	
644	A	3-45	
645	B	3-46	
646	D	3-47	
647	B	3-47	
648	D	3-48	
649	D	3-49	
650	A-C-E	4-6	
651	A-C-E	4-1	
652	A-C-E	4-1	
653	A-C-E	4-2, 4-5, 4-6	
654	A-C-E	4-2, 4-5, 4-6	
655	A-C-E	4-2, 4-5, 4-6	
656	A-C-E	4-2, 4-5	
657	A-C-E	4-4, 4-5, 4-6	
658	A-C-E	4-2, 4-4, 4-5	
659	A-C-E	4-2, 4-5, 4-6	
660	A-C-E	4-2, 4-4, 4-5	

Number	Answer	LEEDPASS Page Number	Remarks
661	A-C-E	4-2, 4-4	
662	A-C-E	4-2, 4-3, 4-4	
663	A-C-E	4-3, 4-4	
664	A-C-E	4-3, 4-4, 4-7	
665	A-C-E	4-3, 4-4, 4-5	
666	A-C-E	4-3, 4-5	
667	A-C-E	4-3, 4-4	
668	A-C-E	4-3, 4-6, 4-7	
669	A-C-E	4-6, 4-7	
670	A-C-E	4-7	
671	A-C-E	4-6, 4-7	
672	A-C-E	5-1	
673	A-C-E	5-1, 5-2	
674	A-C-E	5-2, 5-3	
675	A-C-E	5-2, 5-3	
676	A-C	5-4	
677	A-C-E	5-5	
678	A-C-E	5-5, 5-6	
679	A-B-C	5-6, 5-8, 5-9	
680	A-B-E	5-10, 5-11	

Number	Answer	LEEDPASS Page Number	Remarks
681	A-B-C	5-9, 5-10, 5-11	
682	A-B-E	5-6, 5-7, 5-11	
683	A-B	5-7, 5-8	
684	A-C-E	5-8, 5-10, 5-12	
685	A-B-E	5-10, 5-12	
686	A-D	5-4	
687	A-B-C	5-6, 5-7, 5-12	
688	A-D-E	3-9	
689	A-D-E	3-10	
690	A-D-E	3-11	
691	A-C-E	3-43	
692	B-C-E	3-8	
693	C	3-47	
694	A-C-E	3-1, 3-2, 3-10	
695	A-C-E	3-1, 3-9, 3-11	
696	A-C-E	3-9, 3-11	
697	A-C-E	3-5, 3-11, 3-16	
698	A-C-E	3-3, 3-12, 3-16	
699	A-C-E	3-11, 3-15, 3-18	
700	A-C-E	3-4, 3-6, 3-12	

Number	Answer	LEEDPASS Page Number	Remarks
701	A-C-E	3-11, 3-13, 3-16	
702	A-C-E	3-4, 3-5, 3-13,	
703	A-C-E	3-9, 3-19, 3-23	
704	A-C-E	3-5, 3-17, 3-27	
705	A-C-E	3-9, 3-11, 3-13	
706	A-C-E	3-20, 3-28, 3-33	
707	A-C-E	3-20, 3-25, 3-26	
708	A-C-E	3-28, 3-32, 3-34	
709	A-C-E	3-23, 3-28, 3-29	
710	A-C-E	3-23, 3-28, 3-33	
711	A-C-E	3-34, 3-38, 3-40	
712	A-C-E	3-29, 3-39, 3-40	
713	A-C-E	3-35, 3-38, 3-42	
714	A-C-E	3-39, 3-40, 3-42	
715	A-C-E	3-29, 3-30, 3-36	
716	A-C-E	3-29, 3-30, 3-37	
717	A-C-E	3-30, 3-31, 3-32	
718	A-C-E	3-44, 3-46, 3-47	
719	A-C-E	3-45, 3-48, 3-49	
720	A-C-E	3-38, 3-45, 3-48	

Number	Answer	LEEDPASS Page Number	Remarks
721	A-B-C		GENERAL INFORMATION
722	C-D-E		GENERAL INFORMATION
723	C-D		GENERAL INFORMATION
724	B-D		GENERAL INFORMATION
725	D		GENERAL INFORMATION
726	C-D		GENERAL INFORMATION
727	A-D		GENERAL INFORMATION
728	A-B-E		GENERAL INFORMATION
729	A-D		GENERAL INFORMATION
730	A-E		GENERAL INFORMATION
731	A-B-E		GENERAL INFORMATION
732	A-D		GENERAL INFORMATION
733	A-D		GENERAL INFORMATION
734	A-D		GENERAL INFORMATION
735	A-C-D		GENERAL INFORMATION
736	C		GENERAL INFORMATION
737	A-C-D		GENERAL INFORMATION
738	A		GENERAL INFORMATION
739	C		GENERAL INFORMATION
740	D		GENERAL INFORMATION

Number	Answer	LEEDPASS Page Number	Remarks
741	B-E		GENERAL INFORMATION
742	A-E		GENERAL INFORMATION
743	A-D		GENERAL INFORMATION
744	A-D		GENERAL INFORMATION
745	C		USGBC Reference Guide Page 160
746	D		USGBC Reference Guide Page 166
747	C		USGBC Reference Guide Page 166
748	C		USGBC Reference Guide Page 169
749	D		USGBC Reference Guide Page 169
750	A-C-E		USGBC Reference Guide Page 169
751	A-B		USGBC Reference Guide Page 169
752	E		USGBC Reference Guide Page 182
753	A-B-C		USGBC Reference Guide Page 188
754	A-B		USGBC Reference Guide Page 188
755	D		USGBC Reference Guide Page 184
756	A-B-D		USGBC Reference Guide Page 188
757	A-C		USGBC Reference Guide Page 188
758	C-D-E	3-16, 3-27, 3-35	
759	B-C-D		USGBC Reference Guide Page 205
760	A-B-E		USGBC Reference Guide Page 205

Number	Answer	LEEDPASS Page Number	Remarks
761	A-B-C		USGBC Reference Guide Page 216
762	B-D		USGBC Reference Guide Page 235
763	B		USGBC Reference Guide Page 240
764	A		USGBC Reference Guide Page 250
765	A-B-E		USGBC Reference Guide Page 250
766	C-D		USGBC Reference Guide Page 251
767	C-D		USGBC Reference Guide Page 255
768	A-B		USGBC Reference Guide Page 257
769	A-B		USGBC Reference Guide Page 265
770	B		USGBC Reference Guide Page 266
771	A-B-C		USGBC Reference Guide Page 274
772	A-B-C		USGBC Reference Guide Page 275
773	B-C-D		USGBC Reference Guide Page 295
774	A-B-C		USGBC Reference Guide Page 324
775	A-B		USGBC Reference Guide Page 331
776	A-C-D		USGBC Reference Guide Page 330
777	A-C-E		USGBC Reference Guide Page 332
778	A-B-C		USGBC Reference Guide Page 402
779	B-D		USGBC Reference Guide Page 265
780	B		USGBC Reference Guide Page 95

Number	Answer	LEEDPASS Page Number	Remarks
781	B		USGBC Reference Guide Page 130
782	A-B-C		USGBC Reference Guide Page 137
783	A-B-C		USGBC Reference Guide Page 138
784	A-C-D		USGBC Reference Guide Page 139
785	B		USGBC Reference Guide Page 148
786	A-C-E		USGBC Reference Guide Page 195
787	A-B-C		USGBC Reference Guide Page 243
788	A		USGBC Reference Guide Page 273
789	A-C		USGBC Reference Guide Page 52
790	B-C-D		USGBC Reference Guide Page 53
791	A-B-D		USGBC Reference Guide Page 365
792	A-B-C		USGBC Reference Guide Page 367
793	A-B-C		USGBC Reference Guide Page 387
794	C		USGBC Reference Guide Page 387
795	A-B-C-D		USGBC Reference Guide Page 397
796	A-C-D	2-3	
797	A-B	2-9	
798	A		USGBC Reference Guide Page 143
799	B-C-D		USGBC Reference Guide Page 339
800	A-B-C-D	3-21	

LEEDPASS

(Chapter 13)

COMMON ABBREVIATIONS

COMMON ABBREVIATIONS

A/C	*Air Conditioning Unit*
ACH	*Air Change per Hour*
AHU	*Air Handling Unit*
ANSI	*American National Standard Institute*
ASHRAE	*American Society of Heating Refrigeration and Air conditioning Engineers*
ASTM	*American Society of Testing & Materials*
AWEA	*American Wind Energy Association*
BcxA	*Building Commissioning Association*
BMP	*Best Management Practice*
BOD	*Basis Of Design*
CBECS	*Commercial Building Energy Consumption Survey*
CDVR	*Corrected Design Ventilation Rate*
CEC	*California Energy Commission*
CERCLA	*Comprehensive Environmental Response, Compensation and Liability Act*
CF	*Cubic Feet*
CFC	*Chlorofluorocarbons*
CFM	*Cubic Feet per Minute*
CFR	*Code Federal of Regulation*
CFS	*Cubic Feet per Second*

COMMON ABBREVIATIONS

CIBSE	*Chartered Institution of Building Services Engineers*
CIWMB	*California Integrated Waste management Board*
CO	*Carbon Monoxide*
COC	*Chain Of Custody*
COP	*Coefficient of Performance*
Const	*Construction*
CRI	*Carpet & Rug Institute*
CRS	*Center for Resource Solution*
CU	*Coefficient of Utilization*
CxA	*Commissioning Authority*
DEC	*Design Energy Cost*
DHS	*California Department of Health Services*
DOE	*Department Of Energy*
ECB	*Energy Cost Budget*
ECM	*Energy Conservation Measures*
EEM	*Energy Efficiency Measures*
EER	*Energy Efficiency Rating*
EIA	*Energy Information Administration*
EMP	*Energy Modeling Protocol*
EMS	*Energy Management System*

COMMON ABBREVIATIONS

EPA	*Environmental Protection Agency*
ESC	*Erosion and Sedimentation Control*
ETS	*Environmental Tobacco Smoke*
EVO	*Efficiency Valuation Organization*
Fc	*Foot-candle*
FEMA	*Federal Emergency Management Agency*
FPT	*Functional Performance Testing*
FSC	*Forest Stewardship Council*
FTE	*Full Time Equivalent*
G/L	*Grams per Litter*
GPF	*Gallon Per Flush*
GPM	*Gallon Per Minute*
GS	*Green Seal*
GWP	*Global Warning Potential*
HCFC	*Hydrochloroflurocarbons*
HFC	*Hydroflurocarbons*
HVAC	*Heating, Ventilation, Air Conditioning*
IAQ	*Indoor Air Quality*
IESNA	*Illuminating Engineering Society of North America*
IMEX	*Industrial Material Exchange*

COMMON ABBREVIATIONS

IPMVP	*International Performance Measurement and Verification Protocol*
ISO	*International Organization for Standardization*
LAV	*Lavatory*
LCA	*Life Cycle Analysis*
LCC	*Life Cycle Cost*
LCGWP	*Life Cycle Direct Global Warning Potential*
LCODP	*Life Cycle Ozone Deletion Potential*
LEED	*Leadership in Energy and Environmental Design*
LPD	*Lighting Power Density*
Lr	*Refrigerant Leakage Rate*
M&V	*Measurement and Verification*
MDF	*Medium Density Fiberboard*
MEP	*Mechanical, Electrical and Plumbing*
MERV	*Minimum Efficiency Reporting Value*
Mr	*End-of-life Refrigerant*
MSD	*Medium Safety Data Sheet*
n/a	*Not applicable*
NBI	*New Building Institute*
NC	*New Construction*
NFRC	*National Fenestration Rating Council*

COMMON ABBREVIATIONS

NPDES	*National Pollutant Discharge Elimination System*
O&M	*Operation and Maintenance*
ODP	*Ozone Depleting Potential*
OPR	*Owner Project Requirements*
OSA	*Out Side Air*
Pa	*Pascal (pressure unit)*
PCH	*Phenylcychlohexene*
PM	*Particulate Matter*
PMV	*Predicted Mean Vote*
PPM	*Parts Per Million*
PRM	*Performance Rating Model*
RA	*Return Air*
Rc	*Refrigerant Charge*
RCRA	*Resource Conservation and Recovery Act*
REC	*Renewable Energy Certificate*
RH	*Relative Humidity*
SC	*Shading Coefficient*
SBIC	*Sustainable Building Industry Council*
SHGC	*Solar Heat Gain Coefficient*
SCAQMD	*South Coast Air Quality Management District*

COMMON ABBREVIATIONS

SHGC	*Solar Heat Gain Coefficient*
SMACNA	*Sheet Metal and Air conditioning contractors' National Association*
Sq.ft	*Square feet*
SRI	*Solar Reflectance Index*
TSS	*Total Suspended Solid*
TARP	*Technology Acceptance Reciprocity Partnership*
TVOC	*Total Volatile Organic Compounds*
UL	*Urinal (Plumbing Fixture)*
USAD	*US Agricultural Department*
USGBC	*U.S. Green Building Council*
UV	*Ultra Violet*
VOC	*Volatile Organic Compound*
WC	*Water Closet*
ZEV	*Zero Emission Vehicle*

LEEDPASS

(Chapter 14)

STUDY NOTES

LEEDPASS
Study Notes

LEEDPASS
Study Notes